Law, Authority and Society

*Readings in
Ancient and Medieval
Social Thought*

Edited by

Michael E. Burke

Robert L. Pigeon

COMBINED BOOKS
Pennsylvania

Library of Congress Cataloging-in-Publication Data
Burke, Michael E., and Pigeon, Robert L.
    Law, authority, and society : readings in ancient and medieval
    social thought / edited by Michael E. Burke and Robert L. Pigeon.
        p. cm.
    ISBN 0-938289-53-5
    1. Law, Ancient. 2. Law—History. 3. Sociological
jurisprudence—History. I. Burke, Michael E., 1942– .
    II. Pigeon, Robert L.
K190.L38   1995   95-34404
340'.112—dc20   CIP

Combined Books Edition   1   2   3   4   5

For information, address: Combined Books, Inc., 151 East 10th
Avenue, Conshohocken, PA 19428.

TRANSLATION ACKNOWLEDGMENTS: Thomas Aquinas, "Treatise on Law"
from Summa Theologica by the Fathers of the English Dominican Province,
1912-1936; Thomas Aquinas, On Kingship, selection by Michael B. Foster in
Masters of Political Thought; Aristotle, Politics by Benjamin Jowett; Augustine,
selections from City of God by M. Dods, J.J. Smith and G. Wilson; Augustine,
Confessions by Edward Bouverie Pusey; Augustine, "Letters on True Faith" from
Letters of St. Augustine by J.G. Cunningham; Cicero, On Duties by Michael Grant,
(courtesy Penguin Books, Inc., New York, 1960); Cicero, On Law by C.D. Yonge;
Hammurabi, Law Code by L.W. King; John of Salisbury, Policraticus by John
Dickinson; Martin Luther, On Temporal Authority by J.J. Schindel (courtesy of
Fortress Press, 1962); Machiavelli, The Prince by W.K. Marriott; Thomas More,
Utopia by Ralph Robinson; Old and New Testament selections from the English
Revised Version (1885) and the American Standard version (1901) of the original
King James Version; Plato, Crito and Republic by Benjamin Jowett; Sophocles,
Antigone by Richard Crawley; Thucydides, "Pericles' Funeral Speech" from History
of the Peloponnesian War by Richard Crawley.

Contents

Preface

Every human society has laws that impose rules and define the norms of individual behavior. No one would deny that some actions are virtuous, others evil. Not everyone, however, has agreed about the source of the laws that ought to govern our actions. Modern Western society accepts law as subject to change, and debates whether individual conscience or the will of the majority should take precedence. We also assume that laws and lawmakers are accountable to their public, and that legitimate authority to enforce law emanates from those subject to law. This perspective has been rare, however, in human experience. Most societies—and most of the authors included in this volume—have searched for more absolute norms of human behavior, and pondered whether to find law in divine revelation, in human reason, or in tradition.

The relationship between the individual and society has also been a dominant theme in Western thought. Both the classical and Christian traditions that comprise the readings in this volume recognize the integrity of the individual, that individual men and women possess a unique nature by virtue of their humanity. At the same time, these same traditions have recognized that individuals live in a society, a society that itself may make certain demands on the individual. The Christian tradition of an all-powerful God who has dictated the nature of good and evil complicates further the inherent tension between individual and society. Thus law, the rules by which societies define justice, and authority, wherein societies determine who can legitimately define what is lawful, are at the essence of any society.

The selections that follow propose visions of law, individual autonomy, community, and justice that are often very different from the conventional wisdom of today. We do not expect our readers to accept every premise, every argument, every conclusion. We do hope, however, that readers will approach each text in its own terms—and its own historical context—and not allow the values of contemporary America to become the only criteria by which they are judged. For despite the passage of time, the ideas they contain remain an integral part of both the Western tradition and our own intellectual identity.

The readings in this volume are excerpted from the original. We have endeavored to offer selections of sufficient length to enable the reader to appreciate the flavor as well as the substance, and to enter into the arguments as well as the conclusions. At the same time, we have deleted digressions and examples not directly relevant to our themes, and have edited the translations in order to make them more accessible to the modern reader. We have resisted the temptation to include interpretative introductions to the selections so that the reader will approach the text in its own terms, not through the lens of another's understanding. The selections are presented in approximate chronological order to demonstrate the evolution of Western thought. The reader should keep in mind that in most cases the authors of the texts themselves were familiar with selections that precede them.

This collection was inspired by the Villanova University Core Humanities Seminar, *Ancient, Medieval, and Renaissance Thought*, in an effort to provide students with a solid, comprehensive collection of original texts. Individual selections were chosen to focus on our common theme: the nature of law, authority and society. Thus the readings, taken together, are intended not as a random selection of excerpts from so-called Great Books, but rather to reflect significant moments in the evolution in pre-modern Western notions of law, authority, and the nature of society.

We are indebted to our former students in the Villanova Core Humanities Seminars whose constructive advice and criticism have proven invaluable in selecting compelling texts and excerpts, and in editing the selections for greater clarity. We particularly want to thank Villanova undergraduates Deanna Albanese and Michele Laganella for their helpful suggestions and thorough review of the manuscript, and History graduate student Kristen Spader-Rathsam for her meticulous copy-editing.

1. Hammurabi, *Law Code*

The Law Code of Hammurabi is the oldest extant legal code in the West. Probably compiled during the reign of Hammurabi (1728-1686 B.C.E.) in ancient Babylonia, it presumably reflected existing practice throughout the Near East. It is notable for its comprehensive character, and for the impact it had on later legal practice in the region. The original code of some three hundred articles was written on an eight-foot stone column.

1. If any one accuses another and puts a punishment upon him, but he cannot prove it, then the accuser shall be put to death.

2. If anyone bring an accusation against a man, and the accused go to the river and leap into the river, if he sink in the river his accuser shall take possession of his house. But if the river prove that the accused is not guilty, and he escape unhurt, then he who had brought the accusation shall be put to death, while he who leaped into the river shall take possession of the house that had belonged to his accuser.

3. If anyone bring an accusation of any crime before the elders, and does not prove what he has charged, he shall, if it be a capital offense charged, be put to death.

4. If he request of the elders to impose a fine of grain or money, he shall receive the fine that the action produces.

5. If a judge try a case, reach a decision, and present his judgment in writing; if later error shall appear in his decision, and it be through the judge's own fault, then he shall pay twelve times the

fine set by him in the case, and he shall be publicly removed from the judge's bench, and never again shall he sit there to render judgement.

6. If a man has stolen goods from a temple, or house, he shall be put to death; and he that has received the stolen property from him shall be put to death.

7. If anyone buy from the son or the slave of another man, without witnesses or a contract, silver or gold, a male or female slave, an ox or a sheep, an ass or anything, or if he take it in charge, he is considered a thief and shall be put to death.

8. If anyone steal cattle or sheep, or an ass, or a pig or a goat, if it belong to a god or to the court, the thief shall pay thirtyfold therefore; if they belonged to a freed man of the king he shall pay tenfold; if the thief has nothing with which to pay he shall be put to death.

14. If anyone steal the minor son of another, he shall be put to death.

15. If anyone take a male or female slave of the court, or a male or female slave of a freed man, outside the city gates, he shall be put to death.

16. If anyone receive into his house a runaway male or female slave of the court, or of a freedman, and does not bring it out at the public proclamation of the major domus, the master of the house shall be put to death.

17. If anyone find runaway male or female slaves in the open country and bring them to their masters, the master of the slaves shall pay him two shekels of silver.

18. If such a slave will not name his owner, his captor shall bring him to the palace where he shall be examined as to his past and returned to his owner.

19. If the captor has secreted the slave in his house and afterward it happens that the slave has been caught in his possession, he shall be put to death.

20. If the slave has fled from the hands of his captor, the latter shall swear to the owner of the slave and he shall be free from blame.

21. If anyone break a hole into a house (break in to steal), he shall be put to death before that hole and be buried.

22. If anyone is committing a robbery and is caught, then he shall be put to death.

23. If the robber is not caught, then he who was robbed shall claim under oath the amount of his loss; then the community shall...compensate him for the goods stolen.

24. If a life has been lost, the city or district magistrate shall pay one mina of silver to the deceased's relatives.

25. If fire break out in a house, and some one who comes to put it out cast his eye upon the property of the owner of the house, and take the property of the master of the house, he shall be thrown into that same fire.

26. If a chieftain or a man (common soldier), who has been ordered to go upon the king's highway for war does not go, but hires a mercenary, if he withholds the compensation, then shall this officer or man be put to death, and he who represented him shall take possession of his house.

27. If a chieftain or man be captured in battle, and if his fields and garden be given to another and he take possession, if he return and reaches his place, his field and garden shall be returned to him.

42. If anyone take over a field to till it, and obtain no harvest therefrom, it must be proved that he did no work on the field, and he must deliver grain, just as his neighbor raised, to the owner of the field.

43. If he did not till the field, but let it lie fallow, he shall give grain like his neighbor's to the owner of the field, and the field which he let lie fallow he must plow and sow and return to its owner.

44. If anyone take over a field lying in waste to make it arable, but is lazy, and does not make it arable, he shall plow the fallow field in the fourth year, harrow it and till it, and give it back to its owner, and for each ten gan (a measure of area) ten gur of grain shall be paid.

45. If a man rent his field for tillage for a fixed rental, and receive

the rent of his field, but bad weather come and destroy the harvest, the injury falls upon the tiller of the soil.

46. If he [the owner] does not receive a fixed rental for his field, but rents it on half or third shares of the harvest, the grain on the field shall be divided proportionately between the tiller and the owner.

47. If the tiller, because he did not succeed in the first year, has had the soil tilled by others, the owner may raise no objection; the field has been cultivated and he receives the harvest according to agreement.

48. If anyone owe a debt for a loan, and a storm destroys the grain, or the harvest fails, or the grain does not grow for lack of water; in that year he need not give his creditor any grain, he washes his debt tablet in water and pays no rent for this year.

53. If anyone be too lazy to keep his dam [irrigation ditch] in proper condition, and does not so keep it; if then the dam breaks and all the fields be flooded, then he whose dam broke shall be sold for money, and the money shall replace the corn which he has caused to be ruined.

54. If he be not able to replace the corn, then he and his possessions shall be divided among the farmers whose corn he has flooded.

55. If anyone opens his ditches to water his crop, but is careless, and the water floods the field of his neighbor, then he shall pay his neighbor corn for his loss.

57. If a shepherd, without the permission of the owner of the field, and without the knowledge of the owner of the sheep, lets the sheep into a field to graze, then the owner of the field shall harvest his crop, and the shepherd, who had pastured his flock there without permission of the owner of the field, shall pay to the owner twenty gur of corn for every ten gan.

108. If a tavern keeper (female) does not accept corn according to gross weight in payment of drink, but takes money, and the price of the drink is less than that of the corn, she shall be convicted and thrown into the water.

109. If conspirators meet in the house of a tavern keeper, and these conspirators are not captured and delivered to the court, the tavern keeper shall be put to death.

117. If anyone fail to meet a claim for debt, and sell himself, his wife, his son, and daughter for money or give them away to forced labor: they shall work for three years in the house of the man who bought them, or the proprietor, and in the fourth year they shall be set free.

118. If he give a male or female slave away for forced labor, and the merchant sublease them, or sell them for money, no objection can be raised.

119. If anyone fail to meet a claim for debt, and he sell the maid servant who has borne him children for money, the money which the merchant has paid shall be repaid to him by the owner of the slave and she shall be freed.

128. If a man take a woman to wife, but have no intercourse with her, this woman is no wife to him.

129. If a man's wife be surprised (in flagrante delicto) with another man, both shall be tied and thrown into the water, but the husband may pardon his wife and the king his slaves.

130. If a man violate the wife (betrothed or child-wife) of another man, who has never known a man, and still lives in her father's house, and sleep with her and be surprised, this man shall be put to death, but the wife is blameless.

131. If a man bring a charge against one's wife, but she is not surprised with another man, she must take an oath and then may return to her house.

132. If the "finger is pointed" at a man's wife about another man, but she is not caught sleeping with the other man, she shall jump into the river for her husband.

133. If a man has been taken captive, and his house was maintained for his wife [by his family], but his wife has left his house and entered into another man's house; because that woman has not preserved her body and has entered into the house of another, that woman shall be prosecuted and shall be drowned.

134. If a man has been taken captive, but his house was not maintained for his wife, and his wife has entered the house of another, that woman has no blame.

135. If a man has been taken captive, but his house was not maintained for his wife, and she has entered into the house of another, and has borne him children, if in the future her first husband shall return, that woman shall return to her first husband, but the children shall follow their own father.

136. If anyone leave his house, run away, and then his wife go to another house, if then he return, and wishes to take his wife back: because he fled from his home and ran away, the wife of this runaway shall not return to her husband.

137. If a man wish to separate from a woman who has borne him children, or from his wife who has borne him children: then he shall give that wife her dowry, and a part of the usufruct of field, garden, and property, so that she can rear her children. When she has brought up her children, a portion of all that is given to the children, equal as that of one son, shall be given to her. She may then marry the man of her heart.

138. If a man wishes to separate from his wife who has borne him no children, he shall give her the amount of her purchase money and the dowry which she brought from her father's house, and let her go.

141. If a man's wife, who lives in his house, wishes to leave it, plunges into debt, tries to ruin her house, neglects her husband, and is judicially convicted: if her husband offer her release, she may go on her way, and he gives her nothing as a gift of release. If her husband does not wish to release her, and if he take another wife, she shall remain as servant in her husband's house.

142. If a woman quarrel with her husband, and say: "You are not congenial to me," the reasons for her prejudice must be presented. If she is guiltless, and there is no fault on her part, but he leaves and neglects her, then no guilt attaches to this woman, she shall take her dowry and go back to her father's house.

143. If she is not innocent, but leaves her husband, and ruins

her house, neglecting her husband, this woman shall be cast into the water.

144. If a man take a wife and this woman give her husband a maidservant, and she bear him children, but this man wishes to take another wife, this shall not be permitted to him; he shall not take a second wife.

145. If a man take a wife, and she bear him no children, and he intend to take another wife: if he take this second wife, and bring her into the house, this second wife shall not be allowed equality with his wife.

146. If a man take a wife and she give this man a maidservant as wife and she bear him children, and then this maid assume equality with the wife: because she has borne him children her master shall not sell her for money, but he may keep her as a slave, reckoning her among the maidservants.

147. If she have not borne him children, then her mistress may sell her for money.

148. If a man take a wife, and she be seized by disease, if he then desire to take a second wife he shall not put away his wife, who has been attacked by disease, but he shall keep her in the house which he has built and support her so long as she lives.

149. If this woman does not wish to remain in her husband's house, then he shall compensate her for the dowry that she brought with her from her father's house, and she may go.

154. If a man be guilty of incest with his daughter, he shall be driven from the place (exiled).

155. If a man betroth a girl to his son, and his son have intercourse with her, but he (the father) afterward defile her, and be surprised, then he shall be bound and cast into the water (drowned).

156. If a man betroth a girl to his son, but his son has not known her, and if then he defile her, he shall pay her half a gold mina, and compensate her for all that she brought out of her father's house. She may marry the man of her heart.

157. If anyone be guilty of incest with his mother after his father, both shall be burned.

159. If a man, who has presented a gift to the house of his prospective father-in-law and has given the bride-price, has afterward looked upon another woman and has said to his father-in-law, "I will not marry your daughter;" the father of the girl shall keep whatever he has brought as a present.

160. If a man has presented a gift to the house of his prospective father-in-law, and has given the bride-price, but the father of the girl has said, "I will not give you my daughter," the father shall return double all that was presented him.

161. If a man has brought a gift to the house of his prospective father-in-law, and has given the bride-price, but his comrade has slandered him and his father-in-law has said to the suitor, "You shall not marry my daughter," [the father] shall return double all that was presented him. Further, the comrade shall not marry the girl.

162. If a man has married a wife, and she has borne him children, and that woman has gone to her fate, her father shall lay no claim to her dowry. Her dowry is her children's only.

163. If a man has married a wife, and she has not borne him children, and that woman has gone to her fate; if his father-in-law has returned to him the bride-price, which that man brought into the house of his father-in-law, her husband shall have no claim on the dowry of that woman. Her dowry belongs to her father's house.

164. If the father-in-law has not returned the bride-price, the husband shall deduct the amount of her bride-price from her dowry, and shall return her dowry to her father's house.

165. If a man has presented a field, garden, or house to his son, the first in his eyes, and has written him a deed of gift; after the father has gone to his fate, when the brothers share, he shall keep the present his father gave him, and over and above shall share equally with them in the goods of his father's estate.

166. If a man has taken wives for the other sons be had, but has not taken a wife for his young son, after the father has gone to his

16

fate, when the brothers share, they shall set aside from the goods of their father's estate money, as a bride-price, for their younger brother, who has not married a wife, over and above his share, and they shall cause him to take a wife.

167. If a man has taken a wife, and she has borne him children and that woman has gone to her fate, and he has taken a second wife, and she also has borne children; after the father has gone to his fate, the sons shall not share according to mothers, but each family shall take the dowry of its mother, and all shall share the goods of their father's estate equally,

168. If a man has determined to disinherit his son and has declared before the judge, "I cut off my son," the judge shall inquire into the son's past, and, if the son has not committed a grave misdemeanor such as should cut him off from sonship, the father shall not disinherit his son.

169. If he has committed a grave crime against his father, which cuts off from sonship, for the first offense he shall pardon him. If he has committed a grave crime a second time, the father shall cut off his son from sonship.

170. If man has had children borne to him by his wife, and also by a maid, if the father in his lifetime has said, "My sons," to the children his maid bore him, and has reckoned them with the sons of his wife; then after the father has gone to his fate, the children of the wife and of the maid shall share equally. The children of the wife shall apportion the shares and make their own selections.

171. And if the father, in his lifetime, has not said, "My sons," to the children whom the maid bore him, after the father has gone to his fate, the children of the maid shall not share with the children of the wife in the goods of their father's house. The maid and her children, however, shall obtain their freedom. The children of the wife have no claim for service on the children of the maid.

The wife shall take her dowry, and any gift that her husband has given her and for which he has written a deed of gift and she shall dwell in her husband's house as long as she lives, she shall enjoy it, she shall not sell it. After her death it is her children's.

172. If her husband has not given her a gift, her dowry shall be given her in full, and, from the goods of her husband's estate, she shall take a share equal to that of one son.

If her children have persecuted her in order to have her leave the house, and the judge has inquired into her past, and laid the blame on the children, that woman shall not leave her husband's house. If that woman has determined to leave, she shall relinquish to her children the gift her husband gave her, she shall take the dowry of her father's estate, and the husband of her choice may marry her.

183. If a man give his daughter by a concubine a dowry, and a husband, and a deed; if then her father die, she shall receive no portion from the paternal estate.

184. If a man does not give a dowry to his daughter by a concubine, and no husband; if then her father die, her brother shall give her a dowry according to her father's wealth and secure a husband for her.

188. If an artisan has undertaken to rear a child and teaches him his craft, he can not be demanded back.

189. If he has not taught him his craft, this adopted son may return to his father's house.

194. If a man give his child to a nurse and the child die in her hands, but the nurse unbeknown to the father and mother nurse another child, then they shall convict her of having nursed another child without the knowledge of the father and mother and her breasts shall be cut off.

195. If a son strike his father, his hands shall be hewn off.

196. If a man put out the eye of another man, his eye shall be put out. [An eye for an eye]

197. If he break another man's bone, his bone shall be broken.

198. If he put out the eye of a freed man, or break the bone of a freed man, he shall pay one gold mina.

199. If he put out the eye of a man's slave, or break the bone of a man's slave, he shall pay one-half of its value.

200. If a man knock out the teeth of his equal, his teeth shall be knocked out. [A tooth for a tooth]

201. If he knock out the teeth of a freed man, he shall pay one-third of a gold mina.

202. If anyone strike the body of a man higher in rank than he, he shall receive sixty blows with an ox whip in public.

203. If a free-born man strike the body of another free-born man or equal rank, he shall pay one gold mina.

204. If a freed man strike the body of another freed man, he shall pay ten shekels in money.

205. If the slave of a freed man strike the body of a freed man, his ear shall be cut off.

206. If during a quarrel one man strike another and wound him, then he shall swear, "I did not injure him wittingly," and pay the physicians.

207. If the man die of his wound, he shall swear similarly, and if he (the deceased) was a free-born man, he shall pay half a mina in money.

208. If he was a freed man, he shall pay one-third of a mina.

209. If a man strike a free-born woman so that she lose her unborn child, he shall pay ten shekels for her loss.

210. If the woman die, his daughter shall be put to death.

211. If a woman of the free class lose her child by a blow, he shall pay five shekels in money.

212. If this woman die, he shall pay half a mina.

213. If he strike the maidservant of a man, and she lose her child, he shall pay two shekels in money.

214. If this maidservant die, he shall pay one-third of a mina.

215. If a physician make a large incision with an operating knife and cure it, or if he open a tumor (over the eye) with an operating knife, and saves the eye, he shall receive ten shekels in money.

216. If the patient be a freed man, he receives five shekels.

217. If he be the slave of some one, his owner shall give the physician two shekels.

218. If a physician make a large incision with the operating knife, and kill him, or open a tumor with the operating knife, and cut out the eye, his hands shall be cut off.

219. If a physician make a large incision in the slave of a freed man, and kill him, he shall replace the slave with another slave.

220. If he had opened a tumor with the operating knife, and put out his eye, he shall pay half his value.

221. If a physician heal the broken bone or diseased soft part of a man, the patient shall pay the physician five shekels in money.

222. If he were a freed man he shall pay three shekels.

223. If he were a slave his owner shall pay the physician two shekels.

224. If a veterinary surgeon perform a serious operation on an ass or an ox, and cure it, the owner shall pay the surgeon one-sixth of a shekel as a fee.

225. If he perform a serious operation on an ass or ox, and kill it, he shall pay the owner one-fourth of its value.

228. If a builder build a house for some one and complete it, he shall give him a fee of two shekels in money for each sar of surface.

229 If a builder build a house for some one, and does not construct it properly, and the house which he built fall in and kill its owner, then that builder shall be put to death.

230. If it kill the son of the owner the son of that builder shall be put to death.

231. If it kill a slave of the owner, then he shall pay slave for slave to the owner of the house.

232. If it ruin goods, he shall make compensation for all that has been ruined, and inasmuch as he did not construct properly this house which he built and it fell, he shall re-erect the house from his own means.

233. If a builder build a house for some one, even though he has not yet completed it; if then the walls seem toppling, the builder must make the walls solid from his own means.

282. If a slave say to his master: "You are not my master," if they convict him his master shall cut off his ear.

2. Book of Genesis

The first five books of the Old Testament, or Hebrew Scripture, form the Torah, the story of the establishment of God's Law and the Covenant between God and his chosen people. It was probably written in the twelfth century B.C.E. *The laws of the Torah came to be known as Mosaic Law.*

The first chapters of Genesis describe the creation of the world and tell the story of Adam and Eve.

In the beginning God created the heaven and the earth. And the earth was without form, and void; and darkness was upon the face of the deep. And the Spirit of God moved upon the face of the waters.

God said, "Let there be light;" and there was light. God saw the light, that it was good; and God divided the light from the darkness. And God called the light Day, and the darkness he called Night. And the evening and the morning were the first day.

Then God said, "Let there be a firmament in the midst of the waters, and let it divide the waters from the waters." So God made the firmament, and divided the waters which were under the firmament from the waters which were above the firmament; and it was so. God called the firmament Heaven. And the evening and the morning were the second day.

And God said, "Let the waters under the heaven be gathered together in one place, and let the dry land appear;" and it was so. And God called the dry land Earth; and the gathering together of the waters Seas; and God saw that it was good. And God said, "Let the earth bring forth grass, the herb yielding seed, and the fruit tree yielding fruit after its kind, whose seed is in itself, upon the earth;" and it was so. And the earth brought forth grass, and herb yielding seed, and the tree yielding fruit after his kind, whose seed was in itself; and God saw that it was good. And the evening and the morning were the third day.

And God said, "Let there be lights in the firmament of the heaven to divide the day from the night; and let them be for signs, and for seasons, and for days, and years. And let them be for lights in the firmament of the heaven to give light upon the earth;" and it was so. And God made two great lights; the greater light to rule the day, and the lesser light to rule the night; he made the stars also. And God set them in the firmament of the heaven to give light upon the earth. And to rule over the day and over the night, and to divide the light from the darkness; and God saw that it was good. And the evening and the morning were the fourth day.

And God said, "Let the waters bring forth abundantly the moving creature that have life, and fowl that may fly above the earth in the open firmament of heaven." And God created great whales, and every living creature that moves, which the waters brought forth abundantly, after their kind, and every winged fowl after his kind; and God saw that it was good. And God blessed them, saying, "Be fruitful, and multiply, and fill the waters in the seas, and let fowl multiply on the earth." And the evening and the morning were the fifth day.

And God said, "Let the earth bring forth the living creature after his kind, cattle, and creeping thing, and beast of the earth after his kind;" and it was so. And God made the beast of the earth after his kind, and cattle after their kind, and every thing that creeps upon the earth after his kind; and God saw that it was good.

And God said, "Let us make man in our image, after our likeness; and let them have dominion over the fish of the sea, and over the fowl of the air, and over the cattle, and over all the earth, and over every creeping thing that creeps upon the earth."

So God created man in his own image, in the image of God he created him; male and female created he them.

And God blessed them, and God said to them, "Be fruitful, and multiply, and fill the earth, and subdue it; and have dominion over the fish of the sea, and over the fowl of the air, and over every living thing that moves upon the earth." And God said, Behold, "I have given you every herb bearing seed, which is upon the face of all the earth, and every tree, in the which is the fruit of a tree yielding seed; to you it shall be for meat. And to every beast of the earth, and to every fowl of the air, and to every thing that creeps upon the earth, wherein there is life, I have given every green herb for meat;" and it was so. And God saw every thing that he had made, and, behold, it was very good. And the evening and the morning were the sixth day.

Thus the heavens and the earth were finished, and all the host of them. And on the seventh day God ended his work which he had made; and he rested on the seventh day from all his work which he had made. And God blessed the seventh day, and sanctified it; because that on it he had rested from all his work which God created and made.

These are the generations of the heavens and of the earth when they were created, in the day that the Lord God made the earth and the heavens. And every plant of the field before it was in the earth, and every herb of the field before it grew; for the Lord God had not caused it to rain upon the earth, and there was not a man to till the ground. But there went up a mist from the earth, and watered the whole face of the ground. And the Lord God formed man of the dust of the ground, and breathed into his nostrils the breath of life; and man became a living soul. The Lord God planted a garden eastward in Eden; and there he put the man whom he had formed. And out of the ground made the Lord God to grow every tree that is pleasant to the sight, and good for food; the tree of life also in the midst of the garden, and the tree of knowledge of good and evil.

And the Lord God took the man, and put him into the garden

of Eden to dress it and to keep it. And the Lord God commanded the man, saying, "Of every tree of the garden you may freely eat. But of the tree of the knowledge of good and evil, you shall not eat of it; for in the day that you eat thereof you shall surely die."

And the Lord God said, "It is not good that the man should be alone; I will make a help mate for him."

And out of the ground the Lord God formed every beast of the field, and every fowl of the air; and brought them to Adam to see what he would call them; and whatever Adam called every living creature, that was the name thereof. And Adam gave names to all cattle, and to the fowl of the air, and to every beast of the field; but for Adam there was not found a help mate for him.

And the Lord God caused a deep sleep to fall upon Adam, and he slept; and he took one of his ribs, and closed up the flesh instead thereof. And the rib, which the Lord God had taken from man, he made a woman, and brought her to the man. And Adam said, "This is now bone of my bones, and flesh of my flesh; she shall be called Woman, because she was taken out of Man. Therefore shall a man leave his father and his mother, and shall cleave to his wife; and they shall be one flesh."

And they were both naked, the man and his wife, and were not ashamed.

Now the serpent was more subtle than any beast of the field which the Lord God had made. And he said to the woman, "Yea, has God said, 'You shall not eat of every tree of the garden?'" And the woman said to the serpent, "We may eat of the fruit of the trees of the garden. But of the fruit of the tree which is in the midst of the garden, God has said, 'You shall not eat of it, neither shall you touch it, less you die.'"

And the serpent said to the woman, "You shall not surely die. For God knows that in the day you eat thereof, then your eyes shall be opened, and you shall be as gods, knowing good and evil." And when the woman saw that the tree was good for food, and that it was pleasant to the eyes, and a tree to be desired to make one wise, she took of the fruit thereof, and did eat, and gave also to her husband with her; and he did eat. And the eyes of them both were opened, and they knew that they were naked; and they sewed fig leaves together, and made themselves aprons.

And they heard the voice of the Lord God walking in the garden in the cool of the day; and Adam and his wife hid themselves from the presence of the Lord God among the trees of the garden. And the Lord God called to Adam, and said to him, "Where are you?" And he said, "I heard your voice in the garden, and I was afraid, because I was naked; and I hid myself." And he said, "Who told you that you were naked? Have you eaten of the tree, whereof I commanded you that you should not eat?" And the man said, "The woman whom you gave to be with me, she gave me of the tree, and I did eat." And the Lord God said to the woman, "What is this that you have done?" And the woman said, "The serpent beguiled me, and I ate."

And the Lord God said to the serpent, "Because you have done this, you are cursed above all cattle, and above every beast of the field; upon your belly shall you go, and dust shall you eat all the days of your life. And I will put enmity between you and the woman, and between your seed and her seed; it shall bruise your head, and you shall bruise his heel."

To the woman he said, "I will greatly multiply your sorrow and your conception; in sorrow you shall bring forth children; and your desire shall be to your husband, and he shall rule over you."

And to Adam he said, "Because you have hearkened to the voice of your wife, and have eaten of the tree, of which I commanded you, saying, 'You shall not eat of it;' cursed is the ground for your sake; in sorrow shall you eat of it all the days of your life. Thorns also and thistles shall it bring forth to you; and you shall eat the herb of the field. In the sweat of your face shall you eat bread, until you return to the ground; for out of it were you taken; for dust you are, and to dust shall you return."

3. Book of Exodus

Exodus, the second book of the Torah, is the narrative of the Jews' liberation from Egypt and its aftermath. In this passage God delivers the essence of his Law, the Ten Commandments, and then elaborates at some length on how the law is to be applied in specific situations. The Jews were to become God's chosen people by virtue of their adherence to the law.

And God spoke all these words, saying, "I am the Lord your God, who has brought you out of the land of Egypt, out of the house of bondage. You shall have no other gods before me. You shall not make for yourself any graven image, or any likeness of any thing that is in heaven above, or that is in the earth beneath, or that is in the water under the earth. You shall not bow down to them, nor serve them; for I the Lord your God am a jealous God, visiting the iniquity of the fathers upon the children into the third and fourth generation of those that hate me; and showing mercy to thousands of those that love me, and keep my commandments.

"You shall not take the name of the Lord your God in vain; for the Lord will not hold him guiltless that takes his name in vain.

"Remember the Sabbath day, to keep it holy. Six days shall you labor, and do all your work; but the seventh day is the Sabbath of the Lord your God; in it you shall not do any work, you, nor your son, nor your daughter, your manservant, nor your maidservant, nor your cattle, nor your stranger that is within your gates; for in six days the Lord made heaven and earth, the sea, and all that is in them, and rested the seventh day; therefore the Lord blessed the Sabbath day, and hallowed it.

"Honor your father and your mother; that your days may be long upon the land which the Lord your God gives you.

"You shall not kill.

"You shall not commit adultery.

"You shall not steal.

"You shall not bear false witness against your neighbor.

"You shall not covet your neighbor's house, you shall not covet your neighbor's wife, nor his manservant, nor his maidservant, nor his ox, nor his ass, nor any thing that is your neighbor's."

And all the people saw the thunderings, and the lightnings, and the noise of the trumpet and the mountain smoking; and when the people saw it, they went away, and stood afar off. And they said to Moses, "Speak you with us, and we will hear; but let not God speak with us, less we die." And Moses said to the people, "Fear not; for God is come to test you, and that his fear may be before your faces, that you sin not." And the people stood afar off, and Moses drew near the thick darkness where God was.

And the Lord said to Moses, "Thus you shall say to the children of Israel, 'You have seen that I have talked with you from heaven. You shall not make gods of silver, neither shall you make gods of gold. An altar of earth you shall make for me, and shall sacrifice there your burnt offerings, and your peace offerings, your sheep, and your oxen; in all places where I record my name I will come to you, and I will bless you. And if you will make me an altar of stone, you shall not build it of hewn stone; for if you lift up your tool upon it, you have polluted it. Neither shall you go up by steps to my altar, that your nakedness be not discovered.'

"Now these are the judgments which you shall set before them. If you buy a Hebrew servant, six years he shall serve; and in the seventh he shall go out free for nothing. If he came in by himself, he shall go out by himself; if he was married, then his wife shall go out with him. If his master has given him a wife, and she has born him sons or daughters; the wife and her children shall be her master's, and he shall go out by himself. And if the servant shall plainly say, 'I love my master, my wife, and my children; I will not go out free;' Then his master shall bring him before the judges; he shall also bring him to the door, or to the door post; and his master shall bore his ear through with an awl; and he shall serve him forever.

"And if a man sells his daughter to be a maidservant, she shall not go out as the menservants do. If she pleases not her master, who has betrothed her to himself, then shall he let her be redeemed; to sell her to a strange nation he shall have no power, seeing he has dealt deceitfully with her. And if he have betrothed her to his son, he shall deal with her after the manner of daughters. If he takes another wife; her food, her raiment, and her duty of marriage, shall he not diminish. And if he does not these three things for her, then shall she go out free without money.

"He that strikes a man, so that he dies, shall be surely put to death. And if a man lie not in wait, but God delivers him into his hand; then I will appoint you a place where he shall flee. But if a man comes presumptuously upon his neighbor, to slay him with deceit; you shall take him from my altar, that he may die. And he that strikes his father, or his mother, shall be surely put to death.

"And he that steals a man, and sells him, or if he be found in his hand, he shall surely be put to death.

"And he that curses his father, or his mother, shall surely be put to death.

"And if men engage in strife, and one strikes another with a stone, or with his fist, and he does not die, but keeps his bed; if he rises again, and walks abroad upon his staff, then shall he that struck him be acquitted; only he shall pay for the loss of his time, and shall cause him to be thoroughly healed.

"And if a man strikes his servant, or his maid, with a rod, and he dies under his hand; he shall be surely punished. But if he lives a day or two, he shall not be punished; for he is his property.

"If men strive, and hurt a woman with child, so that her fruit depart from her, and yet no injury follow; he shall be surely punished, according as the woman's husband will lay upon him; and he shall pay as the judges determine. And if any injury follows, then you shall give life for life, eye for eye, tooth for tooth, hand for hand, foot for foot, burning for burning, wound for wound, stripe for stripe.

"And if a man strike the eye of his servant, or the eye of his maid so that it perishes; he shall let him go free for his eye's sake. And if he strikes out his manservant's tooth, or his maidservant's tooth; he shall let him go free for his tooth's sake.

"If an ox gore a man or a woman, that they die; then the ox shall be surely stoned, and his flesh shall not be eaten; but the owner of the ox shall be acquitted. But if the ox were inclined to push with his horn in times past, and it has been testified to his owner, and he has not kept him in, but now that he has killed a man or a woman; the ox shall be stoned, and his owner also shall be put to death. If there be laid on him a sum of money, then he shall give for the ransom of his life whatever is laid upon him. Whether he has gored a son, or has gored a daughter, according to this judgment shall it be done to him. If the ox shall push a manservant or a maidservant; he shall give to their master thirty shekels of silver, and the ox shall be stoned.

"And if a man opens a pit, or if a man digs a pit, and does not cover it, and an ox or an ass falls in; the owner of the pit shall make it good, and give money to the owner and the dead beast shall be his.

"And if one man's ox hurts another's so much so that the ox dies; then they shall sell the live ox, and divide the money of it; and the dead ox also they shall also divide. Or if it be known that the ox used to push in times past, and his owner has not kept him in; he shall surely pay ox for ox; and the dead shall be his own.

"If a man shall steal an ox, or a sheep, and kill it, or sell it; he shall restore five oxen for an ox, and four sheep for a sheep....

"And if a man entice a maid that is not betrothed, and lie with her, he shall surely endow her to be his wife. If her father utterly refuses to give her to him, he shall pay money according to the dowry of virgins.

"Whosoever lies with a beast shall surely be put to death.

"He that sacrifices to any god, save the Lord only, he shall be utterly destroyed. You shall neither molest nor oppress a stranger, for you were strangers in the land of Egypt.

"You shall not afflict any widow, or fatherless child. If you afflict them in any manner, and they cry to me, I will surely hear their cry; and my wrath shall be hot, and I will kill you with the sword; and your wives shall be widows, and your children fatherless.

"If you lend money to any of my people that is poor by you, you shall not be to him as an usurer, neither shall you lay upon him usury. If you at all take your neighbor's clothing as pledge, you shall deliver it to him by the time the sun goes down; for that is his covering only, it is his clothing for his skin; wherein shall he sleep? And it shall come to pass, when he cries to me, that I will hear; for I am gracious.

"You shall not revile the gods, nor curse the ruler of your people.

"You shall not delay to offer the first of your ripe fruits, and of your liquors; the firstborn of your sons shall you give to me. Likewise shall you do with your oxen, and with your sheep; seven days it shall be with his mother; on the eighth day you shall give it me.

"And you shall be holy men for me; neither shall you eat any flesh that is torn of beasts in the field; you shall cast it to the dogs.

"You shall not raise a false report; put not your hand with the wicked to be an unrighteous witness. You shall not follow a multitude to do evil....

"If you meet your enemy's ox or his ass going astray, you shall surely bring it back to him again. If you see the ass of him that hates you lying under his burden, and would rather avoid helping him, you shall surely help with him....

"And six years you shall sow your land, and shall gather in the fruits thereof; but the seventh year you shall let it rest and lie still; that the poor of your people may eat; and what they leave the beasts of the field shall eat. In like manner you shall deal with your vineyard, and with your olive yard."

4. *Book of Deuteronomy*

Deuteronomy, the fifth and final book of the Torah, is a reca-pitulation and explanation of the law God gave to his chosen peo-ple through Moses. Some consider Deuteronomy Moses' last testament to the people he had led into the Promised Land.

This selection defines the terms of the covenant between God and his chosen people, including the rewards and sanctions they as a people will experience depending on whether they adhere to the law.

"This day the Lord your God has commanded you to do these statutes and ordinances; you shall therefore be careful to do them with all your heart and with all your soul. You have declared this day the Lord to be your God and that you will walk in his ways, and to keep his statutes, and his commandments, and his ordi-nances, and will obey his voice; and the Lord has declared this day that you be his own people, as he has promised you, and that you should keep all his commandments; and that he will make you high above all nations which he has made, in praise, in name, and in honor; and that you may be a holy people unto the Lord your God, as he has spoken."

Now Moses with the elders of Israel commanded the people, saying, "Keep all the commandments which I command you this day. And on the day when you pass over the Jordan into the land which the Lord your God gives you, you shall set up great stones and plaster them with plaster; and you shall write upon them all the words of this law, when you pass over to enter the land which the Lord your God gives you, a land that flows with milk and honey, as the Lord God of your fathers has promised you. Therefore it shall be when you have gone over the Jordan, that you shall set up these stones, which I command you this day, in mount Ebal, and you shall plaster them with plaster. And there shall you build an altar to the Lord your God, an altar of stones; you shall not lift up any iron tool to them. You shall build the altar of the Lord your God of whole stones; and you shall offer burnt offerings on it to the Lord your God. And you shall offer peace offerings, and shall eat there, and rejoice before the Lord your God. And you shall write upon the stones all the words of this law very plainly."

And Moses and the priests of the Levites spoke to all Israel, saying, "Take heed, and hearken, O Israel; this day you have become the people of the Lord your God. You shall therefore obey the voice of the Lord your God, and do his commandments and his statutes, which I command you this day."

And Moses charged the people the same day, saying, "These shall stand upon mount Gerizim to bless the people, when you have come over the Jordan: Simeon, Levi, Judah, Issachar, Joseph, and Benjamin. And these shall stand upon mount Ebal for the curse: Reuben, Gad, and Asher, and Zebulun, Dan, and Naphtali. And the Levites shall speak, and say to all the men of Israel with a loud voice:

"Cursed be the man who makes any graven or molten image, an abomination to the Lord, a thing made by the hands of craftsmen, and sets it up in a secret place." And all the people shall answer and say, "Amen."

"Cursed be he who dishonors his father or his mother." And all the people shall say, "Amen."

"Cursed be he who removes his neighbor's landmark." And all the people shall say, "Amen."

"Cursed be he who makes the blind move out of the way." And all the people shall say, "Amen."

"Cursed be he who perverts the judgment of the stranger, fatherless, and widow." And all the people shall say, "Amen."

"Cursed be he who lies with his father's wife; because he has uncovered her who is his father's." And all the people shall say, "Amen."

"Cursed be he who lies with any manner of beast." And all the people shall say, "Amen."

"Cursed be he who lies with his sister, the daughter of his father, or the daughter of his mother." And all the people shall say, "Amen."

"Cursed be he who lies with his mother-in-law." And all the people shall say, "Amen."

"Cursed be he who slays his neighbor secretly." And all the people shall say, "Amen."

"Cursed be he who takes a reward for slaying an innocent person." And all the people shall say, "Amen."

"Cursed be he who does not confirm all the words of this law by doing them." And all the people shall say, "Amen."

"And it shall come to pass, if you shall listen diligently to the voice of the Lord your God and observe and do all his commandments which I command you this day, that the Lord your God will set you on high above all the nations of the earth." And all these blessings shall come on you, and overwhelm you, if you just listen to the voice of the Lord your God. Blessed shall you be in the city, and blessed shall you be in the field. Blessed shall be the fruit of your body, and the fruit of your ground, and the fruit of your beasts, the increase of your cattle, and the flocks of your sheep. Blessed shall be your basket and your store. Blessed shall you be when you come in, and blessed shall you be when you go out.

The Lord shall cause your enemies that rise up against you to be defeated before your face; they shall come out against you one way, and flee before you seven ways. The Lord shall command the blessing upon you in your storehouses, and in all that you set your hand to do, and he shall bless you in the land which the Lord your God gave you. The Lord shall establish you as a holy people to himself, as he has sworn to you, if you shall keep the commandments of the Lord your God and walk in his ways. And all people of the earth shall see that you are called by the name of the Lord, and they shall be afraid of you. And the Lord shall make you plentiful in goods, in the fruit of your body, and in the fruit of your beasts, and in the fruit of your ground, in the land which the Lord swore to your fathers to give you. The Lord shall open to you his good treasure, the heaven to give rain to your land in his season, and to bless all the work of your hand; and you shall lend to many nations, and you shall not borrow. And the Lord shall make you the head, and not the tail; and you shall be above only, and you shall not be beneath; if only that you listen to the commandments of the Lord your God, which I command you this day, and observe and do them. And you must not go astray from any of the words which I command you this day, to the right hand, or to the left, or to go after other gods to serve them.

"But it shall come to pass, if you will not listen to the voice of the Lord your God, or observe or do all his commandments and his statutes which I command you this day, that all these curses shall come upon you, and overtake you: Cursed shall you be in the city, and cursed shall you be in the field. Cursed shall be your basket and your store. Cursed shall be the fruit of your body, and the fruit of your land, the increase of your cattle, and the flocks of your sheep. Cursed shall you be when you come in, and cursed shall you be when you go out.

"The Lord shall send upon you cursing, vexation, and rebuke, in all that you set your hand to do, until you are destroyed, and until you perish quickly; because of the wickedness of your doings, whereby you have forsaken me. The Lord shall make pestilence cling to you until he has consumed you and stricken you from the land no matter where you go. The Lord shall strike you with a consumption and a fever and an inflammation and an extreme burning, and with the sword, and with blasting, and with mildew; and you shall be pursued until you perish. And the sky that is over your head shall be brass, and the earth that is under you shall be iron. The Lord shall make the rain that comes down from heaven upon your land powder and dust until you are destroyed.

"The Lord shall cause you to be defeated before your enemies; you shall go out one way against them, and flee seven ways before them, and shall be removed from all the kingdoms of the earth. And your dead body shall be meat for all birds of the air and the beasts of the earth, and no one will frighten them away. The Lord will stricken you with the boils of Egypt, and with the ulcers, and with the scab, and with the itch, from which you cannot be healed. The Lord shall smite you with madness, and blindness, and confusion of mind; and you shall grope at noonday, as the blind gropes in the darkness, and you shall not prosper in your ways; and you shall be oppressed and spoiled forever, and no man shall save you. You shall marry a wife, and another man shall lie with her; you shall build a house, and not dwell therein; you shall plant a vineyard, and not gather the grapes. Your ox shall be slain before your eyes, and you shall not eat it; your ass shall be violently taken away before your face, and shall not be restored to you; your sheep shall be given to your enemies, and you shall have none to rescue them. Your sons and your daughters shall be given to another people, and your eyes shall look, and fail with longing for them all the day long; and there shall be no might in your hand. The fruit of your land and all your labors shall be eaten up by a nation which you know not; and you shall be oppressed and crushed always. You shall be driven mad by the sight that your eyes shall see. The Lord shall smite you in the knees and in the legs with sore boils that cannot be healed, from the sole of your foot to the top of your head....

"If you are not careful to do all the words of this law that are written in this book, that you may fear this glorious and fearful name, 'the Lord Your God,' then the Lord will make your plagues great, and the plagues of your seed even greater and longer. Moreover he will bring upon you all the diseases of Egypt, which you were afraid of, and they shall cling to you. Also every sickness and every plague, which is not written in the book of this law, the Lord bring upon you until you are destroyed. And you shall be left few in number, whereas you were once as many as the stars of heaven; because you would not obey the voice of the Lord your God. And it shall come to pass that as the Lord rejoiced over you to do you good and to multiply you, so the Lord will rejoice over you to destroy you and to bring you to nought; and you shall be plucked from off the land wherever you go to possess it. And the Lord shall scatter you among all people, from the one end of the earth to the other; and there you shall serve other gods, which neither you nor your fathers have known, even wood and stone gods. And among these nations shall you shall find no rest, neither shall the sole of your foot have rest; but the Lord shall give you there a trembling heart, and failing of eyes, and sorrow of mind. And your life shall hang in doubt before you, and you shall fear day and night, and shall have no assurance of your life. In the morning you shall say, 'Would God that it were evening!' and in the evening you shall say, 'Would God that it were morning!'..."

These are the words of the covenant, which the Lord commanded Moses to make with the children of Israel in the land of Moab, beside the covenant which he made with them in Horeb.

And Moses called upon all Israel and said to them, "You have seen all that the Lord did before your eyes in the land of Egypt to Pharaoh, and to all his servants, and to all his land, the great trials which your eyes have seen, the signs, and those great miracles. Yet the Lord has not given you a heart to understand, and eyes to see, and ears to hear....Keep therefore the words of this covenant, and do them, that you may prosper in all that you do.

"You stand this day, all of you, before the Lord your God—your patriarchs of your tribes, your elders, and your leaders, with all the men of Israel, your little ones, your wives, and your strangers that are in your camp, from the hewer of your wood to the drawer of your water—that you should enter into a covenant with the Lord your God, and into his oath, which the Lord your God makes with you this day, so that he may establish you today as a people unto himself, and that he may be for you a God, as he has said to you, and as he has sworn to your fathers, to Abraham, to Isaac, and to

Jacob. Nor is it with you only that I do make this covenant and this oath, but with anyone who stands here with us this day before the Lord our God, and also with him who is not here with us this day....

"And it shall come to pass when all these things come upon you, the blessing and the curse which I have set before you, and you call them to mind when you are among all the nations wherever the Lord your God has driven you, and you return to the Lord your God commandments and obey his voice according to all that I command you this day, you and your children, with all your heart, and with all your soul, then the Lord your God will turn your captivity into rescue and have compassion upon you, and will return and gather you from all the nations, wherever the Lord your God has scattered you. If any of you be driven out to the outermost parts of heaven, from there will the Lord your God gather you and from there will he fetch you. And the Lord your God will bring you into the land which your fathers possessed, and you shall possess it; and he will do you good, and multiply you above your fathers. And the Lord your God will circumcise your heart, and the heart of your seed, to love the Lord your God with all your heart, and with all your soul, that you may live. And the Lord your God will put all these curses upon your enemies, and on them that hate you, which persecuted you. And you shall return and obey the voice of the Lord, and do all his commandments which I command you this day. And the Lord your God will make you plentiful in every work of your hand, in the fruit of your body, and in the fruit of your cattle, and in the fruit of your land, for good you do, for the Lord will again rejoice over you for good you do, as he rejoiced over your fathers, if you only listen to the voice of the Lord your God, and keep his commandments and his statutes which are written in this book of the law, and if you turn to the Lord your God with all your heart, and with all your soul.

"For this commandment which I command you this day is not hidden from you, neither is it far off. It is not in heaven, that you should say, 'Who shall go up for us to heaven and bring it to us, that we may hear it, and do it?' Neither is it beyond the sea, that you should say, 'Who shall go over the sea for us, and bring it to us, that we may hear it, and do it?' But the word is very near you, in your mouth, and in your heart, that you may do it.

"See, I have set before you this day life and good, and death and evil. I command you this day to love the Lord your God, to walk in his ways, and to keep his commandments and his statutes and his judgements, that you may live and multiply; and the Lord your God shall bless you in the land which you go to possess. But if your heart turn away, so that you will not hear the law, but shall be drawn away from it, and worship other gods, and serve them, I denounce you this day and you shall surely perish, and you shall not prolong your days on the land that you pass over the Jordan to possess. I call heaven and earth to record this day against you, that I have set before you life and death, blessing and cursing; therefore choose life, that both you and your seed may live, that you may love the Lord your God, and that you may obey his voice, and that you may cleave to him for he is your life and the length of your days, that you may dwell in the land which the Lord swore to your fathers, to Abraham, to Isaac, and to Jacob, to give them."

5. Sophocles, *Antigone*

*A*ntigone *was written by the Greek tragic playwright, Sophocles, in 441* B.C.E. *It embodies the classic conflict between divine
law and human law, and the nature of authority. The play also
raises questions about the position of women in ancient Greece. The
story itself was a familiar one to Greek audiences.*

Characters

ISMENE, daughter of Oedipus

ANTIGONE, daughter of Oedipus

CREON, King of Thebes

HAEMON, son of Creon

TEIRESIAS, a blind prophet

A SENTRY

A MESSENGER

EURYDICE, wife of Creon

CHORUS, of Theban elders

KING'S ATTENDANTS

QUEEN'S ATTENDANTS

A BOY leading Teiresias

SOLDIERS

*Scene: Before the Palace at Thebes. Enter Ismene from the central
door of the Palace. Antigone follows, anxious and urgent; she
closes the door carefully, and comes to join her sister.*

ANTIGONE: O sister! Ismene dear, dear sister Ismene!
You know how heavy the hand of god is upon us;
How we who are left must suffer for our father, Oedipus.
There is no pain, no sorrow, no suffering, no dishonor
We have not shared together, you and I.
And now there is something more. Have you heard this order,
This latest order that the King has proclaimed to the city?
Have you heard how our dearest are being treated like
enemies?

ISMENE: I have heard nothing about any of those we love,
Neither good nor evil—not, I mean, since the death
Of our two brothers, both fallen in a day.
The Argive army, I hear, was withdrawn last night.
I know no more to make me sad or glad.

ANTIGONE: I thought you did not. That's why I brought you out
here,
Where we can't be heard, to tell you something alone.

ISMENE: What is it, Antigone? Black news, I can see already.

ANTIGONE: O Ismene, what do you think? Our two dear broth-
ers...
Creon has given funeral honors to one,
And not to the other; nothing but shame and ignominy.
Eteocles has been buried, they tell me, in state,
With all honorable observances due to the dead.
But Polynices, just as unhappily fallen—the order
Says he is not to be buried, not to be mourned;
To be left unburied, unwept, a feast of flesh
For keen-eyed carrion birds. The noble Creon!
It is against you and me he has made this order.
Yes, against me. And soon he will be here himself

42

To make it plain to those that have not heard it,
And to enforce it. This is no idle threat;
The punishment for disobedience is death by stoning.
So now you know. And now is the time to show
Whether or not you are worthy of your high blood.

ISMENE: My poor Antigone, if this is really true,
What more can I do, or undo, to help you?

ANTIGONE: Will you help me? Will you do something with me?
Will you?

ISMENE: Help you do what, Antigone? What do you mean?

ANTIGONE: Would you help me lift the body...you and me?

ISMENE: You cannot mean...to bury him? Against the order?

ANTIGONE: Is he not my brother, and yours, whether you like it
Or not? I shall never desert him, never.

ISMENE: How could you dare, when Creon has expressly forbidden it?

ANTIGONE: He has no right to keep me from my own.

ISMENE: O sister, sister, do you forget how our father
Perished in shame and misery, his awful sin
Self-proved, blinded by his own self-mutilation?
And then his mother, his wife—for she was both—
Destroyed herself in a noose of her own making.
And now our brothers, both in a single day
Fallen in an awful exaction of death for death,
Blood for blood, each slain by the other's hand.
Now we two left; and what will be the end of us,
If we transgress the law and defy our king?
O think, Antigone; we are women; it is not for us
To fight against men; our rulers are stronger than we,
And we must obey in this, or in worse than this.
May the dead forgive me, I can do no other
But as I am commanded; to do more is madness.

ANTIGONE: No; then I will not ask you for your help.
   Nor would I thank you for it, if you gave it.
   Go your own way; I will bury my brother;
   And if I die for it, what happiness!
   Convicted of reverence—I shall be content
   To lie beside a brother whom I love.
   We have only a little time to please the living,
   But all eternity to love the dead.
   There I shall lie forever. Live, if you will;
   Live, and defy, the holiest laws of heaven.

ISMENE: I do not defy them; but I cannot act
   Against the state. I am not strong enough.

ANTIGONE: Let that be your excuse, then. I will go
   And heap a mound of earth over my brother.

ISMENE: I fear for you, Antigone; I fear—

ANTIGONE: You need not fear for me. Fear for yourself.

ISMENE: At least be secret. Do not breathe a word.
   I'll not betray your secret.

ANTIGONE: Publish it
   To all the world! Else I shall hate you more.

ISMENE: Your heart burns! Mine is frozen at the thought.

ANTIGONE: I know my duty, where true duty lies.

ISMENE: If you can do it; but you're bound to fail.

ANTIGONE: When I have tried and failed, I shall have failed.

ISMENE: No sense in starting on a hopeless task.

ANTIGONE: Oh, I shall hate you if you talk like that!
   And he will hate you, rightly. Leave me alone
   With my own madness. There is no punishment
   Can rob me of my honorable death.

ISMENE: Go then, if you are determined, to your folly.
   But remember that those who love you...love you still.

Ismene goes into the Palace. Antigone leaves the stage by a side exit.
  Enter the Chorus of Theban elders.

CHORUS:
  Hail the sun! the brightest of all that ever
  Dawned on the City of Seven Gates, City of Thebes!
  Hail the golden dawn over Circe's river
  Rising to speed the flight of the white invaders
  Homeward in full retreat!
  The army of Polynices was gathered against us,
  In angry dispute his voice was lifted against us,
  Like a ravening bird of prey he swooped around us
  With white wings flashing, with flying plumes,
  With armed hosts ranked in thousands.
  At the threshold of seven gates in a circle of blood
  His swords stood round us, his jaws were opened against us;
  But before he could taste our blood, or consume us
  He fled, fled with the roar of the dragon behind him,
  And thunder of war in his ears.
  The Father of Heaven abhors the proud tongue's boasting;
  He marked the oncoming torrent, the flashing stream
  Of their golden harness, the clash of their battle gear;
  He heard the invader cry Victory over our ramparts,
  And smote him with fire to the ground.
  Down to the ground from the crest of his hurricane
  onslaught
  He swung, with the fiery brands of his hate brought low:
  Each and all to their doom of destruction appointed
  By the god that fights for us.
  Seven invaders at seven gates, seven defenders
  Spoiled of their bronze for a tribute to Zeus; save two
  Luckless brothers in one fight matched together

45

And in one death laid low.
Great is the victory, great be the joy
In the city of Thebes, the city of chariots.
Now is the time to fill the temples
With glad thanksgiving for warfare ended;
Shake the ground with the night-long dances,
Bacchus afoot and delight abounding.
But see, the King comes here,
Creon, the son of Menoeceus,
Whom the gods have appointed for us
In our recent change of fortune.
What matter is it, I wonder,
That has led him to call us together
By his special proclamation?

The central door is opened, and Creon enters.

CREON: My councilors: now that the gods have brought our city
  Safe through a storm of trouble to tranquillity,
  I have called you especially out of all my people
  To conference together, knowing that you
  Were loyal subjects when King Laius reigned,
  And when King Oedipus so wisely ruled us,
  And again, upon his death, faithfully served
  His sons, until they in turn fell—both slayers, both slain,
  Both stained with brother-blood, dead in a day—
  And I, their next of kin, inherited
  The throne and kingdom which I now possess.
  No other touchstone can test the heart of a man,
  The temper of his mind and spirit, until he be tried
  in the practice of authority and rule.
  For my part, I have always held the view,
  And hold it still, that a king whose lips are sealed

46

By fear, unwilling to seek advice, is damned.
And no less damned is he who puts a friend
Above his country; I have no good word for him.
As god above is my witness, who sees all,
When I see any danger threatening my people,
Whatever it may be, I shall declare it.
No man who is his country's enemy
Shall call himself my friend. Of this I am sure—
Our country is our life; only when she
Rides safely, have we any friends at all.
Such is my policy for our commonweal.
In pursuance of this, I have made a proclamation
Concerning the sons of Oedipus, as follows:
Eteocles, who fell fighting in defense of the city,
Fighting gallantly, is to be honored with burial
And with all the rites due to the noble dead.
The other—you know whom I mean—his brother Polynices,
Who came back from exile intending to burn and destroy
His fatherland and the gods of his fatherland,
To drink the blood of his kin, to make them slaves—
He is to have no grave, no burial,
No mourning from anyone; it is forbidden.
He is to be left unburied, left to be eaten
By dogs and vultures, a horror for all to see.
I am determined that never, if I can help it,
Shall evil triumph over good. Alive
Or dead, the faithful servant of his country
Shall be rewarded.

CHORUS: Creon, son of Menoeceus,
  You have given your judgment for the friend and for the
  enemy.
  As for those that are dead, so for us who remain,
  Your will is law.

CREON: See then that it be kept.

CHORUS: My lord, some younger would be fitter for that task.

CREON: Watchers are already set over the corpse.

CHORUS: What other duty then remains for us?

CREON: Not to connive at any disobedience.

CHORUS: If there were any so mad as to ask for death—

CREON: Aye, that is the penalty. There is always someone
    Ready to be lured to ruin by hope of gain.

He turns to go. A Sentry enters from the side of the stage. Creon
    pauses at the Palace door.

SENTRY: My lord: if I am out of breath, it is not from haste.
    I have not been running. On the contrary, many a time
    I stopped to think and loitered on the way,
    Saying to myself 'Why hurry to your doom,
    Poor fool?' and then I said 'Hurry, you fool.
    If Creon hears this from another man,
    Your head's as good as off.' So here I am,
    As quick as my unwilling haste could bring me;
    In no great hurry, in fact. So now I am here...
    But I'll tell my story...though it may be nothing after all.
    And whatever I have to suffer, it can't be more
    Than what god wills, so I cling to that for my comfort

CREON: Good heavens, man, whatever is the matter?

SENTRY: To speak of myself first—I never did it, sir;
    Nor saw who did; no one can punish me for that.

CREON: You tell your story with a deal of artful precaution.
    It's evidently something strange.

SENTRY: It is.
    So strange, it's very difficult to tell.

CREON: Well, out with it, and let's be done with you.

SENTRY: It's this, sir. The corpse...someone has just
   Buried it and gone. Dry dust over the body
   They scattered, in the manner of holy burial.

CREON: What! Who dared to do it?

SENTRY: I don't know, sir.
   There was no sign of a pick, no scratch of a shovel;
   The ground was hard and dry—no trace of a wheel;
   Whoever it was has left no clues behind him.
   When the Sentry on the first watch showed it us,
   We were amazed. The corpse was covered from sight—
   Not with a proper grave—just a layer of earth—
   As it might be, the act of some pious passer-by.
   There were no tracks of an animal either, a dog
   Or anything that might have come and mauled the body.
   Of course we all started pitching in to each other,
   Accusing each other, and might have come to blows,
   With no one to stop us; for anyone might have done it,
   But it couldn't be proved against him, and all denied it.
   We were all ready to take hot iron in hand
   And go through fire and swear by god and heaven
   We hadn't done it, nor knew of anyone
   That could have thought of doing it, much less done it.
   Well, we could make nothing of it. Then one of our men
   Said something that made all our blood run cold—
   Something we could neither refuse to do, nor do,
   But at our own risk. What he said was 'This
   Must be reported to the King; we can't conceal it.'
   So it was agreed. We drew lots for it, and I,
   Such is my luck, was chosen. So here I am,
   As much against my will as yours, I'm sure;
   A bringer of bad news expects no welcome.

CHORUS: My lord, I fear—I feared it from the first—
   That this may prove to be an act of the gods.

CREON: Enough of that! Or I shall lose my patience.
Don't talk like an old fool, old though you be.
Blasphemy, to say the gods could give a thought
To carrion flesh! Held him in high esteem,
I suppose, and buried him like a benefactor—
A man who came to burn their temples down,
Ransack their holy shrines, their land, their laws?
Is that the sort of man you think gods love?
Not they. No. There's a party of malcontents
In the city, rebels against my word and law,
Shakers of heads in secret, impatient of rule;
They are the people, I see it well enough,
Who have bribed their instruments to do this thing.
Money! Money's the curse of man, none greater.
That's what wrecks cities, banishes men from home,
Tempts and deludes the most well-meaning soul,
Pointing out the way to infamy and shame.
Well, they shall pay for their success.

(To the Sentry)

See to it!
See to it, you! Upon my oath, I swear,
As Zeus is my god above: either you find
The perpetrator of this burial
And bring him here into my sight, or death—
No, not your mere death shall pay the reckoning,
But, for a living lesson against such infamy,
You shall be racked and tortured until you tell
The whole truth of this outrage; so you may learn
To seek your gain where gain is yours to get,
Not try to grasp it everywhere. In wickedness
You'll find more loss than profit.

SENTRY: May I say more?

CREON: No more; each word you say but stings me more.

SENTRY: Stings in your ears, sir, or in your deeper feelings?

CREON: Don't bandy words, fellow, about my feelings.

SENTRY: Though I offend your ears, sir, it is not I
  But he that's guilty that offends your soul.

CREON: Oh, born to argue, were you?

SENTRY: Maybe so;
  But still not guilty in this business.

CREON: Doubly so, if you have sold your soul for money.

SENTRY: To think that thinking men should think so wrongly!

CREON: Think what you will. But if you fail to find
  The doer of this deed, you'll learn one thing:
  Ill-gotten gain brings no one any good.

He goes into the Palace.

SENTRY: Well, heaven send they find him. But whether or no,
  They'll not find me again, that's sure. Once free,
  Who never thought to see another day,
  I'll thank my lucky stars, and keep away.

Exit.

CHORUS:
  Wonders are many on earth, and the greatest of these
  Is man, who rides the ocean and takes his way
  Through the deeps, through wind-swept valleys of perilous
    seas
  That surge and sway.
  He is master of ageless Earth, to his own will bending
  The immortal mother of gods by the sweat of his brow,
- As year succeeds to year, with toil unending

Of mule and plough.
He is lord of all things living; birds of the air,
Beasts of the field, all creatures of sea and land
He taketh, cunning to capture and ensnare
With sleight of hand;
Hunting the savage beast from the upland rocks,
Taming the mountain monarch in his lair,
Teaching the wild horse and the roaming ox
His yoke to bear.
The use of language, the wind-swift motion of brain
He learnt; found out the laws of living together
In cities, building him shelter against the rain
And wintry weather.
There is nothing beyond his power. His subtlety
Meets all chance, all danger conquers.
For every ill he has found its remedy,
Save only death.
O wondrous subtlety of man, that draws
To good or evil ways! Great honor is given
And power to him who upholds his country's laws
And the justice of heaven.
But be that, too rashly daring, walks in sin
In solitary pride to his life's end.
At door of mine shall never enter in
To call me friend.

(Severally, seeing some persons approach from a distance)

O gods! A wonder to see!
Surely it cannot be—
it is no other—
Antigone!
Unhappy maid—

Unhappy Oedipus' daughter; it is she they bring.
Can she have rashly disobeyed
The order of our King?

Enter the Sentry, bringing Antigone guarded by two more soldiers.

SENTRY: We've got her. Here's the woman that did the deed.
We found her in the act of burying him. Where's the King?
CHORUS: He is just coming out of the palace now.

Enter Creon.

CREON: What's this? What am I just in time to see?
SENTRY: My lord, an oath's a very dangerous thing.
Second thoughts may prove us liars. Not long since
I swore I wouldn't trust myself again
To face your threats; you gave me a drubbing the first time.
But there's no pleasure like an unexpected pleasure,
Not by a long way. And so I've come again,
Though against my solemn oath. And I've brought this lady,
Who's been caught in the act of setting that grave in order.
And no casting lots for it this time—the prize is mine
And no one else's. So take her; judge and convict her.
I'm free, I hope, and quit of the horrible business.
CREON: How did you find her? Where have you brought her
from?
SENTRY: She was burying the man with her own hands, and
that's the truth.
CREON: Are you in your senses? Do you know what you are say-
ing?
SENTRY: I saw her myself, burying the body of the man
Whom you said not to bury. Don't I speak plain?

53

CREON: How did she come to be seen and taken in the act?
SENTRY: It was this way.
    After I got back to the place,
    With all your threats and curses ringing my ears,
    We swept off all the earth that covered the body.
    And left it a sodden naked corpse again;
    Then sat up on the hill, on the windward side,
    Keeping clear of the stench of him, as far as we could;
    All of us keeping each other up to the mark,
    With pretty sharp speaking, not to be caught napping this
        time.
    So this went on some hours, until the flaming sun
    Was high in the top of the sky, and the heat was blazing.
    Suddenly a storm of dust, like a plague from heaven,
    Swept over the ground stripping the trees stark bare,
    Filling the sky; you had to shut your eyes
    To stand against it. When at last it stopped,
    There was the girl, screaming like an angry bird
    When it finds its nest left empty and little ones gone.
    Just like that she screamed, seeing the body
    Naked, crying and cursing the ones that had done it.
    Then she picks up the dry earth in her hands,
    And pouring out of a fine bronze urn she's brought
    She makes her offering three times to the dead.
    Soon as we saw it, down we came and caught her.
    She wasn't at all frightened. And so we charged her
    With what she'd done before, and this. She admitted it,
    I'm glad to say—though sorry too, in a way.
    It's good to save your own skin, but a pity
    To have to see another get into trouble,
    Whom you've no grudge against. However, I can't say
    I've ever valued anyone else's life
    More than my own and that's the honest truth.

CREON *(to Antigone)*: Well, what do you say—you, hiding your
head there: Do you admit, or do you deny the deed?

ANTIGONE: I do admit it. I do not deny it.

CREON *(to the Sentry)*: You—you may go. You are discharged
from blame.

Exit Sentry.

Now tell me, in as few words as you can,
Did you know the order forbidding such an act?

ANTIGONE: I knew it, naturally. It was plain enough.

CREON: And yet you dared to contravene it?

ANTIGONE: Yes.
That order did not come from god. Justice,
That dwells with the gods below, knows no such law.
I did not think your edicts strong enough
To overrule the unwritten, unalterable laws
Of god and heaven, you being only a man.
They are not of yesterday or today, but everlasting,
Though where they came from, none of us can tell.
Guilty of their transgression before god
I cannot be, for any man on earth.
I knew that I should have to die, of course,
With or without your order. If it be soon,
So much the better. Living in daily torment
As I do, who would not be glad to die?
This punishment will not be any pain
Only if I had let my mother's son
Lie there unburied, then I could not have borne it.
This I can bear. Does that seem foolish to you?
Or is it you that are foolish to judge me so?

CHORUS: She shows her father's stubborn spirit: foolish

Not to give way when everything's against her.

CREON: Ah, but you'll see. The over-obstinate spirit
Is sooner broken; as the strongest iron will snap
If over-tempered in the fire to brittleness.
A little halter is enough to break
The wildest horse. Proud thoughts do not sit well
Upon subordinates. This girl's proud spirit
Was first in evidence when she broke the law;
And now, to add insult to her injury,
She gloats over her deed. But, as I live,
She shall not flout my orders with impunity.
My sister's child—Aye, were she even nearer,
Nearest and dearest, she should not escape
Full punishment—she, and her sister too,
Her partner, doubtless, in this burying.
Let her be fetched! She was in the house just now;
I saw her, hardly in her right mind either.
Often the thoughts of those who plan dark deeds
Betray themselves before the deed is done.
The criminal who being caught still tries
To make a fair excuse, is damned indeed.

ANTIGONE: Now you have caught me, will you do more than
    kill me?

CREON: No, nothing more; that is all I could wish.

ANTIGONE: Why then delay? There is nothing that you can say
That I should wish to bear, as nothing I say
Can weigh with you. I have given my brother burial.
What greater honor could I wish? All
Would say that what I did was honorable,
But fear locks up their lips. To speak and act
Just as he likes is a king's prerogative.

CREON: You are wrong. None of my subjects thinks as you do.

ANTIGONE: Yes, sir, they do; but dare not tell you so.

CREON: And you are not only alone, but unashamed.

ANTIGONE: There is no shame in honoring my brother.

CREON: Was not his enemy, who died with him, your brother?

ANTIGONE: Yes, both were brothers, both of the same parents.

CREON: You honor one, and so insult the other.

ANTIGONE: He that is dead will not accuse me of that.

CREON: He will, if you honor him no more than the traitor.

ANTIGONE: It was not a slave, but his brother, that died with him.

CREON: Attacking his country, while the other defended it.

ANTIGONE: Even so, we have a duty to the dead.

CREON: Not to give equal honor to good and bad.

ANTIGONE: Who knows? In the country of the dead that may be the law.

CREON: An enemy can't be a friend, even when dead.

ANTIGONE: My way is to share my love, not share my hate.

CREON: Go then, and share your love among the dead.
We'll have no woman's law here, while I live.

Enter Ismene from the Palace.

CHORUS: Here comes Ismene, weeping
In sisterly sorrow; a darkened brow,
Flushed face, and the fair cheek marred with flooding rain.

CREON: You crawling viper! Lurking in my house
To suck my blood! Two traitors unbeknown
Plotting against my throne. Do you admit
To a share in this burying, or deny all knowledge?

ISMENE: I did it—yes—if she will let me say so.
I am as much to blame as she is.

ANTIGONE: No. That is not just. You would not lend a hand
And I refused your help in what I did.

ISMENE: But I am not ashamed to stand beside you
Now in your hour of trial, Antigone.

ANTIGONE: Whose was the deed, death and the dead are witness.
I love no friend whose love is only words.

ISMENE: O sister, sister, let me share your death,
Share in the tribute of honor to him that is dead.

ANTIGONE: You shall not die with me. You shall not claim
That which you would not touch. One death is enough.

ISMENE: How can I bear to live, if you must die?

ANTIGONE: Ask Creon. Is not he the one you care for?

ISMENE: You do yourself no good to taunt me so.

ANTIGONE: Indeed no; even my jests are bitter pains.

ISMENE: But how, O tell me, how can I still help you?

ANTIGONE: Help yourself; I shall not stand in your way.

ISMENE: For pity, Antigone—can I not die with you?

ANTIGONE: You chose; life was your choice, when mine was
death.

ISMENE: Although I warned you that it would be so.

ANTIGONE: Your way seemed right to some, to others mine.

ISMENE: But now both in the wrong, and both condemned.

ANTIGONE: No, no. You live. My heart was long since dead,
So it was right for me to help the dead.

CREON: I do believe the creatures both are mad;
One lately crazed, the other from her birth.

ISMENE: Is it not likely, sir? The strongest mind
Cannot but break under misfortune's blows.

CREON: Yours did, when you threw in your lot with hers.

ISMENE: How could I wish to live without my sister?

CREON: You have no sister. Count her dead already.

ISMENE: You could not take her—kill your own son's bride?

CREON: Oh, there are other fields for him to plough.

ISMENE: No truer troth was ever made than theirs.

CREON: No son of mine shall wed so vile a creature.

ANTIGONE: O Haemon, can your father spite you so?

CREON: You and your paramour, I hate you both.

CHORUS: Sir, would you take her from your own son's arms?

CREON: Not I, but death shall take her.

CHORUS: Be it so. Her death, it seems, is certain.

CREON: Certain it is.
No more delay. Take them, and keep them within—
The proper place for women. None so brave
As not to look for some way of escape
When they see life stand face to face with death.

The women are taken away.

CHORUS:
Happy are they who know not the taste of evil.
From a house that heaven has shaken
The curse departs not
But falls upon all of the blood,
Like the restless surge of the sea when the dark storm drives
The black sand hurled from the deeps
And the Thracian gales boom down
On the echoing shore.
In life and in death is the house of Labdacus stricken.
Generation to generation,
With no atonement,
It is scourged by the wrath of a god.
And now for the dead dust's sake is the light of promise,
The tree's last root, crushed out

By pride of heart and the sin
Of presumptuous tongue.
For what presumption of man can match your power,
O Zeus, that art not subject to sleep or time
Or age, living forever in bright Olympus?
Tomorrow and for all time to come,
As in the past,
This law is immutable:
For mortals greatly to live is greatly to suffer.
Roving ambition helps many a man to good,
And many it falsely lures to light desires,
Until failure trips them unawares, and they fall
On the fire that consumes them. Well was it said,
Evil seems good
To him who is doomed to suffer;
And short is the time before that suffering comes!
But here comes Haemon,
Your youngest son.
Does he come to speak his sorrow
For the doom of his promised bride,
The loss of his marriage hopes?

CREON: We shall know it soon, and need no prophet to tell us.

Enter Haemon.

Son, you have heard, I think, our final judgement
on your late betrothed. No angry words, I hope?
Still friends, in spite of everything my son?

HAEMON: I am your son, sir; by your wise decisions
My life is ruled, and them I shall always obey.
I cannot value any marriage tie
Above your own good guidance.

CREON: Rightly said.

Your father's will should have your heart's first place.
Only for this do fathers pray for sons
Obedient, loyal, ready to strike down
Their fathers' foes, and love their fathers' friends.
To be the father of unprofitable sons
Is to be the father of sorrows, a laughing-stock
To all one's enemies. Do not be fooled, my son,
By lust and the wiles of a woman. You'll have bought
Cold comfort if your wife's a worthless one.
No wound strikes deeper than love that is turned to hate.
This girl's an enemy; away with her,
And let her go and find a mate in Hades.
Once having caught her in a flagrant act—
The one and only traitor in our state—
I cannot make myself a traitor too;
So she must die. Well may she pray to Zeus,
The god of family love. How, if I tolerate
A traitor at home, shall I rule those abroad?
He that is a righteous master of his house
Will be a righteous statesman. To transgress
Or twist the law to one's own pleasure, presume
To order where one should obey, is sinful
And I will have none of it.
He whom the state appoints must be obeyed
To the smallest matter, be it right—or wrong.
And he that rules his household, without a doubt,
Will make the wisest king, or, for that matter,
The staunchest subject. He will be the man
You can depend on in the storm of war,
The most faithful comrade in the day of battle.
There is no more deadly peril than disobedience;
States are devoured by it, homes laid in ruins,
Armies defeated, victory turned to rout.

While simple obedience saves the lives of hundreds
Of honest folk. Therefore, I hold to the law,
And will never betray it—least of all for a woman.
Better be beaten, if need be, by a man,
Than let a woman get the better of us.

CHORUS: To me, as far as an old man can tell,
It seems your Majesty has spoken well.

HAEMON: Father, man's wisdom is the gift of heaven,
The greatest gift of all. I neither am,
Nor wish to be, clever enough to prove you wrong,
Though all men might not think the same as you do.
Nevertheless, I have to be your watchdog,
To know what others say and what they do,
And what they find to praise and what to blame.
Your frown is a sufficient silencer
Of any word that is not for your ears.
But I hear whispers spoken in the dark;
On every side I hear voices of pity
For this poor girl, doomed to the cruellest death,
And most unjust, that ever woman suffered
For an honorable action—burying a brother
Who was killed in battle, rather than leave him naked
For dogs to maul and carrion birds to peck at.
Has she not rather earned a crown of gold?—
Such is the secret talk about the town.
Father, there is nothing I can prize above
Your happiness and well-being. What greater good
Can any son desire? Can any father
Desire more from his son? Therefore I say,
Let not your first thought be your only thought—
Think if there cannot be some other way.
Surely, to think your own the only wisdom,
And yours the only word, the only will,

Betrays a shallow spirit, an empty heart.
It is no weakness for the wisest man
To learn when he is wrong, know when to yield.
So, on the margin of a flooded river
Trees bending to the torrent live unbroken,
While those that strain against it are snapped off.
A sailor has to tack and slacken sheets
Before the gale, or find himself capsized.
So, father, pause, and put aside your anger.
I think, for what my young opinion's worth,
That good as it is to have infallible wisdom,
Since this is rarely found, the next best thing
Is to be willing to listen to wise advice.

CHORUS: There is something to be said, my lord, for his point of
    view,
And for yours as well; there is much to be said on both sides.

CREON: Indeed! Am I to take lessons at my time of life
    From a fellow of his age?

HAEMON: No lesson you need be ashamed of.
    It isn't a question of age, but of right and wrong.

CREON: Would you call it right to admire an act of disobedience?

HAEMON: Not if the act were also dishonorable.

CREON: And was not this woman's action dishonorable?

HAEMON: The people of Thebes think not.

CREON: The people of Thebes!
    Since when do I take my orders from the people of Thebes?

HAEMON: Isn't that rather a childish thing to say?

CREON: No. I am king, and responsible only to myself.

HAEMON: A one-man state? What sort of a state is that?

CREON: Why, does not every state belong to its ruler?

HAEMON: You'd be an excellent king—on a desert island.

CREON: Of course, if you're on the woman's side—

HAEMON: No, no—

Unless you're the woman. It's you I'm fighting for.

CREON: What, villain, when every word you speak is against me?

HAEMON: Only because I know you are wrong, wrong.

CREON: Wrong? To respect my own authority?

HAEMON: What sort of respect tramples on all that is holy?

CREON: Despicable coward! No more will than a woman!

HAEMON: I have nothing to be ashamed of

CREON: Yet you plead her cause.

HAEMON: No, yours, and mine, and that of the gods of the dead.

CREON: You'll never marry her this side of death.

HAEMON: Then, if she dies, she does not die alone.

CREON: Is that a threat, you impudent—

HAEMON: Is it a threat

To try to argue against wrong-headedness?

CREON: You'll learn what wrong-headedness is, my friend, to
your cost.

HAEMON: O father, I could call you mad, were you not my father.

CREON: Don't toady me, boy; keep that for your lady-love.

HAEMON: You mean to have the last word, then?

CREON: I do.

And what is more, by all the gods in heaven,
I'll make you sorry for your impudence.

(Calling to those within)

Bring out that she-devil, and let her die
Now, with her bridegroom by to see it done!

HAEMON: That sight I'll never see. Nor from this hour

Shall you see me again. Let those that will
Be witness of your wickedness and folly.

Exit.

CHORUS: He is gone, my lord, in very passionate haste.
  And who shall say what a young man's wrath may do?
CREON: Let him go! Let him do! Let him rage as never man
    raged,
  He shall not save those women from their doom.
CHORUS: You mean, then, sire, to put them both to death?
CREON: No, not the one whose hand was innocent.
CHORUS: And to what death do you condemn the other?
CREON: I'll have her taken to a desert place
  Where no man ever walked, and there walled up
  Inside a cave, alive, with food enough
  To acquit ourselves of the blood-guiltiness
  That else would lie upon our commonwealth.
  There she may pray to Death, the god she loves,
  And ask release from death; or learn at last
  What hope there is for those who worship death.

Exit.

CHORUS:
  Where is the equal of Love?
  Where is the battle he cannot win,
  The power he cannot outmatch?
  In the farthest corners of earth, in the midst of the sea,
  He is there; he is here
  In the bloom of a fair face
  Lying in wait;

And the grip of his madness
Spares not god or man,
Marring the righteous man,
Driving his soul into mazes of sin
And strife, dividing a house.
For the light that burns in the eyes of a bride of desire
Is a fire that consumes.
At the side of the great gods
Aphrodite immortal
Works her will upon him.

The doors are opened and Antigone enters, guarded.

But here is a sight beyond all bearing,
At which my eyes cannot but weep;
Antigone forth faring
To her bridal-bower of endless sleep.

ANTIGONE: You see me, countrymen, on my last journey,
Taking my last leave of the light of day;
Going to my rest, where death shall take me
Alive across the silent river.
No wedding day; no marriage music;
Death will be all my bridal dower.

CHORUS: But glory and praise go with you, lady,
To your resting place. You go with your beauty
Unmarred by the hand of consuming sickness,
Untouched by the sword, living and free,
As none other that ever died before you.

ANTIGONE: The daughter of Tantalus, a Phrygian maid,
Was doomed to a piteous death on the rock
Of Syphylus, which embraced and imprisoned her,
Merciless as the ivy; rain and snow
Beat down upon her, mingled with her tears,

As she wasted and died. Such was her story,
And such is the sleep that I shall go to.

CHORUS: She was a goddess of immortal birth,
And we are mortals; the greatest the glory,
To share the fate of a god-born maiden,
A living death, but a name undying.

ANTIGONE: Mockery, mockery! By the gods of our fathers,
Must you make me a laughing-stock, while I yet live?
O lordly sons of my city! O Thebes!
Your valleys of rivers, your chariots and horses!
No friend to weep at my banishment
To a rock hewn chamber of endless durance,
In a strange cold tomb alone to linger
Lost between life and death forever.

CHORUS: My child, you have gone your way
To the outermost limit of daring
And have stumbled against Law enthroned.
This is the expiation
You must make for the sin of your father.

ANTIGONE: My father—the thought that sears my soul—
The unending burden of the house of Labdacus.
Monstrous marriage of mother and son...
My father...my parents...O hideous shame!
Whom now I follow, unwed, curse-ridden,
Doomed to this death by the ill-starred marriage
That marred my brother's life.

CHORUS: An act of homage is good in itself, my daughter;
But authority cannot afford to connive at disobedience.
You are the victim of your own self-will.

ANTIGONE: And must go the way that lies before me.
No funeral hymn; no marriage music;
No sun from this day forth, no light,

No friend to weep at my departing.

Enter Creon.

CREON: Weeping and wailing at the door of death!
  There'd be no end of it, if it had force
  To buy death off. Away with her at once
  And close her up in her rock-vaulted tomb.
  Leave her and let her die, if die she must,
  Or live within her dungeon. Though on earth
  Her life is ended from this day, her blood
  Will not be on our hands.

ANTIGONE: So to my grave,
  My bridal-bower, my everlasting prison,
  I go to join those many of my kinsmen
  Who dwell in the mansions of Persephone,
  Last and unhappiest, before my time.
  Yet I believe my father will be there
  To welcome me, my mother greet me gladly,
  And you, my brother, gladly see me come.
  Each one of you my hands have laid to rest,
  Pouring the due libations on your graves.
  It was by this service to your dear body, Polynices,
  I earned the punishment which now I suffer,
  Though all good people know it was for your honor.
  O but I would not have done the forbidden thing
  For any husband or for any son.
  For why? I could have had another husband
  And by him other sons, if one were lost;
  But, father and mother lost, where would I get
  Another brother? For thus preferring you,
  My brother, Creon condemns me and hales me away,
  Never a bride, never a mother, friendless,

68

Condemned alive to solitary death.
What law of heaven have I transgressed? What god
Can save me now? What help or hope have I,
In whom devotion is deemed sacrilege?
If this is god's will, I shall learn my lesson
In death; but if my enemies are wrong,
I wish them no worse punishment than mine.

CHORUS: Still the same tempest in the heart
Torments her soul with angry gusts.

CREON: The more cause then have they that guard her
To hasten their work; or they too suffer.

CHORUS: Alas, that word had the sound of death.

CREON: Indeed there is no more to hope for.

ANTIGONE: Gods of our fathers, my city, my home,
Rulers of Thebes! Time stays no longer.
Last daughter of your royal house
Go I, his prisoner, because I honored
Those things to which honor truly belongs.

Antigone is led away.

CHORUS:
Such was the fate, my child, of Danae
Locked in a brazen bower,
A prison secret as a tomb,
Where there was no day.
Daughter of kings, her royal womb
Garnered the golden shower
Of life from Zeus. So strong is Destiny,
No wealth, no armory, no tower,
No ship that rides the angry sea
Her mastering hand can stay.

And Dryas' son, the proud Edionian king,
Pined in a stony cell
At Dionysus' bidding, pent
To cool his fire?
Until, all his full-blown passion spent,
He came to know right well
What god his ribald tongue was challenging
When he would break the fiery spell
Of the wild Maenads' reveling
And vex the Muses' choir.
It was upon the side
Of Bosphorus, where the Black Rocks stand
By Thracian Salmydessus over the twin tide,
That Thracian Ares laughed to see
How Phineus' angry wife most bloodily
Blinded his two sons' eyes that mutely cried
For vengeance; crazed with jealousy
The woman smote them with the weaving needle in her hand.
Forlorn they wept away
Their sad step childhood's misery
Predestined from their mother's ill-starred marriage day.
She was of old Erechtheid blood,
Cave-dwelling daughter of the north-wind god;
On rocky steeps, as mountain ponies play,
The wild winds nursed her maidenhood.
On her, my child, the grey Fates laid hard hands, as upon
    thee.

Enter Teiresias, the blind prophet, led by a boy.

TEIRESIAS: Gentlemen of Thebes, we greet you, my companion
    and I,
Who share one pair of eyes on our journeys together—

For the blind man goes where his leader tells him to.

CREON: You are welcome, father Teiresias. What's your news?

TEIRESIAS: Aye, news you shall have; and advice, if you can heed it.

CREON: There was never a time when I failed to heed it, father.

TEIRESIAS: And thereby have so far steered a steady course.

CREON: And gladly acknowledge the debt we owe to you.

TEIRESIAS: Then mark me now; for you stand on a razor's edge.

CREON: Indeed? Grave words from your lips, good priest.
    Say on.

TEIRESIAS: I will; and show you all that my skill reveals.
    At my seat of divination, where I sit
    These many years to read the signs of heaven,
    An unfamiliar sound came to my ears
    Of birds in vicious combat, savage cries
    In strange outlandish language, and the whirl
    Of flapping wings; from which I well could picture
    The gruesome warfare of their deadly talons.
    Full of foreboding then I made the test
    Of sacrifice upon the altar fire.
    There was no answering flame; only rank juice
    Oozed from the flesh and dripped among the ashes,
    Smoldering and sputtering; the gall vanished in a puff,
    And the fat ran down and left the haunches bare.
    Thus (through the eyes of my young acolyte,
    Who sees for me, that I may see for others)
    I read the signs of failure in my quest.
    And why? The blight upon us is your doing.
    The blood that stains our altars and our shrines,
    The blood that dogs and vultures have licked up,
    It is none other than the blood of Oedipus
    Spilled from the veins of his ill-fated sin.
    Our fires, our sacrifices, and our prayers

The gods abominate. How should the birds
Give any other than ill-omened voices,
Gorged with the dregs of blood that man has shed?
Mark this my son: all men fall into sin.
But sinning, he is not forever lost
Hapless and helpless, who can make amends
And has not set his face against repentance.
Only a fool is governed by self-will.
Pay to the dead his due. Wound not the fallen.
It is no glory to kill and kill again.
My words are for your good, as is my will,
And should be acceptable, being for your good.

CREON: You take me for your target, reverend sir,
Like all the rest. I know your art of old,
And how you make me your commodity
To trade and traffic in for your advancement.
Trade as you will; but all the silver of Sardis
And all the gold of India will not buy
A tomb for yonder traitor. No. Let the eagles
Carry his carcass up to the throne of Zeus;
Even that would not be sacrilege enough
To frighten me from my determination
Not to allow this burial. No man's act
Has power enough to pollute the goodness of god.
But great and terrible is the fall, Teiresias,
Of mortal men who seek their own advantage
By uttering evil in the guise of good.

TEIRESIAS: Ah, is there any wisdom in the world?

CREON: Why, what is the meaning of that wide-flung taunt?

TEIRESIAS: What prize outweighs the priceless worth of prudence?

CREON: Aye, what indeed? What mischief matches the lack of it?

72

TEIRESIAS: And there you speak of your own symptom, sir.

CREON: I am loath to pick a quarrel with you, priest.

TEIRESIAS: You do so, calling my divination false.

CREON: I say all prophets seek their own advantage.

TEIRESIAS: All kings, say I, seek gain unrighteously.

CREON: Do you forget to whom you say it?

TEIRESIAS: No. Our king and benefactor, by my guidance.

CREON: Clever you may be, but not therefore honest.

TEIRESIAS: Must I reveal my yet unspoken mind?

CREON: Reveal all; but expect no gain from it.

TEIRESIAS: Does that still seem to you my motive, then?

CREON: Nor is my will for sale, sir, in your market.

TEIRESIAS: Then hear this. Ere the chariot of the sun
    Has rounded once or twice his wheeling way,
    You shall have given a son of your own loins
    To death, in payment for death—two debts to pay:
    One for the life that you have sent to death,
    The life you have abominably entombed;
    One for the dead still lying above ground
    Unburied, unhonored, unblest by the gods below.
    You cannot alter this. The gods themselves
    Cannot undo it. It follows of necessity
    From what you have done! Even now the avenging Furies,
    The hunters of Hell that follow and destroy,
    Are lying in wait for you, and will have their prey,
    When the evil you have worked for others falls on you.
    Do I speak this for my gain? The time shall come,
    And soon, when your house will be filled with the lamenta-
        tion
    Of men and of women; and every neighboring city
    Will be goaded to fury against you, for upon them
    Too the pollution falls when the dogs and vultures

Bring the defilement of blood to their hearths and altars.
I have done. You pricked me, and these shafts of wrath
Will find their mark in your heart. You cannot escape
The sting of their sharpness.
Lead me home, my boy.
Let us leave him to vent his anger on younger ears,
Or school his mind and tongue to a milder mood
Than that which now possesses him.
Lead on.

Exit.

CHORUS: He has gone, my lord. He has prophesied terrible
    things.
  And for my part, I that was young, and now am old
  Have never known his prophecies proved false.

CREON: It is true enough; and my heart is torn in two.
  It is hard to give way, and hard to stand and abide
  The coming of the curse. Both ways are hard.

CHORUS: If you would be advised, my good lord Creon.

CREON: What must I do? Tell me, and I will do it.

CHORUS: Release the woman from her rocky prison.
  Set up a tomb for him that lies unburied.

CREON: Is it your wish that I consent to this?

CHORUS: It is, and quickly. The gods do not delay
  The stroke of their swift vengeance on the sinner.

CREON: It is hard, but I must do it. Well I know
  There is no armor against necessity.

CHORUS: Go. Let your own hand do it, and no other.

CREON: I will go this instant.
  Slaves there! One and all.
  Bring spades and mattocks out on the hill!

My mind is made; 'twas I imprisoned her,
And I will set her free. Now I believe
It is by the laws of heaven that man must live.

Exit.

CHORUS:
O Thou whose name is many,
Son of the Thunderer, dear child of his Cadmean bride,
Whose hand is mighty
In Italia,
In the hospitable valley
Of Eleusis,
And in Thebes,
The mother-city of your worshipers,
Where sweet Ismenus gently waters
The soil whence sprang the harvest of the dragon's teeth;
Where torches on the crested mountains gleam,
And by Castalia's stream
The nymph train in your dance rejoices,
When from the ivy-tangled glens
Of Nysa and from vine-clad plains
You come to Thebes where the immortal voices
Sing your glad strains.
Thebes, where you love most to be,
With her, your mother, the fire-stricken one,
Sickens for need of thee.
Healer of all her ills;
Come swiftly o'er the high Parnassian hills,
Come o'er the sighing sea.
The stars, whose breath is fire, delight
To dance for thee; the echoing night
Shall with your praises ring.
Zeus-born, appear! With Thyiads reveling

Come, bountiful
Iacchus, King!

Enter a Messenger, from the side of the stage.

MESSENGER: Hear, men of Cadmus' city, hear and attend,
    Men of the house of Amphion, people of Thebes!
    What is the life of man? A thing not fixed
    For good or evil, fashioned for praise or blame.
    Chance raises a man to the heights, chance casts him down,
    And none can foretell what will be from what is.
    Creon was once an enviable man;
    He saved his country from her enemies,
    Assumed the sovereign power, and bore it well,
    The honored father of a royal house.
    Now all is lost; for life without life's joys
    Is living death; and such a life is his.
    Riches and rank and show of majesty
    And state, where no joy is, are empty, vain
    And unsubstantial shadows, of no weight
    To be compared with happiness of heart.
CHORUS: What is your news? Disaster in the royal house?
MESSENGER: Death; and the guilt of it on living heads.
CHORUS: Who dead? And by what hand?
MESSENGER: Haemon is dead,
    Slain by his own—
CHORUS: His father?
MESSENGER: His own hand.
    His father's act it was that drove him to it.
CHORUS: Then all has happened as the prophet said.
MESSENGER: What's next to do, your worships will decide.

The Palace door opens.

CHORUS: Here comes the Queen, EURYDICE. Poor soul,
  It may be she has heard about her son.

Enter Eurydice, attended by women.

EURYDICE: My friends, I heard something of what you were say-
    ing
  As I came to the door. I was on my way to prayer
  At the temple of Pallas, and had barely turned the latch
  When I caught your talk of some near calamity.
  I was sick with fear and reeled in the arms of my women.
  But tell me what is the matter; what have you heard?
  I am not unacquainted with grief, and I can bear it.

MESSENGER: Madam, it was I that saw it, and will tell you all.
  To try to make it any lighter now
  Would be to prove myself a liar.
  Truth is always best.
  It was thus. I attended your husband,
  The King, to the edge of the field where lay the body
  Of Polynices, in pitiable state, mauled by the dogs.
  We prayed for him to the Goddess of the Roads, and to Pluto,
  That they might have mercy upon him. We washed the re-
    mains
  In holy water, and on a fire of fresh-cut branches
  We burned all that was left of him, and raised
  Over his ashes a mound of his native earth.
  That done, we turned towards the deep rock-chamber
  Of the maid that was married with death.
  Before we reached it,
  One that stood near the accursed place had heard
  Loud cries of anguish, and came to tell King Creon.

As he approached, came strange uncertain sounds
Of lamentation, and he cried aloud:
'Unhappy wretch! Is my foreboding true?
Is this the most sorrowful journey that ever I went?
My son's voice greets me. Go, some of you, quickly
Through the passage where the stones are thrown apart,
Into the mouth of the cave, and see if it be
My son, my own son Haemon that I hear.
If not, I am the sport of gods.
We went and looked, as bidden by our anxious master.
There in the furthest corner of the cave
We saw her hanging by the neck. The rope
Was of the woven linen of her dress.
And, with his arms about her, there stood he
Lamenting his lost bride, his luckless love,
His father's cruelty.
When Creon saw them,
Into the cave he went, moaning piteously.
'O my unhappy boy,' he cried again
'What have you done? What madness brings you here
To your destruction? Come away, my son,
My son, I do beseech you, come away!'
His son looked at him with one angry stare,
Spat in his face, and then without a word
Drew sword and struck out. But his father fled
Unscathed. Whereon the poor demented boy
Leaned on his sword and thrust it deeply home
In his own side, and while his life ebbed out
Embraced the maid in loose enfolding arms,
His spurting blood staining her pale cheeks red.

Eurydice goes quickly back into the Palace.

Two bodies lie together, wedded in death,
Their bridal sleep a witness to the world
How great calamity can come to man
Through man's perversity.

CHORUS: But what is this?
The Queen has turned and gone without a word.

MESSENGER: Yes. It is strange. The best that I can hope
Is that she would not sorrow for her son
Before us all, but vents her grief in private
Among her women. She is too wise, I think,
To take a false step rashly.

CHORUS: It may be.
Yet there is danger in unnatural silence
No less than in excess of lamentation.

MESSENGER: I will go in and see, whether in truth
There is some fatal purpose in her grief
Such silence, as you say, may well be dangerous.

He goes in. Enter Attendants preceding the King.

CHORUS: The King comes here.
What the tongue scarce dares to tell
Must now be known
By the burden that proves too well
The guilt, no other man's
But his alone.

Enter Creon with the body of Haemon.

CREON: The sin, the sin of the erring soul
Drives hard unto death.
Behold the slayer, the slain,

The father, the son.
O the curse of my stubborn will!
Son, newly cut off in the newness of youth,
Dead for my fault, not yours.

CHORUS: Alas, too late you have seen the truth.

CREON: I learn in sorrow. Upon my head
God has delivered this heavy punishment,
Has struck me down in the ways of wickedness,
And trod my gladness under foot.
Such is the bitter affliction of mortal man.

Enter the Messenger from the Palace.

MESSENGER: Sir, you have this and more than this to bear.
Within there's more to know, more to your pain.

CREON: What more? What pain can overtop this pain?

MESSENGER: She is dead—your wife, the mother of him that is
dead—
The death wound fresh in her heart. Alas, poor lady!

CREON: Insatiable Death, will you destroy me yet?
What say you, teller of evil?
I am already dead,
And is there more?
Blood upon blood?
More death? My wife?

The central doors open, revealing the body of Eurydice.

CHORUS: Look then, and see; nothing is hidden now.

CREON: O second horror!
What fate awaits me now?
My child here in my arms...and there, the other...

The son...the mother...

MESSENGER: There at the altar with the whetted knife
    She stood, and as the darkness dimmed her eyes
    Called on the dead, her elder son and this,
    And with her dying breath cursed you, their slayer.

CREON: O horrible...
    Is there no sword for me,
    To end this misery?

MESSENGER: Indeed you bear the burden of two deaths.
    It was her dying word.

CREON: And her last act?

MESSENGER: Hearing her son was dead, with her own hand
    She drove the sharp sword home into her heart.

CREON: There is no man can bear this guilt but I.
    It is true, I killed him.
    Lead me away, away. I live no longer.

CHORUS: 'Twere best, if anything is best in evil times.
    What's soonest done is best when all is ill.

CREON: Come, my last hour and fairest,
    My only happiness...come soon.
    Let me not see another day.
    Away... away...

CHORUS: The future is not to be known; our present care
    Is with the present; the rest is in other hands.

CREON: I ask no more than I have asked.

CHORUS: Ask nothing.
    What is to be, no mortal can escape.

CREON: I am nothing. I have no life.
    Lead me away...
    That have killed unwittingly
    My son, my wife.
    I know not where I should turn,

Where look for help.
My hands have done amiss, my head is bowed
With fate too heavy for me.

Exit.

CHORUS: Of happiness the crown
And chiefest part
Is wisdom, and to hold
The gods in awe.
This is the law
That, seeing the stricken heart
Of pride brought down,
We learn when we are old.

Exeunt

6. Thucydides, *History of the Peloponnesian War,* Pericles' Funeral Oration

Between 431 and 404 B.C.E. *Greece was engulfed in civil war, as Athens and Sparta and their respective allies competed for dominance among the city-states of the Greek peninsula. At stake were not only wealth and influence, but also two competing political models: Athens, an open political society and democracy; and Sparta, an oligarchy. In the selection that follows, Pericles, the Athenian leader and probably its most eminent statesman, praises the unique characteristics of Athenian democracy and the distinctive way of life it represented.*

This selection comes from the History of the Peloponnesian War *by Thucydides (471-400* B.C.E.*), an Athenian general in the war and perhaps the greatest of classical historians. Historians generally agree that it is an accurate reflection of what Pericles said, if not a direct quotation.*

In the same winter the Athenians gave a funeral at the public cost to those who had first fallen in this war. It was a custom of their ancestors, and the manner of it is as follows. Three days before the ceremony, the bones of the dead are laid out in a tent which has been erected; and their friends bring to their relatives such offerings as they please. In the funeral procession cypress coffins are borne in carts, one for each tribe; the bones of the deceased being placed in the coffin of their tribe. Among these is carried one empty bier decked for the missing, that is, for those whose bodies could not be recovered. Any citizen or stranger who pleases, joins in the procession: and the female relatives are there to wail at the burial. The dead are laid in the public sepulcher in the beautiful suburb of the city where those who fall in war are always buried; with the exception of those slain at Marathon, who for their singular and extraordinary valor were interred on the spot where they fell. After the bodies have been laid in the earth, a man chosen by the *polis*, of approved wisdom and eminent reputation, pronounces over them an appropriate panegyric; after which all retire. Such is the manner of the burying; and throughout the whole of the war, whenever the occasion arose, the established custom was observed. Meanwhile these were the first that had fallen, and Pericles, son of Xanthippus, was chosen to pronounce their eulogy. When the proper time arrived, he advanced from the sepulcher to an elevated platform in order to be heard by as many of the crowd as possible, and spoke as follows:

"Most of my predecessors who have spoken on this occasion have praised the person who made this speech part of the law, telling us that it is well that it should be delivered at the burial of those who fall in battle. For myself, I should have thought that the worth which had displayed itself in deeds would be sufficiently rewarded by honors also shown by deeds; such as you now see in this funeral prepared at the people's cost. And I could have wished that the reputations of many brave men were not to be imperilled in the mouth of a single individual. For it is hard to speak properly upon a subject where it is even difficult to convince your hearers that you are speaking the truth. On the one hand, the friend who is familiar with every fact of the story may think that some point has not been set forth with that fullness which he wishes and knows it to deserve; on the other, he who is a stranger to the matter may be led by envy to suspect exaggeration if he hears anything above his own nature. For men can endure to hear others praised only so long as they can persuade themselves of their own ability to equal the actions recounted: when this point is passed, envy comes in and with it incredulity. However, since our ancestors have stamped this custom with their approval, it becomes my duty to obey the law and to try to satisfy your several wishes and opinions as best I may.

"I shall begin with our ancestors: it is both just and proper that they should have the honor of the first mention on an occasion like the present. They dwelt in the country without a break in the succession from generation to generation, and handed it down free to the present time by their valor. And if our more remote ancestors deserve praise, much more do our own fathers, who added to their inheritance the empire which we now possess, and spared no pains to be able to leave their acquisitions to us in the present generation. Lastly, there are few parts of our dominions that have not been augmented by those of us here, who are still more or less in the vigor of life; while our city has been furnished by us with everything necessary to enable it to depend on its own resources whether for war or for peace. That part of our history which tells of the military achievements which gave us our several possessions, or of the ready valor with which either we or our fathers stemmed the tide of Hellenic or foreign aggression, is a theme too familiar to my hearers for me to elaborate on, and I shall therefore pass it by. But what was the road by which we reached our position, what was the form of government under which our greatness grew, what were the national habits out of which it sprang; these are questions which I may try to solve before I proceed to my panegyric upon these men; since I think this to be a subject upon which on the present occasion a speaker may properly dwell, and to which the whole assemblage, whether citizens or foreigners, may listen with advantage.

"Our constitution does not copy the laws of neighboring states; we are rather a pattern to others than imitators ourselves. Its administration favors the many instead of the few; this is why it is called a democracy. If we look to the laws, they afford equal justice to all in their private differences; if there is no social standing, advancement in public life comes because of a reputation for capacity, class considerations not being allowed to interfere with merit. Nor again does poverty bar the way; if a man is able to serve the *polis*, he is not hindered by the obscurity of his condition. The freedom which we enjoy in our government extends also to our ordinary life. There, far from exercising a jealous surveillance over each other, we do not feel called upon to be angry with our neighbor for doing what he likes, or even to indulge in those injurious looks which cannot fail to be offensive, although they inflict no positive penalty.

"But all this ease in our private relations does not make us lawless as citizens. Against this fear is our chief safeguard, teaching us to obey the magistrates and the laws, particularly such as those that regard the protection of the injured, whether they are actually on the statute book, or belong to that code which, although unwritten, yet cannot be broken without acknowledged disgrace.

"Further, we provide plenty of means for the mind to refresh itself from business. We celebrate games and sacrifices all the year round, and the elegance of our private establishments forms a daily source of pleasure and helps to banish the unpleasantness; while the magnitude of our city draws the produce of the world into our harbor, so that to the Athenian the fruits of other countries are as familiar a luxury as those of his own.

"If we turn to our military policy, there also we differ from our antagonists. We throw open our city to the world, and never by acts do we exclude foreigners from any opportunity of learning or observing, although the eyes of an enemy may occasionally profit by our liberality; trusting less in system and policy than to the native spirit of our citizens. While in education, where our rivals from their very cradles by a painful discipline seek after manliness, at Athens we live exactly as we please, and yet are just as ready to encounter every legitimate danger. In proof of this it may be noticed that the Spartans do not invade our country alone, but bring with them all their confederates; while we Athenians advance unsupported into the territory of a neighbor, and fighting upon a foreign soil usually vanquish with ease men who are defending their homes. Our united force has never been defeated by any enemy, because we have at once to attend to our navy and to dispatching our citizens by land upon a hundred different services; so that, wherever they engage some small fraction of our strength, a success against a detachment is magnified into a victory over the nation, and a small defeat into a reverse suffered by our entire people. And yet if with habits not of labor but of ease, and courage not of art but of nature, we are still willing to encounter danger, we have the double advantage of escaping the experience of hardships in anticipation and of facing them in the hour of need as fearlessly as those who are never free from them.

"Nor are these the only points in which our city is worthy of admiration. We cultivate refinement without extravagance and knowledge without effeminacy; wealth we employ more for use than for show, and place the real disgrace of poverty not in owning to the fact but in declining the struggle against it. Our public men have, besides politics, their private affairs to attend to, and our ordinary citizens, though occupied with the pursuits of industry, are still fair judges of public matters; for, unlike any other nation, regarding him who takes no part in these duties not as unambitious but as useless, we Athenians are able to judge at all events if we cannot originate, and, instead of looking on discussion as a stumbling-block in the way of action, we think it an indispensable preliminary to any wise action at all. Again, in our enterprises we present the singular spectacle of daring and deliberation, each carried to its highest point, and both united in the same persons; although usually decision is the fruit of ignorance, hesitation of reflection. But the palm of courage will surely be judged most justly to those, who best know the difference between hardship and pleasure and yet are never tempted to shrink from danger.

"In generosity we are equally singular, acquiring our friends by conferring, not by receiving, favors. Yet, of course, the doer of the favor is the firmer friend of the two, in order by continued kindness to keep the recipient in his debt; while the debtor feels less keenly from the very consciousness that the return he makes will be a payment, not a free gift. And it is only the Athenians, who, fearless of consequences, confer their benefits not from calculations of expediency, but in the confidence of liberality.

"In short, I say that as a city we are the school of Hellas, while I doubt if the world can produce a man who, where he has only himself to depend upon, is equal to so many emergencies, and graced by so happy a versatility, as the Athenian. And that this is no mere boast thrown out for the occasion, but plain matter of fact, the power of the *polis* acquired by these habits proves. For Athens alone of her contemporaries is found when tested to be greater than her reputation, and alone gives no occasion to her assailants to blush at the antagonist by whom they have been worsted, or to her subjects to question her title by merit to rule. Rather, the admiration of the present and succeeding ages will be ours, since we have not left our power without witness, but have shown it by mighty proofs; and far from needing a Homer for our panegyrist, or other of his craft whose verses might charm for the moment only for the impression which they gave to melt at the touch of fact, we have forced every sea and land to be the highway of our daring, and everywhere, whether for evil or for good, have left imperishable monuments behind us. Such is the Athens for which these men, in the assertion of their resolve not to lose her, nobly fought and died; and well may every one of their survivors be ready to suffer in her cause.

"Indeed if I have dwelt at some length upon the character of our country, it has been to show that our stake in the struggle is not the same as theirs who have no such blessings to lose, and also that the panegyric of the men over whom I am now speaking might be by definite proofs established. That panegyric is now in a great measure complete; for the Athens that I have celebrated is only what the heroism of these and their like have made her, men whose fame, unlike that of most Hellenes, will be found to be only commensurate with their deserts. And if a test of worth be wanted, it is to be found in their closing scene, and this not only in cases in which it set the final seal upon their merit, but also in those in which it gave the first intimation of their having any. For there is justice in the claim that steadfastness in his country's battles should be as a cloak to cover a man's other imperfections; since the good action has blotted out the bad, and his merit as a citizen more than outweighed his demerits as an individual. But none of these allowed either wealth with its prospect of future enjoyment to unnerve his spirit, or poverty with its hope of a day of freedom and riches to tempt him to shrink from danger. No, holding that vengeance upon their enemies was more to be desired than any personal blessings, and reckoning this to be the most glorious of hazards, they joyfully determined to accept the risk, to make sure of their vengeance, and to let their wishes wait....

"So died these men as became Athenians. You, their survivors, must determine to have as unfaltering a resolution in the field, though you may pray that it may have a happier result. And not contented with ideas derived only from words of the advantages which are bound up with the defense of your country, though these would furnish a valuable text to a speaker even before an audience so alive to them as the present, you must yourselves realize the power of Athens, and feed your eyes upon her from day to day, until love of her fills your hearts; and then, when all her greatness shall break upon you, you must reflect that it was by courage, sense of duty, and a keen feeling of honor in action that men were enabled to win all this, and that no personal failure in an enterprise could make them consent to deprive their country of their valor, but they laid it at her feet as the most glorious contribution that they could offer. For this offering of their lives made in common by all of them, individually they each received that renown which never grows old, and for a sepulcher, not so much that in which their bones have been deposited, but that noblest of shrines wherein their glory is laid up to be eternally remembered upon every occasion on which deed or story shall call for its commemoration. For heroes have the whole earth for their tomb; and in lands far from their own, where the column with its epitaph declares it, there is enshrined in every breast a record unwritten with no tablet to preserve it, except that of the heart. These take as your model and, judging happiness to be the fruit of freedom and freedom of valor, never decline the dangers of war. For it is not the miserable that would most justly be unsparing of their lives; these have nothing to hope for: it is rather they to whom continued life may bring reverses as yet unknown, and to whom a fall, if it came, would be most tremendous in its consequences. And surely, to a man of spirit, the degradation of cowardice must be immeasurably more grievous than the death that strikes him in the midst of his strength and patriotism!

"Comfort, therefore, not condolence, is what I have to offer to the parents of the dead who may be here. Numberless are the chances to which, as they know, the life of man is subject; but fortunate indeed are they who draw for their lot a death so glorious as that which has caused your mourning, and to whom life has been so exactly measured as to terminate in the happiness in which it has been passed. Still I know that this is a hard saying, especially when you will constantly be reminded by seeing in the homes of others blessings of which once you also boasted: for grief is felt not so much for the want of what we have never known, as for the loss of that which we have been long accustomed. Yet you who are still of an age to beget children must bear up in the hope of having others in their stead; not only will they help you to forget those whom you have lost, but will be to the *polis* at once a reinforcement and a security; for never can a fair or just policy be expected of the citizen who does not, like his fellows, bring to the decision the interests and apprehensions of a father. While those of you who have passed your prime must congratulate yourselves with the thought that the best part of your life was fortunate, and that the brief span that remains will be cheered by the fame of the departed. For it is only the love of honor that never grows old; and honor it is, not gain, as some would have it, that rejoices the heart of age and helplessness.

"Turning to the sons or brothers of the dead, I see an arduous struggle before you. When a man is gone, all are accustomed to praising him, and should your merit be ever so transcendent, you will still find it difficult not merely to overtake, but even to approach their renown. The living have envy to contend with, while those who are no longer in our path are honored with a goodwill into which rivalry does not enter. On the other hand, if I must say anything on the subject of female excellence to those of you who will now be in widowhood, it will be all comprised in this brief exhortation. Great will be your glory in not falling short of your natural character; and greatest will be hers who is least talked of among the men, whether for good or for bad.

"My task is now finished. I have performed it to the best of my ability, and in word, at least, the requirements of the law are now satisfied. If deeds be in question, those who are here interred have received part of their honors already, and for the rest, their children will be brought up to manhood at the public expense: the *polis* thus offers a valuable prize, as the garland of victory in this race of valor, for the reward both of those who have fallen and their survivors. And where the rewards for merit are greatest, there are found the best citizens.

"And now that you have brought to a close your lamentations for your relatives, you may depart."

7. Plato, *Crito*

Plato (429-347 B.C.E.*) is one of the giants of Western thought; together with Aristotle, he defined the nature of Western philosophy for two thousand years. His philosophy would strongly influence Christianity, particularly through the writings of St. Augustine. Most of his philosophical works take the form of dialogues in which Socrates is the principal speaker.*

The Crito *is an account of the last days of his mentor, Socrates (470-399* B.C.E.*), who was convicted by a jury of Athenians of impiety and corrupting the young. The dialogue takes place in prison where Socrates is awaiting his execution. His friend, Crito, has arranged his escape. Socrates reflects on whether he would be justified in escaping the punishment decreed by the polis.*

Scene: The prison of Socrates.

SOCRATES: Why have you come at this hour, Crito? It must be quite early.

CRITO: Yes, certainly.

SOCRATES: What is the exact time?

CRITO: The dawn is breaking.

SOCRATES: I wonder the keeper of the prison would let you in.

CRITO: He knows me because I often come, Socrates; moreover, I have done him a kindness.

SOCRATES: And have you only just come?

CRITO: No, I came some time ago.

SOCRATES: Then why did you sit and say nothing, instead of awakening me at once?

CRITO: Why, indeed, Socrates, I myself would rather not have all this sleeplessness and sorrow. But I have been wondering at your peaceful slumbers, and that was the reason why I did not awaken you, because I wanted you to be out of pain. I have always thought you happy in the calmness of your temperament; but never did I see the like of the easy, cheerful way in which you bear this calamity.

SOCRATES: Why, Crito, when a man has reached my age he ought not to be repining at the prospect of death.

CRITO: And yet other old men find themselves in similar misfortunes, and age does not prevent them from repining.

SOCRATES: That may be. But you have not told me why you come at this early hour.

CRITO: I come to bring you a message which is sad and painful; not, as I believe, to yourself but to all of us who are your friends, and saddest of all to me.

SOCRATES: What! I suppose that the ship has come from Delos, on the arrival of which I am to die?

CRITO: No, the ship has not actually arrived, but she will probably be here today, as persons who have come from Sunium tell me that they have left her there; and therefore tomorrow, Socrates, will be the last day of your life.

SOCRATES: Very well, Crito; if such is the will of god, I am willing; but my belief is that there will be a delay of a day.

CRITO: Why do you say this?

SOCRATES: I will tell you. I am to die on the day after the arrival of the ship?

CRITO: Yes; that is what the authorities say.

SOCRATES: But I do not think that the ship will be here until tomorrow; this I gather from a vision which I had last night, or rather only just now, when you fortunately allowed me to sleep.

CRITO: And what was the nature of the vision?

SOCRATES: There came to me the likeness of a woman, fair and

comely, clothed in white raiment, who called to me and said: O
Socrates— "The third day hence, to Phythia shall you go."

CRITO: What a singular dream, Socrates!

SOCRATES: There can be no doubt about the meaning Crito, I
think.

CRITO: Yes; the meaning is only too clear. But, O! my beloved
Socrates, let me entreat you once more to take my advice and
escape. For if you die I shall not only lose a friend who can never
be replaced, but there is another evil: people who do not know you
and me will believe that I might have saved you if I had been willing
to give money, but that I did not care. Now, can there be a worse
disgrace than this—that I should be thought to value money more
than the life of a friend? For the many will not be persuaded that
I wanted you to escape, and that you refused.

SOCRATES: But why, my dear Crito, should we care about the
opinion of the many? Good men, and they are the only persons
who are worth considering, will think of these things truly as they
happened.

CRITO: But do you see. Socrates, that the opinion of the many
must be regarded, as is evident in your own case, because they can
do the very greatest evil to anyone who has lost their good opinion?

SOCRATES: I only wish, Crito, that they could; for then they
could also do the greatest good, and that would be well. But the
truth is, that they can do neither good nor evil: they cannot make
a man wise or make him foolish; and whatever they do is the result
of chance.

CRITO: Well, I will not dispute about that; but please to tell me,
Socrates, whether you are not acting out of regard to me and your
other friends: are you not afraid that if you escape hence we may
get into trouble with the informers for having stolen you away, and
lose either the whole or a great part of our property; or that even
a worse evil may happen to us? Now, if this is your fear, be at ease;
for in order to save you, we ought surely to run this or even a greater
risk; be persuaded, then, and do as I say.

SOCRATES: Yes, Crito, that is one fear which you mention, but by no means the only one.

CRITO: Fear not. There are persons who at no great cost are willing to save you and bring you out of prison; and as for the informers, you may observe that they are far from being exorbitant in their demands; a little money will satisfy them. My means, which are ample, are at your service, and if you worry about spending all mine, here are strangers who will give you the use of theirs; and one of them, Simmias the Theban, has brought a sum of money for this very purpose; and Cebes and many others are willing to spend their money too. I say, therefore, do not on that account hesitate about making your escape, and do not say, as you did in the court, that you will have a difficulty in knowing what to do with yourself if you escape. For men will love you in other places to which you may go, and not in Athens only; there are friends of mine in Thessaly, if you like to go to them, who will value and protect you, and no Thessalian will give you any trouble. Nor can I think that you are justified, Socrates, in betraying your own life when you might be saved; this is playing into the hands of your enemies and destroyers; and moreover I should say that you were betraying your children; for you might bring them up and educate them; instead of which you go away and leave them, and they will have to take their chance; and if they do not meet with the usual fate of orphans, there will be small thanks to you. No man should bring children into the world who is unwilling to persevere to the end in their nurture and education. But you are choosing the easier part, as I think, not the better and manlier, which would rather have become one who professes virtue in all his actions, like yourself. And, indeed, I am ashamed not only of you, but of us who are your friends, when I reflect that this entire business of yours will be attributed to our want of courage. The trial need never have come on, or might have been brought to another issue; and the end of all, which is the crowning absurdity, will seem to have been permitted by us, through cowardice and baseness, who might have saved you, as you might have saved yourself, if we had been good for anything (for there was no difficulty in escaping); and we did not see how disgraceful, Socrates, and also miserable all this will be to us as well as to you. Make your mind up then, or rather have your mind already made up, for the time of deliberation is over, and there is only one thing to be done, which must be done, if at all, this very night, and which any delay will render all but impossible; I beseech you therefore, Socrates, to be persuaded by me, and to do as I say.

SOCRATES: Dear Crito, your zeal is invaluable, if a right one; but if wrong, the greater the zeal the greater the evil; and therefore we ought to consider whether these things shall be done or not. For I am and always have been one of those natures who must be guided by reason, whatever the reason may be which upon reflection appears to me to be the best; and now that this fortune has come upon me, I cannot put away the reasons which I have before given: the principles which I have hitherto honored and revered I still honor, and unless we can find other and better principles on the instant, I am certain not to agree with you; no, not even if the power of the multitude could inflict many more imprisonments, confiscations, deaths, frightening us like children with hobgoblin terrors. But what will be the fairest way of considering the question? Shall I return to your old argument about the opinions of men, some of which are to be regarded, and others, as we were saying, are not to be regarded? Now were we right in maintaining this before I was condemned? And has the argument which was once good now proved to be talk for the sake of talking; in fact an amusement only, and altogether vanity? That is what I want to consider with your help, Crito: whether, under my present circumstances, the argument appears to be in any way different or not; and is to be allowed by me or disallowed. That argument, which, as I believe, is maintained by many who assume to be authorities, was to the effect, as I was saying, that the opinions of some men are to be regarded, and of other men not to be regarded. Now you, Crito, are a disinterested person who are not going to die tomorrow—at least, there is no human probability of this, and you are therefore not liable to be deceived by the circumstances in which you are placed. Tell me, then, whether I am right in saying that some opinions, and the opinions of some men only, are to be valued, and other opinions, and the opinions of other men, are not to be valued. I ask you whether I was right in maintaining this?

CRITO: Certainly.

SOCRATES: The good are to be regarded, and not the bad?

CRITO: Yes.

SOCRATES: And the opinions of the wise are good, and the opinions of the unwise are evil?

CRITO: Certainly.

SOCRATES: And what was said about another matter? Was the disciple in gymnastics supposed to attend to the praise and blame and opinion of every man, or of one man only—his physician or trainer, whoever that was?

CRITO: Of one man only.

SOCRATES: And he ought to fear the censure and welcome the praise of that one only, and not of the many?

CRITO: That is clear.

SOCRATES: And he ought to live and train, and eat and drink in the way which seems good to his single master who has understanding, rather than according to the opinion of all other men put together?

CRITO: True.

SOCRATES: And if he disobeys and disregards the opinion and approval of the one, and regards the opinion of the many who have no understanding, will he not suffer evil?

CRITO: Certainly he will.

SOCRATES: And what will the evil be, whither tending and what affecting, in the disobedient person?

CRITO: Clearly, affecting the body; that is what is destroyed by the evil.

SOCRATES: Very good; and is not this true, Crito, of other things which we need not separately enumerate? In the matter of just and unjust, fair and foul, good and evil, which are the subjects of our present consultation, ought we to follow the opinion of the many and to fear them; or the opinion of the one man who has understanding, and whom we ought to fear and reverence more than all the rest of the world: and whom deserting we shall destroy and injure that principle in us which may be assumed to be improved by justice and deteriorated by injustice; is there not such a principle?

CRITO: Certainly there is, Socrates.

SOCRATES: Take a parallel instance; if, acting under the advice of men who have no understanding, we destroy that which is improvable by health and deteriorated by disease—when that has been destroyed, I say, would life be worth having? And that is—the body?

CRITO: Yes.

SOCRATES: Could we live, having an evil and corrupted body?

CRITO: Certainly not.

SOCRATES: And will life be worth having, if that higher part of man be depraved, which is improved by justice and deteriorated by injustice? Do we suppose that principle, whatever it may be in man, which has to do with justice and injustice, to be inferior to the body?

CRITO: Certainly not.

SOCRATES: More honored, then?

CRITO: Far more honored.

SOCRATES: Then, my friend, we must not regard what the many say of us: but what he, the one man who has understanding of just and unjust, will say, and what the truth will say. And therefore you begin in error when you suggest that we should regard the opinion of the many about just and unjust, good and evil, honorable and dishonorable. Well, someone will say, "But the many can kill us."

CRITO: Yes, Socrates; that will clearly be the answer.

SOCRATES: That is true; but still I find with surprise that the old argument is, as I conceive, unshaken as ever. And I should like to know whether I may say the same of another proposition—that not life, but a good life, is to be chiefly valued?

CRITO: Yes, that also remains.

SOCRATES: And a good life is equivalent to a just and honorable one—that holds also?

CRITO: Yes, that holds.

SOCRATES: From these premises I proceed to argue the question whether I ought or ought not to try to escape without the consent of the Athenians: and if I am clearly right in escaping, then I will make the attempt; but if not, I will abstain. The other considerations which you mention, of money and loss of character, and the duty of educating children, are, I fear, only the doctrines of the multitude, who would be as ready to call people to life, if they were able, as they are to put them to death—and with as little reason. But now, since the argument has thus far prevailed, the only question which remains to be considered is, whether we shall do rightly either in escaping or in suffering others to aid in our escape and paying them in money and thanks, or whether we shall not do rightly; and if the latter, then death or any other calamity which may ensue on my remaining here must not be allowed to enter into the calculation.

CRITO: I think that you are right, Socrates; how then shall we proceed?

SOCRATES: Let us consider the matter together. Refute me if you can, and I will be convinced; or else cease, my dear friend, from repeating to me that I ought to escape against the wishes of the Athenians: for I am extremely desirous to be persuaded by you, but not against my own better judgment. And now please to consider my first position, and do your best to answer me.

CRITO: I will do my best.

SOCRATES: Are we to say that we are never intentionally to do wrong, or that in one way we ought and in another way we ought not to do wrong, or is doing wrong always evil and dishonorable, as I was just now saying, and as has been already acknowledged by us? Are all our former admissions which were made within a few days to be thrown away? And have we, at our age, been earnestly discoursing with one another all our life long only to discover that we are no better than children? Or are we to rest assured, in spite of the opinion of the many, and in spite of consequences whether better or worse, of the truth of what was then said, that injustice is always an evil and dishonor to him who acts unjustly? Shall we affirm that?

CRITO: Yes.

SOCRATES: Then we must do no wrong?

CRITO: Certainly not.

SOCRATES: Nor when injured injure in return, as the many imagine; for we must injure no one at all?

CRITO: Clearly not.

SOCRATES: Again, Crito, may we do evil?

CRITO: Surely not, Socrates.

SOCRATES: And what of doing evil in return for evil, which is the morality of the many—is that just or not?

CRITO: Not just.

SOCRATES: For doing evil to another is the same as injuring him?

CRITO: Very true.

SOCRATES: Then we ought not to retaliate or render evil for evil to anyone, whatever evil we may have suffered from him. But I would have you consider, Crito, whether you really mean what you are saying. For this opinion has never been held, and never will be held, by any considerable number of persons; and those who are agreed and those who are not agreed upon this point have no common ground, and can only despise one another, when they see how widely they differ. Tell me, then, whether you agree with and assent to my first principle, that neither injury nor retaliation nor warding off evil by evil is ever right. And shall that be the premise of our agreement? Or do you decline and dissent from this? For this has been of old and is still my opinion; but, if you are of another opinion, let me hear what you have to say. If, however, you remain of the same mind as formerly, I will proceed to the next step.

CRITO: You may proceed, for I have not changed my mind.

SOCRATES: Then I will proceed to the next step, which may be put in the form of a question: Ought a man to do what he admits to be right, or ought he to betray the right?

CRITO: He ought to do what he thinks right.

SOCRATES: But if this is true, what is the application? In leaving the prison against the will of the Athenians, do I wrong any? or rather do I not wrong those whom I ought least to wrong? Do I not desert the principles which were acknowledged by us to be just? What do you say?

CRITO: I cannot tell, Socrates, for I do not know.

SOCRATES: Then consider the matter in this way: Imagine that I am about to play truant (you may call the proceeding by any name which you like), and the laws and the government come and interrogate me: "Tell us, Socrates," they say; "What are you about? Are you going by an act of yours to overturn us—the laws and the whole *polis*, as far as you are able? Do you imagine that a *polis* can subsist and not be overthrown, in which the decisions of law have no power, but are set aside and overthrown by individuals?" What will be our answer, Crito, to these and the like words? Anyone, and especially a clever rhetorician, will have a good deal to urge about the evil of setting aside the law which requires a sentence to be carried out; and we might reply, "Yes; but the *polis* has injured us and given an unjust sentence." Suppose I say that?

CRITO: Very good, Socrates.

SOCRATES: "And was that our agreement with you?" the law would say, "or were you to abide by the sentence of the *polis*?" And if I were to express astonishment at their saying this, the law would probably add: "Answer, Socrates, instead of opening your eyes: you are in the habit of asking and answering questions. Tell us what complaint you have to make against us which justifies you in attempting to destroy us and the *polis*? In the first place did we not bring you into existence? Your father married your mother by our aid and begat you. Say whether you have any objection to urge against those of us who regulate marriage?" None, I should reply. "Or against those of us who regulate the system of nurture and education of children in which you were trained? Were not the laws, who have the charge of this, right in commanding your father to train you in music and gymnastics?" Right, I should reply. "Well, then, since you were brought into the world and nurtured and educated by us, can you deny in the first place that you are our child and slave, as your fathers were before you? And if this is true you are not on equal terms with us; nor can you think that you have a right to do to us what we are doing to you. Would you have any right to strike or revile or do any other evil to a father or to your master, if you had one, when you have been struck or reviled by him, or received some other evil at his hands?—you would not say this? And because we think right to destroy you, do you think that you have any right to destroy us in return, and your country as far as you are able? And will you, O professor of true virtue, say that you are justified in this? Has a philosopher like you failed to discover that our country is more to be valued and higher and holier far than mother or father or any ancestor, and more to be regarded in the eyes of the gods and of men of understanding? Also to be soothed, and gently and reverently entreated when angry, even more than a father, and if not persuaded, obeyed? And when we are punished by her, whether with imprisonment or stripes, the punishment is to be endured in silence; and if she leads us to wounds or death in battle, thither we follow as is right; neither may anyone yield or retreat or leave his rank, but whether in battle or in a court of law, or in any other place, he must do what his city and his country order him; or he must change their view of what is just: and if he may do no violence to his father or mother, much less may he do violence to his country." What answer shall we make to this, Crito? Do the laws speak truly, or do they not?

CRITO: I think that they do.

SOCRATES: Then the laws will say: "Consider, Socrates, if this is true, that in your present attempt you are going to do us wrong. For, after having brought you into the world, and nurtured and educated you, and given you and every other citizen a share in every good that we had to give, we further proclaim and give the right to every Athenian, that if he does not like us when he has come of age and has seen the ways of the city, and made our acquaintance, he may go where he pleases and take his goods with him; and none of us laws will forbid him or interfere with him. Any of you who does not like us and the city, and who wants to go to a colony or to any other city, may go where he likes, and take his goods with him. But he who has experience of the manner in which we order justice and administer the *polis*, and still remains, has entered into an implied contract that he will do as we command him. And he who disobeys us is, as we maintain, thrice wrong: first, because in disobeying us he is disobeying his parents; secondly, because we are the authors of his education; thirdly, because he has made an agreement with us that he will duly obey our commands; and he neither obeys them nor convinces us that our commands are wrong; and we do not rudely impose them, but give him the alternative of obeying or convincing us; that is what we offer and he does neither. These are the sort of accusations to which, as we were saying, you, Socrates, will be exposed if you accomplish your intentions; you, above all other Athenians." Suppose I ask, why is this? they will justly retort upon me that I above all other men have acknowledged the agreement. "There is clear proof," they will say, "Socrates, that we and the city were not displeasing to you. Of all Athenians you have been the most constant resident in the city, which, as you never leave, you may be supposed to love. For you never went out of the city either to see the games, except once when you went to the Isthmus, or to any other place unless when you were on military service; nor did you travel as other men do. Nor had you any curiosity to know other states or their laws: your affections did not go beyond us and our *polis*; we were your special favorites, and you acquiesced in our government of you; and this is the *polis* in which you begat your children, which is a proof of your satisfaction. Moreover, you might, if you had liked, have fixed the penalty at banishment in the course of the trial—the *polis* which refuses to let you go now would have let you go then. But you pretended that you preferred death to exile, and that you were not grieved at death. And now you have forgotten these fine sentiments, and pay no respect to us, the laws, of whom you are the destroyer; and are doing what only a miserable slave would do, running away and turning your back upon the compacts and agreements which you made as a citizen. And first of all answer this very question: Are we right in saying that you agreed to be governed according to us in deed, and not in word only? Is that true or not?" How shall we answer that, Crito? Must we not agree?

CRITO: There is no help, Socrates.

SOCRATES: Then will they not say: "You, Socrates, are breaking the covenants and agreements which you made with us at your leisure, not in any haste or under any compulsion or deception, but having had seventy years to think of them, during which time you were at liberty to leave the city, if we were not to your mind, or if our covenants appeared to you to be unfair. You had your choice, and might have gone either to Sparta or Crete, which you often praise for their good government, or to some other Hellenic or foreign city. Whereas you, above all other Athenians, seemed to be so fond of the *polis*, or, in other words, of us her laws (for who would like a *polis* that has no laws?), that you never stirred out of her: the halt, the blind, the maimed, were not more stationary in her than you were. And now you run away and forsake your agreements. Not so, Socrates, if you will take our advice; do not make yourself ridiculous by escaping out of the city.

"For just consider, if you transgress and err in this sort of way, what good will you do, either to yourself or to your friends? That your friends will be driven into exile and deprived of citizenship, or will lose their property, is tolerably certain; and you yourself, if you fly to one of the neighboring cities, as, for example, Thebes or Megara, both of which are well-governed cities, will come to them as an enemy, Socrates, and their government will be against you, and all patriotic citizens will cast an evil eye upon you as a subverter of the laws, and you will confirm in the minds of the judges the justice of their own condemnation of you. For he who is a corrupter of the laws is more than likely to be corrupter of the young and foolish portion of mankind. Will you then flee from well-ordered cities and virtuous men? And is existence worth having on these terms? Or will you go to them without shame, and talk to them, Socrates? And what will you say to them? What you say here about virtue and justice and institutions and laws being the best things among men? Would that be decent of you? Surely not. But if you go away from well-governed states to Crito's friends in Thessaly, where there is great disorder and license, they will be charmed to have the tale of your escape from prison, set off with ludicrous particulars of the manner in which you were wrapped in a goatskin or some other disguise, and metamorphosed as the fashion of runaways is—that is very likely; but will there be no one to remind you that in your old age you violated the most sacred laws from a miserable desire of a little more life? Perhaps not, if you keep them in a good temper; but if they are out of temper you will hear many degrading things; you will live, but how?—as the flatterer of all men, and the servant of all men; and doing what?—eating and drinking in Thessaly, having gone abroad in order that you may get a dinner. And where will be your fine sentiments about justice and virtue then? Say that you wish to live for the sake of your children, that you may bring them up and educate them—will you take them into Thessaly and deprive them of Athenian citizenship? Is that the benefit which you would confer upon them? Or are you under the impression that they will be better cared for and educated here if you are still alive, although absent from them; for that your friends will take care of them? Do you fancy that if you are an inhabitant of Thessaly they will take care of them, and if you are an inhabitant of the other world they will not take care of them? Nay; but if they who call themselves friends are truly friends, they surely will.

"Listen, then, Socrates, to us who have brought you up. Think not of life and children first, and of justice afterwards, but of justice first, that you may be justified before the princes of the world below. For neither will you nor any that belong to you be happier or holier or more just in this life, or happier in another, if you do as Crito bids. Now you depart in innocence, a sufferer and not a doer of evil; a victim, not of the laws, but of men. But if you go forth, returning evil for evil, and injury for injury, breaking the covenants and agreements which you have made with us, and wronging those whom you ought least to wrong, that is to say, yourself, your friends, your country, and us, we shall be angry with you while you live, and our brethren, the laws in the world below, will receive you as an enemy; for they will know that you have done your best to destroy us. Listen, then, to us and not to Crito."

This is the voice which I seem to hear murmuring in my ears, like the sound of the flute in the ears of the mystic; that voice, I say, is humming in my ears, and prevents me from hearing any other. And I know that anything more which you will say will be in vain. Yet speak, if you have anything to say.

CRITO: I have nothing to say, Socrates.

SOCRATES: Then let me follow the intimations of the will of god.

8. Plato, *Republic*

The Republic, also written by Plato, is his best-known and longest work. In it Socrates proposes a blueprint for an ideal state, ruled by philosophers. During the course of the dialogue, Plato also raises important questions about human nature, the nature of justice and of law, and the meaning of knowledge. Although the design of his state was anti-democratic and at odds with Athenian values, his ideas on education, equality, knowledge and justice have had an enormous impact on Western thought.

The scene is set in the house of Cephalus at the Piraeus; and the whole dialogue is narrated by Socrates the day after it actually took place to Timaeus, Hermocrates, Critias, and a nameless person, who are introduced in the Timaeus.

I went down yesterday to the Piraeus with Glaucon, the son of Ariston, that I might offer up my prayers to the goddess; and also because I wanted to see in what manner they would celebrate the festival, which was a new thing. I was delighted with the procession of the inhabitants; but that of the Thracians was equally, if not more, beautiful. When we had finished our prayers and viewed the spectacle, we turned in the direction of the city; and at that instant Polemarchus, the son of Cephalus, chanced to catch sight of us from a distance as we were starting on our way home, and told his servant to run and bid us wait for him. The servant took hold of me by the cloak behind, and said, Polemarchus desires you to wait.

I turned round, and asked him where his master was.

"There he is," said the youth, "coming after you, if you will only wait."

"Certainly we will," said Glaucon; and in a few minutes Polemarchus appeared, and with him Adeimantus, Glaucon's brother, Niceratus, the son of Nicias, and several others who had been at the procession.

Polemarchus said to me, "I perceive, Socrates, that you and your companion are already on your way to the city."

"You are not far wrong," I said.

"But do you see," he rejoined, "how many we are?"

"Of course."

"And are you stronger than all these? For if not, you will have to remain where you are."

"May there not be the alternative," I said, "that we may persuade you to let us go?"

"But can you persuade us if we refuse to listen to you?" he said.

"Certainly not," replied Glaucon.

"Then we are not going to listen; of that you may be assured."

Adeimantus added, "Has no one told you of the torch-race on horseback in honor of the goddess which will take place in the evening?"

"With horses!" I replied. "That is a novelty. Will horsemen carry torches and pass them one to another during the race?"

"Yes," said Polemarchus; "and not only so, but a festival will be celebrated at night, which you certainly ought to see. Let us rise soon after supper and see this festival; there will be a gathering of young men, and we will have a good talk. Stay then, and do not be perverse."

Glaucon said, "I suppose, since you insist, that we must."

"Very good," I replied.

Accordingly we went with Polemarchus to his house; and there we found his brothers Lysias and Euthydemus, and with them Thrasymachus the Chalcedonian, Charmantides the Paeanian, and Cleitophon, the son of Aristonymus. There too was Cephalus, the father of Polemarchus, whom I had not seen for a long time, and I thought him very much aged. He was seated on a cushioned chair, and had a garland on his head, for he had been sacrificing in the court; and there were some other chairs in the room arranged in a semicircle, upon which we sat down by him. He saluted me eagerly, and then he said, "You don't come to see me, Socrates, as often as you ought. If I were still able to go and see you I would not ask you to come to me. But at my age I can hardly get to the city, and therefore you should come more often to the Piraeus. For, let me tell you that the more the pleasures of the body fade away, the greater to me are the pleasure and charm of conversation. Do not, then, deny my request, but make our house your resort and keep company with these young men; we are old friends, and you will be quite at home with us."

I replied, "There is nothing which for my part I like better, Cephalus, than conversing with aged men; for I regard them as travelers who have gone a journey which I too may have to go, and of whom I ought to inquire whether the way is smooth and easy or rugged and difficult. And this is a question which I should like to ask of you, who have arrived at that time which the poets call the 'threshold of old age'. Is life harder toward the end, or what report do you give of it?"

"I will tell you, Socrates," he said, "what my own feeling is. Men of my age flock together; we are birds of a feather, as the old proverb says; and at our meetings the tale of my acquaintance commonly is: I cannot eat, I cannot drink; the pleasures of youth and love are fled away; there was a good time once, but now that is gone, and life is no longer life. Some complain of the slights which are put upon them by relations, and they will tell you sadly of how many evils their old age is the cause. But to me, Socrates, these complainers seem to blame that which is not really in fault. For if old age were the cause, I too, being old, and every other old man would have felt as they do. But this is not my own experience, nor that of others whom I have known. How well I remember the aged poet Sophocles, when in answer to the question, 'How does love suit with age, Sophocles—are you still the man you were?' 'Peace,' he replied; 'most gladly have I escaped the thing of which you speak; I feel as if I had escaped from a mad and furious master.' His words have often occurred to my mind since, and they seem as good to me now as at the time when he uttered them. For certainly old age has a great sense of calm and freedom; when the passions relax their hold, then, as Sophocles says, we are freed from the grasp not of one mad master only, but of many. The truth is, Socrates, that these regrets, and also the complaints about relations, are to be attributed to the same cause, which is not old age, but men's characters and tempers; for he who is of a calm and happy nature will hardly feel the pressure of age, but to him who is of an opposite disposition youth and age are equally a burden."

I listened in admiration, and wanting to draw him out, that he might go on—"Yes, Cephalus," I said; "but I rather suspect that people in general are not convinced by you when you speak thus; they think that old age sits lightly upon you, not because of your happy disposition, but because you are rich, and wealth is well known to be a great comforter."

"You are right," he replied; "they are not convinced; and there is something in what they say; not, however, so much as they imagine. I might answer them as Themistocles answered the Seriphian who was abusing him and saying that he was famous, not for his own merits but because he was an Athenian, 'If you had been a native of my country or I of yours, neither of us would have been famous.' And to those who are not rich and are impatient of old age, the same reply may be made; for to the good poor man old age cannot be a light burden, nor can a bad rich man ever have peace with himself."

"May I ask, Cephalus, whether your fortune was for the most part inherited or acquired by you?"

"Acquired! Socrates; do you want to know how much I acquired? In the art of making money I have been midway between my father and grandfather; for my grandfather, whose name I bear, doubled and trebled the value of his patrimony, that which he inherited being much what I possess now; but my father, Lysanias, reduced the property below what it is at present; and I shall be satisfied if I leave to these my sons not less, but a little more, than I received."

"That was why I asked you the question," I replied, "because I see that you are indifferent about money, which is a characteristic rather of those who have inherited their fortunes than of those who have acquired them; the makers of fortunes have a second love of money as a creation of their own, resembling the affection of authors for their own poems, or of parents for their children, besides that natural love of it for the sake of use and profit which is common to them and all men. And hence they are very bad company, for they can talk about nothing but the praises of wealth."

"That is true," he said.

"Yes, that is very true, but may I ask another question? What do you consider to be the greatest blessing which you have reaped from your wealth?"

"One," he said, "of which I could not expect easily to convince others. For let me tell you, Socrates, that when a man thinks himself to be near death, fears and cares enter into his mind which he never had before; the tales of a world below and the punishment which is exacted there of deeds done here were once a laughing matter to him, but now he is tormented with the thought that they may be true, either from the weakness of age, or because he is now drawing nearer to that other place, he has a clearer view of these things; suspicions and alarms crowd thickly upon him, and he begins to reflect and consider what wrongs he has done to others. And when he finds that the sum of his transgressions is great he will many a time like a child start up in his sleep for fear, and he is filled with a dark foreboding. But to him who is conscious of no sin, sweet hope, as Pindar charmingly says, is the kind nurse of his age; 'Hope,' he says, 'cherishes the soul of him who lives in justice and holiness, and is the nurse of his age and the companion of his journey—hope which is mightiest to sway the restless soul of man.'

"How admirable are his words! And the great blessing of riches,

I do not say to every man, but to a good man, is that he has had no occasion to deceive or to defraud others, either intentionally or unintentionally; and when he departs to the world below he is not in any apprehension about offerings due to the gods or debts which he owes to men. Now to this peace of mind the possession of wealth greatly contributes; and therefore I say, that, setting one thing against another, of the many advantages which wealth has to give, to a man of sense this is in my opinion the greatest."

"Well said, Cephalus," I replied; "but as concerning justice, what is it?—to speak the truth and to pay your debts—no more than this? And even to this are there not exceptions? Suppose that a friend when in his right mind has deposited arms with me and he asks for them when he is not in his right mind, ought I to give them back to him? No one would say that I ought or that I should be right in doing so, any more than they would say that I ought always to speak the truth to one who is in his condition."

"You are quite right," he replied.

"But then," I said, "speaking the truth and paying your debts is not a correct definition of justice."

"Quite correct, Socrates, if Simonides is to be believed," said Polemarchus, interposing.

"I fear," said Cephalus, "that I must go now, for I have to look after the sacrifices, and I hand over the argument to Polemarchus and the company."

"Is not Polemarchus your heir?" I said.

"To be sure," he answered, and went away laughing to the sacrifices.

"Tell me then, O you heir of the argument, what did Simonides say, and according to you, truly say, about justice?"

"He said that the repayment of a debt is just, and in saying so he appears to me to be right."

"I shall be sorry to doubt the word of such a wise and inspired man, but his meaning, though probably clear to you, is the reverse of clear to me. For he certainly does not mean, as we were just now saying, that I ought to return a deposit of arms or of anything else to one who asks for it when he is not in his right senses; and yet a deposit cannot be denied to be a debt."

"True."

"Then when the person who asks me is not in his right mind I am by no means to make the return?"

"Certainly not."

"When Simonides said that the repayment of a debt was justice, he did not mean to include that case?"

"Certainly not; for he thinks that a friend ought always to do good to a friend, and never evil."

"You mean that the return of a deposit of gold which is to the injury of the receiver, if the two parties are friends, is not the repayment of a debt—that is what you would imagine him to say?"

"Yes."

"And are enemies also to receive what we owe to them?"

"To be sure," he said, "they are to receive what we owe them; and an enemy, as I take it, owes to an enemy that which is due or proper to him—that is to say, evil."

"Simonides, then, after the manner of poets, would seem to have spoken darkly of the nature of justice; for he really meant to say that justice is the giving to each man what is proper to him, and this he termed a debt."

"That must have been his meaning," he said.

"By heaven!" I replied; "and if we asked him what due or proper thing is given by medicine, and to whom, what answer do you think that he would make to us?"

"He would surely reply that medicine gives drugs and meat and drink to human bodies."

"And what due or proper thing is given by cookery, and to what?"

"Seasoning to food."

"And what is that which justice gives, and to whom?"

"If, Socrates, we are to be guided at all by the analogy of the preceding instances, then justice is the art which gives good to friends and evil to enemies."

"That is his meaning, then?"

"I think so."

"And who is best able to do good to his friends and evil to his enemies in time of sickness?"

"The physician."

"Or when they are on a voyage, amid the perils of the sea?"

"The pilot."

"And in what sort of actions or with a view to what result is the just man most able to do harm to his enemy and good to his friend?"

"In going to war against the one and in making alliances with the other."

"But when a man is well, my dear Polemarchus, there is no need of a physician?"

"No."

"And he who is not on a voyage has no need of a pilot?"

"No."

"Then in time of peace justice will be of no use?"

"I am very far from thinking so."

"You think that justice may be of use in peace as well as in war?"

"Yes."

"Like husbandry for the acquisition of corn?"

"Yes."

"Or like shoe making for the acquisition of shoes—that is what you mean?"

"Yes."

"And what similar use or power of acquisition has justice in time of peace?"

"In contracts, Socrates, justice is of use."

"And by contracts you mean partnerships?"

"Exactly."

"But is the just man or the skillful player a more useful and better partner at a game of checkers?"

"The skillful player."

"And in the laying of bricks and stones is the just man a more useful or better partner than the builder?"

"Quite the reverse."

"Then in what sort of partnership is the just man a better partner than the harp-player, as in playing the harp the harp player is certainly a better partner than the just man?"

"In a money partnership."

"Yes, Polemarchus, but surely not in the use of money; for you do not want a just man to be your counselor in the purchase or sale of a horse; a man who is knowing about horses would be better for that, would he not?"

"Certainly."

"And when you want to buy a ship, the shipwright or the pilot would be better?"

"True."

"Then what is that joint use of silver or gold in which the just man is to be preferred?"

"When you want a deposit to be kept safely."

"You mean when money is not wanted, but allowed to lie?"

"Precisely."

"That is to say, justice is useful when money is useless?"

"That is the inference."

"And when you want to keep a pruning-hook safe, then justice is useful to the individual and to the *polis*; but when you want to use it, then the art of the vine-dresser?"

"Clearly."

"And when you want to keep a shield or a lyre, and not to use them, you would say that justice is useful; but when you want to use them, then the art of the soldier or of the musician?"

"Certainly."

"And so of all other things—justice is useful when they are useless, and useless when they are useful?"

"That is the inference."

"Then justice is not good for much. But let us consider this further point. Is not he who can best strike a blow in a boxing match or in any kind of fighting best able to ward off a blow?"

"Certainly."

"And he who is most skillful in preventing or escaping from a disease is best able to create one?"

"True."

"And he is the best guard of a camp who is best able to steal a march upon the enemy?"

"Certainly."

"Then he who is a good keeper of anything is also a good thief?"

"That, I suppose, is to be inferred."

"Then if the just man is good at keeping money, he is good at stealing it."

"That is implied in the argument."

"Then after all, the just man has turned out to be a thief. And this is a lesson which I suspect you must have learnt out of Homer; for he, speaking of Autolycus, the maternal grandfather of Odysseus, who is a favorite of his, affirms that 'He was excellent above all men in theft and perjury.' And so, you and Homer and Simonides are agreed that justice is an art of theft; to be practiced, however, 'for the good of friends and for the harm of enemies'—that was what you were saying?"

"No, certainly not that, though I do not now know what I did say; but I still stand by the latter words."

"Well, there is another question. By friends and enemies do we mean those who are so really, or only in seeming?"

"Surely," he said, "a man may be expected to love those whom he thinks good, and to hate those whom he thinks evil."

"Yes, but do not persons often err about good and evil; many who are not good seem to be so, and conversely?"

"That is true."

"Then to them the good will be enemies and the evil will be their friends? True."

"And in that case they will be right in doing good to the evil and evil to the good?"

"Clearly."

"But the good are just and would not do an injustice?"

"True."

"Then according to your argument it is just to injure those who do no wrong?"

"Nay, Socrates; the doctrine is immoral."

"Then I suppose that we ought to do good to the just and harm to the unjust?"

"I like that better."

"But see the consequence. Many a man who is ignorant of human nature has friends who are bad friends, and in that case he ought to do harm to them; and he has good enemies whom he ought to benefit; but, if so, we shall be saying the very opposite of that which we affirmed to be the meaning of Simonides."

"Very true," he said; "and I think that we had better correct an error into which we seem to have fallen in the use of the words 'friend' and 'enemy.'"

"What was the error, Polemarchus?" I asked.

"We assumed that he is a friend who seems to be or who is thought good."

"And how is the error to be corrected?"

"We should rather say that he is a friend who is, as well as seems, good; and that he who seems only and is not good, only seems to be and is not a friend; and of an enemy the same may be said."

"You would argue that the good are our friends and the bad our enemies?"

"Yes."

"And instead of saying simply as we did at first, that it is just to do good to our friends and harm to our enemies, we should further say, 'It is just to do good to our friends when they are good, and harm to our enemies when they are evil?'"

"Yes, that appears to me to be the truth."

"But ought the just to injure anyone at all?"

"Undoubtedly he ought to injure those who are both wicked and his enemies."

"When horses are injured, are they improved or deteriorated?"

"The latter."

"Deteriorated, that is to say, in the good qualities of horses, not of dogs?"

"Yes, of horses."

"And dogs are deteriorated in the good qualities of dogs, and not of horses?"

"Of course."

"And will not men who are injured be deteriorated in that which is the proper virtue of man?"

"Certainly."

"And that human virtue is justice?"

"To be sure."

"Then men who are injured are of necessity made unjust?"

"That is the result."

"But can the musician by his art make men unmusical?"

"Certainly not."

"Or the horseman by his art make them bad horsemen?"

"Impossible."

"And can the just by justice make men unjust, or speaking generally, can the good by virtue make them bad?"

"Assuredly not."

"Any more than heat can produce cold?"

"It cannot."

"Or drought moisture?"

"Clearly not."

"Nor can the good harm anyone?"

"Impossible."

"And the just is the good?"

"Certainly."

"Then to injure a friend or anyone else is not the act of a just man, but of the opposite, who is the unjust?"

"I think that what you say is quite true, Socrates."

"Then if a man says that justice consists in the repayment of debts, and that good is the debt which a just man owes to his friends, and evil the debt which he owes to his enemies—to say this is not wise; for it is not true, if, as has been clearly shown, the injuring of another can be in no case just."

"I agree with you," said Polemarchus.

"Then you and I are prepared to take up arms against anyone who attributes such a saying to Simonides or Bias or Pittacus, or any other wise man or seer?"

"I am quite ready to do battle at your side," he said.

"Shall I tell you whose I believe the saying to be?"

"Whose?"

"I believe that Periander or Perdiccas or Xerxes or Ismenias the Theban, or some other rich and mighty man, who had a great opinion of his own power, was the first to say that justice is 'doing good to your friends and harm to your enemies.'"

"Most true," he said.

"Yes," I said; "but if this definition of justice also breaks down, what other can be offered?"

Several times in the course of the discussion Thrasymachus had made an attempt to get the argument into his own hands, and had been put down by the rest of the company, who wanted to hear the end. But when Polemarchus and I had done speaking and there was a pause, he could no longer hold his peace; and, gathering himself up, he came at us like a wild beast, seeking to devour us. We were quite panic-stricken at the sight of him.

He roared out to the whole company, "What folly, Socrates, has taken possession of you all? And why do you readily fall behind one another? I say that if you want really to know what justice is, you should not only ask but answer, and you should not seek honor to yourself from the refutation of an opponent, but have your own answer; for there is many a one who can ask and cannot answer. And now I will not have you say that justice is duty or advantage or profit or gain or interest, for this sort of nonsense will not do for me; I must have clearness and accuracy."

I was panic-stricken at his words, and could not look at him without trembling. Indeed I believe that if I had not fixed my eye upon him, I should have been struck dumb, but when I saw his fury rising, I looked at him first, and was therefore able to reply to him.

"Thrasymachus," I said, with a quiver, "don't be hard on us. Polemarchus and I may have been guilty of a little mistake in the argument, but I can assure you that the error was not intentional. If we were seeking for a piece of gold, you would not imagine that we were wasting time and so losing our chance of finding it. And why, when we are seeking for justice, a thing more precious than many pieces of gold, do you say that we are weakly yielding to one another and not doing our utmost to get at the truth? Nay, my good friend, we are most willing and anxious to do so, but the fact is that we cannot. And if so, you people who know all things should pity us and not be angry with us."

"How characteristic of Socrates!" he replied, with a bitter laugh; "that's your ironical style! Did I not foresee—have I not already told you, that whatever he was asked he would refuse to answer, and try irony or any other shuffle, in order that he might avoid answering?"

"You are a philosopher, Thrasymachus," I replied, "and well know that if you ask a person what numbers make up twelve, taking care to prohibit him whom you ask from answering twice six, or three times four, or six times two, or four times three, 'for this sort of nonsense will not do for me'—then obviously, if that is your way of putting the question, no one can answer you. But suppose that he were to retort, 'Thrasymachus, what do you mean? If one of these numbers which you interdict be the true answer to the question, am I falsely to say some other number which is not the right one?—Is that your meaning?' How would you answer him?"

"Just as if the two cases were at all alike!" he said.

"Why should they not be?" I replied; "and even if they are not, but only appear to be so to the person who is asked, ought he not to say what he thinks, whether you and I forbid him or not?"

"I presume then that you are going to make one of the interdicted answers?"

"I dare say that I may, notwithstanding the danger, if upon reflection I approve of any of them."

"But what if I give you an answer about justice that is better," he said, "than any of these? What do you deserve to have done to you?"

"Done to me!—as becomes the ignorant, I must learn from the wise—that is what I deserve to have done to me."

"What, and no payment! A pleasant notion!"

"I will pay when I have the money," I replied.

"But you have, Socrates," said Glaucon, "and you, Thrasymachus, need be under no anxiety about money, for we will all make a contribution for Socrates."

"Yes," he replied, "and then Socrates will do as he always does —refuse to answer himself, but take and pull to pieces the answer of someone else."

"Why, my good friend," I said, "how can anyone answer who knows, and says that he knows, just nothing; and who, even if he has some faint notions of his own, is told by a man of authority not to utter them? The natural thing is, that the speaker should be someone like yourself who professes to know and can tell what he knows. Will you then kindly answer, for the edification of the company and of myself?"

Glaucon and the rest of the company joined in my request, and Thrasymachus, as anyone might see, was in reality eager to speak; for he thought that he had an excellent answer, and would distinguish himself. But at first he affected to insist on my answering; at length he consented to begin. "Behold," he said, "the wisdom of Socrates; he refuses to teach himself, and goes about learning of others, to whom he never even says, 'Thank you.'"

"That I learn of others," I replied, "is quite true; but that I am ungrateful I wholly deny. Money I have none, and therefore I pay in praise, which is all I have; and how ready I am to praise anyone who appears to me to speak well you will very soon find out when you answer; for I expect that you will answer well."

"Listen, then," he said; "I proclaim that justice is nothing else than the interest of the stronger. And now why do you not praise me? But of course you won't."

"Let me first understand you," I replied. "Justice, as you say, is the interest of the stronger. What, Thrasymachus, is the meaning of this? You cannot mean to say that because Polydamas is stronger than we are, and finds the eating of beef conducive to his bodily strength, that to eat beef is therefore equally for us who are weaker?"

"That's abominable of you, Socrates; you take the words in the sense which is most damaging to the argument."

"Not at all, my good sir," I said; "I am trying to understand them; and I wish that you would be a little clearer."

"Well," he said, "have you never heard that forms of government differ—there are tyrannies, and there are democracies, and there are aristocracies?"

"Yes, I know."

"And the government is the ruling power in each *polis?*"

"Certainly."

"And the different forms of government make laws democratic, aristocratic, tyrannical, with a view to their several interests; and these laws, which are made by them for their own interests, are the justice which they deliver to their subjects, and him who transgresses them they punish as a breaker of the law, and unjust. And that is what I mean when I say that in all states there is the same principle of justice, which is the interest of the government; and as the government must be supposed to have power, the only reasonable conclusion is that everywhere there is one principle of justice, which is the interest of the stronger."

"Now I understand you," I said; "and whether you are right or not I will try to discover. But let me remark that in defining justice you have yourself used the word 'interest,' which you forbade me to use. It is true, however, that in your definition the words 'of the stronger' are added."

"A small addition, you must allow," he said.

"Great or small, never mind about that; we must first inquire whether what you are saying is the truth. Now we are both agreed that justice is interest of some sort, but you go on to say 'of the stronger'; about this addition I am not so sure, and must therefore consider further."

"Proceed."

"I will; and first tell me, do you admit that it is just for subjects to obey their rulers?"

"I do."

"But are the rulers of states absolutely infallible, or are they sometimes liable to err."

"To be sure," he replied, "they are liable to err?"

"Then in making their laws they may sometimes make them rightly, and sometimes not?"

"True."

"When they make them rightly, they make them agreeably to their interest; when they are mistaken, contrary to their interest; you admit that?"

"Yes."

"And the laws which they make must be obeyed by their subjects—and that is what you call justice?"

"Doubtless."

"Then justice, according to your argument, is not only obedience to the interest of the stronger, but the reverse?"

"What is that you are saying?" he asked.

"I am only repeating what you are saying, I believe. But let us consider, Have we not admitted that the rulers may be mistaken about their own interest in what they command, and also that to obey them is justice? Has not that been admitted?"

"Yes."

"Then you must also have acknowledged justice not to be for the interest of the stronger, when the rulers unintentionally command things to be done which are to their own injury. For if, as you say, justice is the obedience which the subject renders to their commands, in that case, O wisest of men, is there any escape from the conclusion that the weaker are commanded to do, not what is for their interest, but what is for the injury of the stronger?"

"Nothing can be clearer, Socrates," said Polemarchus.

"Yes," said Cleitophon, interposing, "if you are allowed to be his witness."

"But there is no need of any witness," said Polemarchus, "for Thrasymachus himself acknowledges that rulers may sometime command what is not for their own interest, and that for subjects to obey them is justice."

"Yes, Polemarchus—Thrasymachus said that for subjects to do what was commanded by their rulers is just."

"Yes, Cleitophon, but he also said that justice is the interest of the stronger, and, while admitting both these propositions, he further acknowledged that the stronger may command the weaker who are his subjects to do what is not for his own interest; whence follows that justice is the injury quite as much as the interest of the stronger."

"But," said Cleitophon, "he meant by the interest of the stronger what the stronger thought to be his interest—this was what the weaker had to do; and this was affirmed by him to be justice."

"Those were not his words," rejoined Polemarchus.

"Never mind," I replied, "if he now says that they are, let us accept his statement. Tell me, Thrasymachus, I said, did you mean by justice what the stronger thought to be his interest, whether really so or not?"

"Certainly not," he said. "Do you suppose that I call him who is mistaken the stronger at the time when he is mistaken?"

"Yes," I said, "my impression was that you did so, when you admitted that the ruler was not infallible, but might be sometimes mistaken."

"You argue like an informer, Socrates. Do you mean, for example, that he who is mistaken about the sick is a physician in that he is mistaken? Or that he who errs in arithmetic or grammar is an arithmetician or grammarian at the time when he is making the mistake, in respect of the mistake? True, we say that the physician or arithmetician or grammarian has made a mistake, but this is only a way of speaking; for the fact is that neither the grammarian nor any other person of skill ever makes a mistake in so far as he is what his name implies; then none of them err unless their skill fails them, and then they cease to be skilled artists. No artist or sage or ruler errs at the time when he is what his name implies; though he is commonly said to err, and I adopted the common mode of speaking. But to be perfectly accurate, since you are such a lover of accuracy, we should say that the ruler, in so far as he is a ruler, is unerring, and, being unerring, always commands that which is for his own interest; and the subject is required to execute his commands; and therefore, as I said at first and now repeat, justice is the interest of the stronger."

"Indeed, Thrasymachus, and do I really appear to you to argue like an informer?"

"Certainly," he replied.

"And do you suppose that I ask these questions with any design of injuring you in the argument?"

"Nay," he replied, "'suppose' is not the word—I know it; but you will be found out, and by sheer force of argument you will never prevail."

"I shall not make the attempt, my dear man; but to avoid any misunderstanding occurring between us in future, let me ask, in what sense do you speak of a ruler whose interests are justly executed by an inferior—is he a ruler in the popular or in the strict sense of the term?"

"In the strictest of all senses," he said. "And now cheat and play the informer if you can; I ask no quarter at your hands. But you never will be able, never."

"And do you imagine," I said, "that I am such a madman as to try and cheat Thrasymachus? I might as well shave a lion."

"Why," he said, "you made the attempt a minute ago, and you failed."

"Enough," I said, "of these civilities. It will be better that I should ask you a question. Is the physician, taken in that strict sense of which you are speaking, a healer of the sick or a maker of money? And remember that I am now speaking of the true physician."

"A healer of the sick," he replied.

"And the pilot—that is to say, the true pilot—is he a captain of sailors or a mere sailor?"

"A captain of sailors."

"The circumstance that he sails in the ship is not to be taken into account; neither is he to be called a sailor; the name pilot by which he is distinguished has nothing to do with sailing, but is significant of his skill and of his authority over the sailors."

"Very true," he said.

"Now," I said, "every art has an interest?"

"Certainly."

"For which the art has to consider and provide?"

"Yes, that is the aim of art."

"And the interest of any art is the perfection of it—this and nothing else?"

"What do you mean?"

"I mean what I may illustrate negatively by the example of the body. Suppose you were to ask me whether the body is self-sufficing or has wants, I should reply, 'Certainly the body has wants; for the body may be ill and require to be cured, and has therefore interests to which the art of medicine ministers; and this is the origin and intention of medicine, as you will acknowledge.' Am I not right?"

"Quite right," he replied.

"But is the art of medicine or any other art faulty or deficient in any quality in the same way that the eye may be deficient in sight or the ear fail of hearing, and therefore requires another art to provide for the interests of seeing and hearing—has art in itself, I say, any similar liability to fault or defect, and does every art require another supplementary art to provide for its interests, and that another and another without end? Or have the arts to look only after their own interests? Or have they no need either of themselves or of another?—having no faults or defects, they have no need to correct them, either by the exercise of their own art or of any other; they have only to consider the interest of their subject-matter. For every art remains pure and faultless while remaining true—that is to say, while perfect and unimpaired. Take the words in your precise sense, and tell me whether I am not right."

"Yes, clearly."

"Then medicine does not consider the interest of medicine, but the interest of the body?"

"True," he said.

"Nor does the art of horsemanship consider the interests of the art of horsemanship, but the interests of the horse; neither do any other arts care for themselves, for they have no needs; they care only for that which is the subject of their art?"

"True," he said.

"But surely, Thrasymachus, the arts are the superiors and rulers of their own subjects?"

To this he assented with a good deal of reluctance.

"Then," I said, "no science or art considers or enjoins the interest of the stronger or superior, but only the interest of the subject and weaker?"

He made an attempt to contest this proposition also, but finally acquiesced.

"Then," I continued, "no physician, in so far as he is a physician, considers his own good in what he prescribes, but the good of his patient; for the true physician is also a ruler having the human body as a subject, and is not a mere money-maker; that has been admitted?"

"Yes."

"And the pilot likewise, in the strict sense of the term, is a ruler of sailors, and not a mere sailor?"

"That has been admitted."

"And such a pilot and ruler will provide and prescribe for the interest of the sailor who is under him, and not for his own or the ruler's interest?"

He gave a reluctant "Yes."

"Then," I said, "Thrasymachus, there is no one in any rule who, in so far as he is a ruler, considers or enjoins what is for his own interest, but always what is for the interest of his subject or suitable to his art; to that he looks, and that alone he considers in everything which he says and does."

When we had got to this point in the argument, and everyone saw that the definition of justice had been completely upset, Thrasymachus, instead of replying to me, said, "Tell me, Socrates, have you got a nurse?"

"Why do you ask such a question," I said, "when you ought rather to be answering?"

"Because she leaves you to snivel, and never wipes your nose; she has not even taught you to know the shepherd from the sheep."

"What makes you say that?" I replied.

"Because you fancy that the shepherd tends the sheep or oxen with a view to their own good and not to the good of himself or his master; and you further imagine that the rulers of states, if they are true rulers, never think of their subjects as sheep, and that they are not studying their own advantage day and night. Oh, no; and so entirely astray are you in your ideas about the just and unjust as not even to know that justice and the just are in reality another's good; that is to say, the interest of the ruler and stronger, and the loss of the subject and servant; and injustice the opposite; for the unjust is lord over the truly simple and just; he is the stronger, and his subjects do what is for his interest, and minister to his happiness, which is very far from being their own. Consider further, most foolish Socrates, that the just is always a loser in comparison with the unjust. First of all, in private contracts: wherever the unjust is the partner of the just you will find that, when the partnership is dissolved, the unjust man has always more and the just less. Secondly, in their dealings with the *polis*: when there is an income-tax, the just man will pay more and the unjust less on the same amount of income; and when there is anything to be received the one gains nothing and the other much. Observe also what happens when they take an office; there is the just man neglecting his affairs and perhaps suffering other losses, and getting nothing out of the public, because he is just; moreover he is hated by his friends and acquaintance for refusing to serve them in unlawful ways. But all this is reversed in the case of the unjust man. I am speaking, as before, of injustice on a large scale in which the advantage of the unjust is most apparent; and my meaning will be most clearly seen if we turn to that highest form of injustice in which the criminal is the happiest of men, and the sufferers or those who refuse to do injustice are the most miserable—that is to say tyranny, which by fraud and force takes away the property of others, not little by little but wholesale; comprehending in one, things sacred as well as profane, private and public; for which acts of wrong, if he were detected perpetrating any one of them singly, he would be punished and incur great disgrace—they who do such wrong in particular cases are called robbers of temples, and man-stealers and burglars and swindlers and thieves. But when a man besides taking away the money of the citizens has made slaves of them, then, instead of these names of reproach, he is termed happy and blessed, not only by the citizens but by all who hear of his having achieved the consummation of injustice. For mankind censure injustice, fearing that they may be the victims of it and not because they shrink from committing it. And thus, as I have shown, Socrates, injustice, when on a sufficient scale, has more strength and freedom and mastery than justice; and, as I said at first, justice is the interest of the stronger, whereas injustice is a man's own profit and interest."

Thrasymachus, when he had thus spoken, having deluged our ears with his words, had a mind to go away. But the company would not let him; they insisted that he should remain and defend his position; and I myself added my own humble request that he would not leave us. "Thrasymachus," I said to him, "excellent man, how suggestive are your remarks! And are you going to run away before you have fairly taught or learned whether they are true or not? Is the attempt to determine the way of man's life so small a matter in your eyes—to determine how life may be passed by each one of us to the greatest advantage?"

"And do I differ from you, he said, as to the importance of the inquiry?"

"You appear rather," I replied, "to have no care or thought about us, Thrasymachus—whether we live better or worse from not knowing what you say you know, is to you a matter of indifference. Pray, friend, do not keep your knowledge to yourself; we are a large party; and any benefit which you confer upon us will be amply rewarded. For my own part I openly declare that I am not convinced, and that I do not believe injustice to be more gainful than justice, even if uncontrolled and allowed to have free play. For, granting that there may be an unjust man who is able to commit injustice either by fraud or force, still this does not convince me of the superior advantage of injustice, and there may be others who are in the same predicament with myself. Perhaps we may be wrong; if so, you in your wisdom should convince us that we are mistaken in preferring justice to injustice."

"And how am I to convince you," he said, "if you are not already convinced by what I have just said; what more can I do for you? Would you have me put the proof bodily into your souls?"

"Heaven forbid!" I said; "I would only ask you to be consistent; or, if you change, change openly and let there be no deception. For I must remark, Thrasymachus, if you will recall what was previously said, that although you began by defining the true physician in an exact sense, you did not observe a like exactness when speaking of the shepherd; you thought that the shepherd as a shepherd tends the sheep not with a view to their own good, but like a mere diner or banqueter with a view to the pleasures of the table; or, again, as a trader for sale in the market, and not as a shepherd. Yet surely the art of the shepherd is concerned only with the good of his subjects; he has only to provide the best for them, since the perfection of the art is already insured whenever all the requirements of it are satisfied. And that was what I was saying just now about the ruler. I conceived that the art of the ruler, considered as a ruler, whether in a *polis* or in private life, could only regard the good of his flock or subjects; whereas you seem to think that the rulers in states, that is to say, the true rulers, like being in authority."

"Think! Nay, I am sure of it."

"Then why in the case of lesser offices do men never take them willingly without payment, unless under the idea that they govern for the advantage not of themselves but of others? Let me ask you a question: Are not the several arts different, by reason of their each having a separate function? And, my dear illustrious friend, do say what you think, that we may make a little progress."

"Yes, that is the difference," he replied.

"And each art gives us a particular good and not merely a general one—medicine, for example, gives us health; navigation, safety at sea, and so on?"

"Yes," he said.

"And the art of payment has the special function of giving pay; but we do not confuse this with other arts, any more than the art of the pilot is to be confused with the art of medicine, because the health of the pilot may be improved by a sea voyage. You would not be inclined to say, would you? that navigation is the art of medicine, at least if we are to adopt your exact use of language?"

"Certainly not."

"Or because a man is in good health when he receives pay you would not say that the art of payment is medicine?"

"I should not."

"Nor would you say that medicine is the art of receiving pay because a man takes fees when he is engaged in healing?"

"Certainly not."

"And we have admitted," I said, "that the good of each art is specially confined to the art?"

"Yes."

"Then, if there be any good which all artists have in common, that is to be attributed to something of which they all have the common use?"

"True," he replied.

"And when the artist is benefited by receiving pay the advantage is gained by an additional use of the art of pay, which is not the art professed by him?"

He gave a reluctant assent to this.

"Then the pay is not derived by the several artists from their respective arts. But the truth is, that while the art of medicine gives health, and the art of the builder builds a house, another art attends them which is the art of pay. The various arts may be doing their own business and benefiting that over which they preside, but would the artist receive any benefit from his art unless he were paid as well?"

"I suppose not."

"But does he therefore confer no benefit when he works for nothing?"

"Certainly, he confers a benefit."

"Then now, Thrasymachus, there is no longer any doubt that neither arts nor governments provide for their own interests; but, as we were before saying, they rule and provide for the interests of their subjects who are the weaker and not the stronger—to their good they attend and not to the good of the superior.

"And this is the reason, my dear Thrasymachus, why, as I was just now saying, no one is willing to govern; because no one likes to take in hand the reformation of evils which are not his concern, without remuneration. For, in the execution of his work, and in giving his orders to another, the true artist does not regard his own interest, but always that of his subjects; and therefore in order that rulers may be willing to rule, they must be paid in one of three modes of payment, money, or honor, or a penalty for refusing."

"What do you mean, Socrates?" said Glaucon. "The first two modes of payment are intelligible enough, but what the penalty is I do not understand, or how a penalty can be a payment."

"You mean that you do not understand the nature of this payment which to the best men is the great inducement to rule?

Of course you know that ambition and avarice are held to be, as indeed they are, a disgrace?"

"Very true."

"And for this reason," I said, "money and honor have no attraction for them; good men do not wish to be openly demanding payment for governing and so to get the name of hirelings, nor by secretly helping themselves out of the public revenues to get the name of thieves. And not being ambitious they do not care about honor. Wherefore necessity must be laid upon them, and they must be induced to serve from the fear of punishment. And this, as I imagine, is the reason why the forwardness to take office, instead of waiting to be compelled, has been deemed dishonorable. Now the worst part of the punishment is that he who refuses to rule is liable to be ruled by one who is worse than himself. And the fear of this, as I conceive, induces the good to take office, not because they would, but because they cannot help—not under the idea that they are going to have any benefit or enjoyment themselves, but as a necessity, and because they are not able to commit the task of ruling to anyone who is better than themselves, or indeed as good. For there is reason to think that if a city were composed entirely of good men, then to avoid office would be as much an object of contention as to obtain office is at present; then we should have plain proof that the true ruler is not meant by nature to regard his own interest, but that of his subjects; and everyone who knew this would choose rather to receive a benefit from another than to have the trouble of conferring one. So far am I from agreeing with Thrasymachus that justice is the interest of the stronger. This latter question need not be further discussed at present; but when Thrasymachus says that the life of the unjust is more advantageous than that of the just, his new statement appears to me to be of a far more serious character. Which of us has spoken truly? And which sort of life, Glaucon, do you prefer?"

"I for my part deem the life of the just to be the more advantageous," he answered.

"Did you hear all the advantages of the unjust which Thrasymachus was rehearsing?"

"Yes, I heard him," he replied, "but he has not convinced me."

"Then shall we try to find some way of convincing him, if we can, that he is saying what is not true?"

"Most certainly," he replied.

"If," I said, "he makes a set speech and we make another recounting all the advantages of being just, and he answers and we rejoin, there must be a numbering and measuring of the goods which are claimed on either side, and in the end we shall want judges to decide; but if we proceed in our inquiry as we lately did, by making admissions to one another, we shall unite the offices of judge and advocate in our own persons."

"Very good," he said.

"And which method do I understand you to prefer?" I said.

"That which you propose."

"Well, then, Thrasymachus," I said, "suppose you begin at the beginning and answer me. You say that perfect injustice is more gainful than perfect justice?"

"Yes, that is what I say, and I have given you my reasons."

"And what is your view about them? Would you call one of them virtue and the other vice?"

"Certainly."

"I suppose that you would call justice virtue and injustice vice?"

"What a charming notion! So likely too, seeing that I affirm injustice to be profitable and justice not."

"What else then would you say?"

"The opposite," he replied.

"And would you call justice vice?"

"No, I would rather say sublime simplicity."

"Then would you call injustice malignity?"

"No; I would rather say discretion."

"And do the unjust appear to you to be wise and good?"

"Yes," he said; "at any rate those of them who are able to be

136

perfectly unjust, and who have the power of subduing states and nations; but perhaps you imagine me to be talking of highwaymen.

"Even this profession, if undetected, has advantages, though they are not to be compared with those of which I was just now speaking."

"I do not think that I misapprehend your meaning, Thrasymachus," I replied; "but still I cannot hear without amazement that you class injustice with wisdom and virtue, and justice with the opposite."

"Certainly I do so class them."

"Now," I said, "you are on more substantial and almost unanswerable ground; for if the injustice which you were maintaining to be profitable had been admitted by you as by others to be vice and deformity, an answer might have been given to you on received principles; but now I perceive that you will call injustice honorable and strong, and to the unjust you will attribute all the qualities which were attributed by us before to the just, seeing that you do not hesitate to rank injustice with wisdom and virtue."

"You have guessed most infallibly," he replied.

"Then I certainly ought not to shrink from going through with the argument so long as I have reason to think that you, Thrasymachus, are speaking your real mind; for I do believe that you are now in earnest and are not amusing yourself at our expense."

"I may be in earnest or not, but what is that to you? To refute the argument is your business."

"Very true," I said; "that is what I have to do. But will you be so good as answer yet one more question? Does the just man try to gain any advantage over the just?"

"Far otherwise; if he did he would not be the simple amusing creature which he is."

"And would he try to go beyond just action?"

"He would not."

"And how would he regard the attempt to gain an advantage over the unjust; would that be considered by him as just or unjust?"

"He would think it just, and would try to gain the advantage; but he would not be able."

"Whether he would or would not be able," I said, "is not to the point. My question is only whether the just man, while refusing to have more than another just man, would wish and claim to have more than the unjust?"

"Yes, he would."

"And what of the unjust—does he claim to have more than the just man and to do more than is just?"

"Of course," he said, "for he claims to have more than all men."

"And the unjust man will strive and struggle to obtain more than the just man or action, in order that he may have more than all?"

"True."

"We may put the matter thus," I said, "the just does not desire more than his like, but more than his unlike, whereas the unjust desires more than both his like and his unlike?"

"Nothing," he said, "can be better than that statement."

"And the unjust is good and wise, and the just is neither?"

"Good again," he said.

"And is not the unjust like the wise and good, and the just unlike them?"

"Of course," he said, "he who is of a certain nature is like others of the same nature; he who is not, is not."

"Each of them," I said, "is like others of similar nature?"

"Certainly," he replied.

"Very good, Thrasymachus," I said; "and now to take the case of the arts. You would admit that one man is a musician and another not a musician?"

"Yes."

"And which is wise and which is foolish?"

"Clearly the musician is wise, and he who is not a musician is foolish."

"And he is good in as far as he is wise, and bad in as far as he is foolish?"

"Yes."

"And you would say the same sort of thing of the physician?"

"Yes."

"And do you think, my excellent friend, that a musician when he adjusts the lyre would desire or claim to exceed or go beyond a musician in the tightening and loosening the strings?"

"I do not think that he would."

"But he would claim to exceed the non-musician?"

"Of course."

"And what would you say of the physician? In prescribing meats and drinks would he wish to go beyond another physician or beyond the practice of medicine?"

"He would not."

"But he would wish to go beyond the non-physician?"

"Yes."

"And about knowledge and ignorance in general; see whether you think that any man who has knowledge ever would wish to have the choice of saying or doing more than another man who has knowledge. Would he not rather say or do the same as his like in the same case?"

"That, I suppose, can hardly be denied."

"And what of the ignorant? would he not desire to have more than either the knowing or the ignorant?"

"I dare say."

"And the knowing is wise?"

"Yes."

"And the wise is good?"

"True."

"Then the wise and good will not desire to gain more than his like, but more than his unlike and opposite?"

"I suppose so."

"Whereas the bad and ignorant will desire to gain more than both?"

"Yes."

"But did we not say, Thrasymachus, that the unjust goes beyond both his like and unlike? Were not these your words?"

139

"They were."

"And you also said that the just will not go beyond his like, but his unlike?"

"Yes."

"Then the just is like the wise and good, and the unjust like the evil and ignorant?"

"That is the inference."

"And each of them is such as his like is?"

"That was admitted."

"Then the just has turned out to be wise and good, and the unjust evil and ignorant."

Thrasymachus made all these admissions, not fluently, as I repeat them, but with extreme reluctance; it was a hot summer's day, and the perspiration poured from him in torrents; and then I saw what I had never seen before, Thrasymachus blushing. As we were now agreed that justice was virtue and wisdom, and injustice vice and ignorance, I proceeded to another point.

"Well," I said, "Thrasymachus, that matter is now settled; but were we not also saying that injustice had strength—do you remember?"

"Yes, I remember," he said, "but do not suppose that I approve of what you are saying or have no answer; if, however, I were to answer, you would be quite certain to accuse me of haranguing; therefore either permit me to have my say out, or if you would rather ask, do so, and I will answer 'Very good,' as they say to story-telling old women, and will nod 'Yes' and 'No.'"

"Certainly not," I said, "if contrary to your real opinion."

"Yes," he said, "I will, to please you, since you will not let me speak. What else would you have?"

"Nothing in the world," I said; "and if you are so disposed I will ask and you shall answer."

"Proceed."

"Then I will repeat the question which I asked before, in order that our examination of the relative nature of justice and injustice may be carried on regularly. A statement was made that injustice is stronger and more powerful than justice, but now justice, having been identified with wisdom and virtue, is easily shown to be stronger than injustice, if injustice is ignorance; this can no longer be questioned by anyone. But I want to view the matter, Thrasymachus, in a different way. You would not deny that a *polis* may be unjust and may be unjustly attempting to enslave other states, or may have already enslaved them, and may be holding many of them in subjection?"

"True," he replied; "and I will add that the best and most perfectly unjust *polis* will be most likely to do so."

"I know," I said, "that such was your position; but what I would further consider is, whether this power which is possessed by the superior *polis* can exist or be exercised without justice or only with justice."

"If you are right in your view, and justice is wisdom, then only with justice; but if I am right, then without justice."

"I am delighted, Thrasymachus, to see you not only nodding assent and dissent, but making answers which are quite excellent."

"That is out of civility to you," he replied.

"You are very kind," I said; "and would you have the goodness also to inform me, whether you think that a *polis*, or an army, or a band of robbers and thieves, or any other gang of evildoers could act at all if they injured one another? No, indeed, he said, they could not."

"But if they abstained from injuring one another, then they might act together better?"

"Yes."

"And this is because injustice creates divisions and hatreds and fighting, and justice imparts harmony and friendship; is not that true, Thrasymachus?"

"I agree," he said, "because I do not wish to quarrel with you."

"How good of you," I said; "but I should like to know also whether injustice, having this tendency to arouse hatred, wherever existing, among slaves or among freemen, will not make them hate one another and set them at variance and render them incapable of common action?"

"Certainly."

"And even if injustice be found in two only, will they not quarrel and fight, and become enemies to one another and to the just?"

"They will."

"And suppose injustice abiding in a single person, would your wisdom say that she loses or that she retains her natural power?"

"Let us assume that she retains her power."

"Yet is not the power which injustice exercises of such a nature that wherever she takes up her abode, whether in a city, in an army, in a family, or in any other body, that body is, to begin with, rendered incapable of united action by reason of sedition and distraction? And does it not become its own enemy and at variance with all that opposes it, and with the just? Is not this the case?"

"Yes, certainly."

"And is not injustice equally fatal when existing in a single person—in the first place rendering him incapable of action because he is not at unity with himself, and in the second place making him an enemy to himself and the just? Is not that true, Thrasymachus?"

"Yes. And, O my friend, I said, surely the gods are just?"

"Granted that they are. But, if so, the unjust will be the enemy of the gods, and the just will be their friends?"

"Feast away in triumph, and take your fill of the argument; I will not oppose you, lest I should displease the company. Well, then, proceed with your answers, and let me have the remainder of my repast. For we have already shown that the just are clearly wiser and better and abler than the unjust, and that the unjust are incapable of common action; nay, more, that to speak as we did of men who are evil acting at any time vigorously together, is not strictly true, for, if they had been perfectly evil, they would have laid hands upon one another; but it is evident that there must have been some remnant of justice in them, which enabled them to combine; if there had not been they would have injured one another as well as their victims; they were but half-villains in their enterprises; for had they been whole villains, and utterly unjust, they would have been utterly incapable of action. That, as I believe, is the truth of the matter, and not what you said at first. But whether the just have a better and happier life than the unjust is a further question which we also proposed to consider. I think that they have, and for the reasons which I have given; but still I should like to examine further, for no light matter is at stake, nothing less than the rule of human life."

"Proceed."

"I will proceed by asking a question. Would you not say that a horse has some end?"

"I should."

"And the end or use of a horse or of anything would be that which could not be accomplished, or not so well accomplished, by any other thing?"

"I do not understand," he said.

"Let me explain. Can you see, except with the eye?"

"Certainly not."

"Or hear, except with the ear?"

"No. These, then, may be truly said to be the ends of these organs?"

"They may."

"But you can cut off a vine-branch with a dagger or with a chisel, and in many other ways?"

"Of course."

"And yet not so well as with a pruning-hook made for the purpose?"

"True."

"May we not say that this is the end of a pruning-hook?"

"We may."

"Then now I think you will have no difficulty in understanding my meaning when I asked the question whether the end of anything would be that which could not be accomplished, or not so well accomplished, by any other thing?"

"I understand your meaning," he said, "and assent."

"And that to which an end is appointed has also an excellence? Need I ask again whether the eye has an end?"

"It has."

"And has not the eye an excellence?"

"Yes."

"And the ear has an end and an excellence also?"

"True."

"And the same is true of all other things; they have each of them an end and a special excellence?"

"That is so."

"Well, and can the eyes fulfill their end if they are wanting in their own proper excellence and have a defect instead?"

"How can they," he said, "if they are blind and cannot see?"

"You mean to say, if they have lost their proper excellence, which is sight; but I have not arrived at that point yet. I would rather ask the question more generally, and only inquire whether the things which fulfill their ends fulfill them by their own proper excellence, and fail of fulfilling them by their own defect?"

"Certainly," he replied.

"I might say the same of the ears; when deprived of their own proper excellence they cannot fulfill their end?"

"True."

"And the same observation will apply to all other things?"

"I agree."

"Well; and has not the soul an end which nothing else can fulfill? for example, to superintend and command and deliberate and the like. Are not these functions proper to the soul, and can they rightly be assigned to any other?"

"To no other."

"And is not life to be reckoned among the ends of the soul?"

"Assuredly," he said.

"And has not the soul an excellence also?"

"Yes."

"And can she or can she not fulfill her own ends when deprived of that excellence?"

"She cannot."

"Then an evil soul must necessarily be an evil ruler and superintendent, and the good soul a good ruler?"

"Yes, necessarily."

"And we have admitted that justice is the excellence of the soul, and injustice the defect of the soul?"

"That has been admitted."

"Then the just soul and the just man will live well, and the unjust man will live ill?"

"That is what your argument proves."

"And he who lives well is blessed and happy, and he who lives ill the reverse of happy?"

"Certainly."

"Then the just is happy, and the unjust miserable?"

"So be it."

"But happiness, and not misery, is profitable?"

"Of course."

"Then, my blessed Thrasymachus, injustice can never be more profitable than justice."

"Let this, Socrates," he said, "be your entertainment at the Bendidea."

"For which I am indebted to you," I said, "now that you have grown gentle toward me and have left off scolding. Nevertheless, I have not been well entertained; but that was my own fault and not yours. As an epicure snatches a taste of every dish which is successively brought to table, he not having allowed himself time to enjoy the one before, so have I gone from one subject to another without having discovered what I sought at first, the nature of justice. I left that inquiry and turned away to consider whether justice is virtue and wisdom, or evil and folly; and when there arose a further question about the comparative advantages of justice and injustice, I could not refrain from passing on to that. And the result of the whole discussion has been that I know nothing at all. For I know not what justice is, and therefore I am not likely to know whether it is or is not a virtue, nor can I say whether the just man is happy or unhappy."

With these words I was thinking that I had made an end of the discussion; but the end, in truth, proved to be only a beginning. For Glaucon, who is always the most pugnacious of men, was dissatisfied at Thrasymachus's retirement; he wanted to have the battle out. So he said to me, "Socrates, do you wish really to persuade us, or only to seem to have persuaded us, that to be just is always better than to be unjust?"

"I should wish really to persuade you," I replied, "if I could."

"Then you certainly have not succeeded. Let me ask you now, How would you arrange goods—are there not some which we welcome for their own sakes, and independently of their consequences, as, for example, harmless pleasures and enjoyments, which delight us at the time, although nothing follows from them?"

"I agree in thinking that there is such a class," I replied.

"Is there not also a second class of goods, such as knowledge, sight, health, which are desirable not only in themselves, but also for their results?"

"Certainly," I said.

"And would you not recognize a third class, such as gymnastic, and the care of the sick, and the physician's art; also the various ways of money-making—these do us good but we regard them as disagreeable; and no one would choose them for their own sakes, but only for the sake of some reward or result which flows from them?"

"There is," I said, "this third class also. But why do you ask?"

"Because I want to know in which of the three classes you would place justice?"

"In the highest class," I replied, "among those goods which he who would be happy desires both for their own sake and for the sake of their results."

"Then the many are of another mind; they think that justice is to be reckoned in the troublesome class, among goods which are to be pursued for the sake of rewards and of reputation, but in themselves are disagreeable and rather to be avoided."

"I know," I said, "that this is their manner of thinking, and that this was the thesis which Thrasymachus was maintaining just now, when he censured justice and praised injustice. But I am too stupid to be convinced by him."

"I wish," he said, "that you would hear me as well as him, and then I shall see whether you and I agree. For Thrasymachus seems to me, like a snake, to have been charmed by your voice sooner than he ought to have been; but to my mind the nature of justice and injustice has not yet been made clear. Setting aside their rewards and results, I want to know what they are in themselves, and how they inwardly work in the soul. If you please, then, I will revive the argument of Thrasymachus. And first I will speak of the nature and origin of justice according to the common view of them. Secondly, I will show that all men who practice justice do so against their will, of necessity, but not as a good. And thirdly, I will argue that there is reason in this view, for the life of the unjust is after all better far than the life of the just—if what they say is true, Socrates, since I myself am not of their opinion. But still I acknowledge that I am perplexed when I hear the voices of Thrasymachus and myriads of others dinning in my ears; and, on the other hand, I have never yet heard the superiority of justice to injustice maintained by anyone in a satisfactory way. I want to hear justice praised in respect of itself; then I shall be satisfied, and you are the person from whom I think that I am most likely to hear this; and therefore I will praise the unjust life to the utmost of my power, and my manner of speaking will indicate the manner in which I desire to hear you too praising justice and censuring injustice. Will you say whether you approve of my proposal?"

"Indeed I do; nor can I imagine any theme about which a man of sense would more often wish to converse."

"I am delighted," he replied, "to hear you say so, and shall begin by speaking, as I proposed, of the nature and origin of justice.

"They say that to do injustice is, by nature, good; to suffer injustice, evil; but that the evil is greater than the good. And so when men have both done and suffered injustice and have had experience of both, not being able to avoid the one and obtain the other, they think that they had better agree among themselves to have neither; hence there arise laws and mutual covenants; and that which is ordained by law is termed by them lawful and just. This they affirm to be the origin and nature of justice; it is a mean or compromise, between the best of all, which is to do injustice and not be punished, and the worst of all, which is to suffer injustice without the power of retaliation; and justice, being at a middle point between the two, is tolerated not as a good, but as the lesser evil, and honored by reason of the inability of men to do injustice. For no man who is worthy to be called a man would ever submit to such an agreement if he were able to resist; he would be mad if he did. Such is the received account, Socrates, of the nature and origin of justice.

"Now that those who practice justice do so involuntarily and because they have not the power to be unjust will best appear if we imagine something of this kind; having given both to the just and the unjust power to do what they will, let us watch and see whither desire will lead them; then we shall discover in the very act the just and unjust man to be proceeding along the same road, following their interest, which all natures deem to be their good, and are only diverted into the path of justice by the force of law. The liberty which we are supposing may be most completely given to them in the form of such a power as is said to have been possessed by Gyges, the ancestor of Croesus the Lydian. According to the tradition, Gyges was a shepherd in the service of the King of Lydia; there was a great storm, and an earthquake made an opening in the earth at the place where he was feeding his flock. Amazed at the sight, he descended into the opening, where, among other marvels, he beheld a hollow brazen horse, having doors, at which he, stooping and looking in, saw a dead body of stature, as appeared to him, more than human and having nothing on but a gold ring; this he took from the finger of the dead and reascended. Now the shepherds met together, according to custom, that they might send their monthly report about the flocks to the King; into their assembly he came having the ring on his finger, and as he was sitting among them he chanced to turn the collet of the ring inside his hand, when instantly he became invisible to the rest of the company and they began to speak of him as if he were no longer present. He was astonished at this, and again touching the ring he turned the collet outward and reappeared; he made several trials of the ring, and always with the same result—when he turned the collet inward he became invisible, when outward he reappeared. Whereupon he contrived to be chosen one of the messengers who were sent to the court; where as soon as he arrived he seduced the Queen, and with her help conspired against the King and slew him and took the kingdom. Suppose now that there were two such magic rings, and the just put on one of them and the unjust the other; no man can be imagined to be of such an iron nature that he would stand fast in justice. No man would keep his hands off what was not his own when he could safely take what he liked out of the market, or go into houses and lie with anyone at his pleasure, or kill or release from prison whom he would, and in all respects be like a god among men. Then the actions of the just would be as the actions of the unjust; they would both come at last to the same point. And this we may truly affirm to be a great proof that a man is just, not willingly or because he thinks that justice is any good to him individually, but of necessity, for wherever anyone thinks that he can safely be unjust, there he is unjust. For all men believe in their hearts that injustice is far more profitable to the individual than justice, and he who argues as I have been supposing, will say that they are right. If you could imagine anyone obtaining this power of becoming invisible, and never doing any wrong or touching what was another's, he would be thought by the onlookers to be a most wretched idiot, although they would praise him to one another's faces, and keep up appearances with one another from a fear that they too might suffer injustice. Enough of this.

"Now, if we are to form a real judgment of the life of the just and unjust, we must isolate them; there is no other way; and how is the isolation to be effected? I answer, Let the unjust man be entirely unjust, and the just man entirely just; nothing is to be taken away from either of them, and both are to be perfectly furnished for the work of their respective lives. First, let the unjust be like other distinguished masters of craft; like the skillful pilot or physician, who knows intuitively his own powers and keeps within their limits, and who, if he fails at any point, is able to recover himself. So let the unjust make his unjust attempts in the right way, and lie hidden if he means to be great in his injustice (he who is found out is nobody); for the highest reach of injustice is, to be deemed just when you are not. Therefore I say that in the perfectly unjust man we must assume the most perfect injustice; there is to be no deduction, but we must allow him, while doing the most unjust acts, to have acquired the greatest reputation for justice. If he has taken a false step he must be able to recover himself; he must be one who can speak with effect, if any of his deeds come to light, and who can force his way where force is required by his courage and strength, and command of money and friends. And at his side let us place the just man in his nobleness and simplicity, wishing, as Aeschylus says, to be and not to seem good. There must be no seeming, for if he seem to be just he will be honored and rewarded, and then we shall not know whether he is just for the sake of justice or for the sake of honor and rewards; therefore, let him be clothed in justice only, and have no other covering; and he must be imagined in a *polis* of life the opposite of the former. Let him be the best of men, and let him be thought the worst; then he will have been put to the proof; and we shall see whether he will be affected by the fear of infamy and its consequences. And let him continue thus to the hour of death; being just and seeming to be unjust. When both have reached the uttermost extreme, the one of justice and the other of injustice, let judgment be given which of them is the happier of the two."

"Heavens! my dear Glaucon," I said, "how energetically you polish them up for the decision, first one and then the other, as if they were two statues."

"I do my best," he said. "And now that we know what they are like there is no difficulty in tracing out the sort of life which awaits either of them. This I will proceed to describe; but as you may think the description a little too coarse, I ask you to suppose, Socrates, that the words which follow are not mine. Let me put them into the mouths of the eulogists of injustice. They will tell you that the just man who is thought unjust will be scourged, racked, bound—will have his eyes burnt out; and, at last, after suffering every kind of evil, he will be impaled. Then he will understand that he ought to seem only, and not to be, just. For the unjust is pursuing a reality; he does not live with a view to appearances—he wants to be really unjust and not to seem only just. In the first place, he is thought just, and therefore bears rule in the city; he can marry whom he will, and give in marriage to whom he will; also he can trade and deal where he likes, and always to his own advantage, because he has no misgivings about injustice; and at every contest, whether in public or private, he gets the better of his antagonists, and gains at their expense, and is rich, and out of his gains he can benefit his friends, and harm his enemies; moreover, he can offer sacrifices, and dedicate gifts to the gods abundantly and magnificently, and can honor the gods or any man whom he wants to honor in a far better style than the just, and therefore he is likely to be dearer than they are to the gods. And thus, Socrates, gods and men are said to unite in making the life of the unjust better than the life of the just."

I was going to say something in answer to Glaucon, when Adeimantus, his brother, interposed, "Socrates," he said, "you do not suppose that there is nothing more to be urged?"

"Why, what else is there?" I answered.

"The strongest point of all has not been even mentioned," he replied.

"Well, then, according to the proverb, 'Let brother help brother'—if he fails in any part, do you assist him; although I must confess that Glaucon has already said quite enough to lay me in the dust, and take from me the power of helping justice."

"Nonsense," he replied. "But let me add something more. There is another side to Glaucon's argument about the praise and censure of justice and injustice, which is equally required in order to bring out what I believe to be his meaning. Parents and tutors are always telling their sons and their wards that they are to be just; but why? Not for the sake of justice, but for the sake of character and reputation; in the hope of obtaining for him who is reputed just some of those offices, marriages, and the like which Glaucon has enumerated among the advantages accruing to the unjust from the reputation of justice. More, however, is made of appearances by this class of persons than by the others; for they throw in the good opinion of the gods, and will tell you of a shower of benefits which the heavens, as they say, rain upon the pious. Some extend their rewards yet further; the posterity, as they say, of the faithful and just shall survive to the third and fourth generation. This is the style in which they praise justice. But about the wicked there is another strain; they bury them in a slough in Hades, and make them carry water in a sieve; also while they are yet living they bring them to infamy, and inflict upon them the punishments which Glaucon described as the portion of the just who are reputed to be unjust; nothing else does their invention supply. Such is their manner of praising the one and censuring the other.

"Once more, Socrates, I will ask you to consider another way of speaking about justice and injustice. The universal voice of mankind is always declaring that justice and virtue are honorable, but grievous and toilsome; and that the pleasures of vice and injustice are easy of attainment, and are only censured by law and opinion. They say also that honesty is for the most part less profitable than dishonesty; and they are quite ready to call wicked men happy, and to honor them both in public and private when they are rich or in any other way influential, while they despise and overlook those who may be weak and poor, even though acknowledging them to be better than the others. But most extraordinary of all is their mode of speaking about virtue and the gods; they say that the gods apportion calamity and misery to many good men, and good and happiness to the wicked. And mendicant prophets go to rich men's doors and persuade them that they have a power committed to them by the gods of making an atonement for a man's own or his ancestor's sins by sacrifices or charms, with rejoicing and feasts; and they promise to harm an enemy, whether just or unjust, at a small cost; with magic arts and incantations binding heaven, as they say, to execute their will; according to which they perform their ritual, and persuade not only individuals, but whole cities, that expiations and atonements for sin may be made by sacrifices and amusements which fill a vacant hour, and are equally at the service of the living and the dead; the latter sort they call mysteries, and they redeem us from the pains of hell, but if we neglect them no one knows what awaits us."

He proceeded, "And now when the young hear all this said about virtue and vice, and the way in which gods and men regard them, how are their minds likely to be affected, my dear Socrates—those of them, I mean, who are quick-witted, and, like bees on the wing, light on every flower, and from all that they hear are prone to draw conclusions as to what manner of persons they should be and in what way they should walk if they would make the best of life? Probably the youth will say to himself in the words of Pindar, 'Can I by justice or by crooked ways of deceit ascend a loftier tower which may be a fortress to me all my days?' For what men say is that, if I am really just and am not also thought just, profit there is none, but the pain and loss on the other hand are unmistakable. But if, though unjust, I acquire the reputation of justice, a heavenly life is promised to me. Since then, as philosophers prove, appearance tyrannizes over truth and is lord of happiness, to appearance I must devote myself. I will describe around me a picture and shadow of virtue to be the vestibule and exterior of my house; behind I will trail the subtle and crafty fox, as Archilochus, greatest of sages, recommends. But I hear someone exclaiming that the concealment of wickedness is often difficult; to which I answer, Nothing great is without price. Nevertheless, the argument indicates that if we would be happy with this direction we should proceed. With a view to concealment we will establish secret brotherhoods and political clubs. And there are professors of rhetoric who teach the art of persuading courts and assemblies; and so, partly by persuasion and partly by force, I shall make unlawful gains and not be punished. Still I hear a voice saying that the gods cannot be deceived, neither can they be compelled. But what if there are no gods? Or, suppose them to have no care of human things—why in either case should we mind about concealment? And even if there are gods, and they do care about us, yet we know of them only from tradition and the genealogies of the poets; and these are the very persons who say that they may be influenced and turned by 'sacrifices and soothing entreaties and by offerings.' Let us be consistent, then, and believe both or neither. If the poets speak truly, why, then, we had better be unjust, and offer of the fruits of injustice; for if we are just, although we may escape the vengeance of heaven, we shall lose the gains of injustice; but, if we are unjust, we shall keep the gains, and by our sinning and praying, and praying and sinning, the gods will be propitiated, and we shall not be punished. 'But there is a world below in which either we or our posterity will suffer for our unjust deeds.' Yes, my friend, that will be the reflection, but there are mysteries and atoning deities, and these have great power. That is what mighty cities declare; and the children of the gods, who were their poets and prophets, bear a like testimony.

"On what principle, then, shall we any longer choose justice rather than the worst injustice? when, if we only unite the latter with a deceitful regard to appearances, we shall fare to our mind both with gods and men, in life and after death, as the most numerous and the highest authorities tell us. Knowing all this,

Socrates, how can a man who has any superiority of mind or person or rank or wealth, be willing to honor justice; or indeed to refrain from laughing when he hears justice praised? And even if there should be someone who is able to disprove the truth of my words, and who is satisfied that justice is best, still he is not angry with the unjust, but is very ready to forgive them, because he also knows that men are not just of their own free will; unless, peradventure, there be someone whom the divinity within him may have inspired with a hatred of injustice, or who has attained knowledge of the truth—but no other man. He only blames injustice, who, owing to cowardice or age or some weakness, has not the power of being unjust. And this is proved by the fact that when he obtains the power, he immediately becomes unjust as far as he can be.

"The cause of all this, Socrates, was indicated by us at the beginning of the argument, when my brother and I told you how astonished we were to find that of all the professing panegyrists of justice—beginning with the ancient heroes of whom many memorials have been preserved for us, and ending with the men of our own time—no one has ever blamed injustice or praised justice except with a view to the glories, honors, and benefits which flow from them. No one has ever adequately described either in verse or prose the true essential nature of either of them abiding in the soul, and invisible to any human or divine eye; or shown that of all the things of a man's soul which he has within him, justice is the greatest good, and injustice the greatest evil. Had this been the universal strain, had you sought to persuade us of this from our youth upward, we should not have been on the watch to keep one another from doing wrong, but everyone would have been his own watchman, because afraid, if he did wrong, of harboring in himself the greatest of evils. I dare say that Thrasymachus and others would seriously hold the language which I have been merely repeating, and words even stronger than these about justice and injustice, grossly, as I conceive, perverting their true nature. But I speak in this vehement manner, as I must frankly confess to you, because I want to hear from you the opposite side; and I would ask you to show not only the superiority which justice has over injustice, but what effect they have on the possessor of them which makes the one to be a good and the other an evil to him. And please, as Glaucon requested of you, to exclude reputations; for unless you take away from each of them his true reputation and add on the false, we shall say that you do not praise justice, but the appearance of it; we shall think that you are only exhorting us to keep injustice dark, and that you really agree with Thrasymachus in thinking that justice is another's good and the interest of the stronger, and that injustice is a man's own profit and interest, though injurious to the weaker. Now as you have admitted that justice is one of that highest class of goods which are desired, indeed, for their results, but in a far greater degree for their own sakes—like sight or hearing or knowledge or health, or any other real and natural and not merely conventional good—I would ask you in your praise of justice to regard one point only; I mean the essential good and evil which justice and injustice work in the possessors of them. Let others praise justice and censure injustice, magnifying the rewards and honors of the one and abusing the other; that is a manner of arguing which, coming from them, I am ready to tolerate, but from you who have spent your whole life in the consideration of this question, unless I hear the contrary from your own lips, I expect something better. And therefore, I say, not only prove to us that justice is better than injustice, but show what either of them do to the possessor of them, which makes the one to be a good and the other an evil, whether seen or unseen by gods and men."

I had always admired the genius of Glaucon and Adeimantus, but on hearing these words I was quite delighted, and said, "Sons of an illustrious father, that was not a bad beginning of the elegiac verses which the admirer of Glaucon made in honor of you after you had distinguished yourselves at the battle of Megara, 'Sons of Ariston,' he sang, 'divine offspring of an illustrious hero.' The epithet is very appropriate, for there is something truly divine in being able to argue as you have done for the superiority of injustice, and remaining unconvinced by your own arguments. And I do believe that you are not convinced—this I infer from your general character, for had I judged only from your speeches I should have mistrusted you. But now, the greater my confidence in you, the greater is my difficulty in knowing what to say. For I am in a strait between two; on the one hand I feel that I am unequal to the task; and my inability is brought home to me by the fact that you were not satisfied with the answer which I made to Thrasymachus, proving, as I thought, the superiority which justice has over injustice. And yet I cannot refuse to help, while breath and speech remain to me; I am afraid that there would be an impiety in being present when justice is evil spoken of and not lifting up a hand in her defense. And therefore I had best give such help as I can."

Glaucon and the rest entreated me by all means not to let the question drop, but to proceed in the investigation. They wanted to arrive at the truth, first, about the nature of justice and injustice, and secondly, about their relative advantages. I told them what I really thought, that the inquiry would be of a serious nature, and would require very good eyes. "Seeing then," I said, "that we are no great wits, I think that we had better adopt a method which I may illustrate thus; suppose that a short-sighted person had been asked by someone to read small letters from a distance; and it occurred to someone else that they might be found in another place which was larger and in which the letters were larger—if they were the same and he could read the larger letters first, and then proceed to the lesser —this would have been thought a rare piece of good-fortune."

"Very true," said Adeimantus; "but how does the illustration apply to our inquiry?"

"I will tell you," I replied; "justice, which is the subject of our inquiry, is, as you know, sometimes spoken of as the virtue of an individual, and sometimes as the virtue of a *polis*."

"True," he replied.

"And is not a *polis* larger than an individual?"

"It is."

"Then in the larger the quantity of justice is likely to be larger and more easily discernible. I propose therefore that we inquire into the nature of justice and injustice, first as they appear in the *polis*, and secondly in the individual, proceeding from the greater to the lesser and comparing them."

"That," he said, "is an excellent proposal."

"And if we imagine the *polis* in process of creation, we shall see the justice and injustice of the *polis* in process of creation also."

"I dare say."

"When the *polis* is completed there may be a hope that the object of our search will be more easily discovered."

"Yes, far more easily."

"But ought we to attempt to construct one?" I said; "for to do so, as I am inclined to think, will be a very serious task. Reflect therefore."

"I have reflected," said Adeimantus, "and am anxious that you should proceed."

"A *polis*," I said, "arises, as I conceive, out of the needs of mankind; no one is self-sufficing, but all of us have many wants. Can any other origin of a *polis* be imagined?"

"There can be no other."

"Then, as we have many wants, and many persons are needed to supply them, one takes a helper for one purpose and another for another; and when these partners and helpers are gathered together in one habitation the body of inhabitants is termed a *polis*."

"True," he said.

"And they exchange with one another, and one gives, and another receives, under the idea that the exchange will be for their good."

"Very true."

"Then," I said, "let us begin and create the idea of a *polis*, keeping in mind that the true creator is necessity, who is the mother of our invention."

"Of course," he replied.

"Now the first and greatest of necessities is food, which is the condition of life and existence."

"Certainly."

"The second is a dwelling, and the third clothing and the like."

"True."

"And now let us see how our city will be able to supply this great demand. We may suppose that one man is a husbandman, another a builder, someone else a weaver—shall we add to them a shoemaker, or perhaps some other purveyor to our bodily wants?"

"Quite right."

"The barest notion of a *polis* must include four or five men."

"Clearly."

"And how will they proceed? Will each bring the result of his labors into a common stock?—the individual husbandman, for example, producing for four, and laboring four times as long and as much as he need in the provision of food with which he supplies others as well as himself; or will he have nothing to do with others and not be at the trouble of producing for them, but provide for himself alone a fourth of the food in a fourth of the time, and in the remaining three-fourths of his time be employed in making a house or a coat or a pair of shoes, having no partnership with others, but supplying himself all his own wants?"

Adeimantus thought that he should aim at producing food only and not at producing everything.

"Probably," I replied, "that would be the better way; and when I hear you say this, I am myself reminded that we are not all alike; there are diversities of natures among us which are adapted to different occupations."

"Very true."

"And will you have a work better done when the workman has many occupations, or when he has only one?"

"When he has only one."

"Further, there can be no doubt that a work is spoiled when not done at the right time?"

"No doubt."

"For business is not disposed to wait until the doer of the

business is at leisure; but the doer must follow up what he is doing, and make the business his first object."

"He must."

"And if so, we must infer that all things are produced more plentifully and easily and of a better quality when one man does one thing which is natural to him and does it at the right time, and leaves other things."

"Undoubtedly."

"Then more than four citizens will be required; for the husbandman will not make his own plough or mattock, or other implements of agriculture, if they are to be good for anything. Neither will the builder make his tools—and he, too, needs many; and in like manner the weaver and shoemaker."

"True."

"Then carpenters and smiths and many other artisans will be sharers in our little *polis*, which is already beginning to grow?"

"True."

"Yet even if we add shepherds and other herdsmen, in order that our husbandmen may have oxen to plough with, and builders as well as husbandmen may have draft cattle, and tanners and weavers fleeces and hides—still our *polis* will not be very large."

"That is true; yet neither will it be a very small *polis* which contains all these."

"Then, again, there is the situation of the city—to find a place where nothing need be imported is well-nigh impossible."

"Impossible."

"Then there must be another class of citizens who will bring the required supply from another city?"

"There must."

"But if the trader goes empty-handed, having nothing which they require who would supply his need, he will come back empty-handed."

"That is certain."

"And therefore what they produce at home must be not only

enough for themselves, but such both in quantity and quality as to accommodate those from whom their wants are supplied."

"Very true."

"Then more husbandmen and more artisans will be required?"

"They will."

"Not to mention the importers and exporters, who are called merchants?"

"Yes."

"Then we shall want merchants?"

"We shall."

"And if merchandise is to be carried over the sea, skillful sailors will also be needed, and in considerable numbers?"

"Yes, in considerable numbers."

"Then, again, within the city, how will they exchange what they produce? To secure such an exchange was, as you will remember, one of our principal objects when we formed them into a society and constituted a *polis*."

"Clearly they will buy and sell."

"Then they will need a market-place, and a money-token for purposes of exchange."

"Certainly."

"Suppose now that a husbandman or an artisan brings some production to market, and he comes at a time when there is no one to exchange with him—is he to leave his calling and sit idle in the market-place?"

"Not at all; he will find people there who, seeing the want, undertake the office of salesmen. In well-ordered states they are commonly those who are the weakest in bodily strength, and therefore of little use for any other purpose; their duty is to be in the market, and to give money in exchange for goods to those who desire to sell, and to take money from those who desire to buy."

"This want, then, creates a class of retail-traders in our *polis*. Is not 'retailer' the term which is applied to those who sit in the market-place engaged in buying and selling, while those who wander from one city to another are called merchants?"

"Yes," he said.

"And there is another class of servants, who are intellectually hardly on the level of companionship; still they have plenty of bodily strength for labor, which accordingly they sell, and are called, if I do not mistake, hirelings, 'hire' being the name which is given to the price of their labor."

"True."

"Then hirelings will help to make up our population?"

"Yes."

"And now, Adeimantus, is our *polis* matured and perfected?"

"I think so."

"Where, then, is justice, and where is injustice, and in what part of the *polis* did they spring up?"

"Probably in the dealings of these citizens with one another. I cannot imagine that they are more likely to be found anywhere else."

"I dare say that you are right in your suggestion," I said; "we had better think the matter out, and not shrink from the inquiry.

"Let us then consider, first of all, what will be their way of life, now that we have thus established them. Will they not produce corn and wine and clothes and shoes, and build houses for themselves? And when they are housed, they will work, in summer, commonly, stripped and barefoot, but in winter substantially clothed and shod. They will feed on barley-meal and flour of wheat, baking and kneading them, making noble cakes and loaves; these they will serve up on a mat of reeds or on clean leaves, themselves reclining the while upon beds strewn with yew or myrtle. And they and their children will feast, drinking of the wine which they have made, wearing garlands on their heads, and singing the praises of the gods, in happy converse with one another. And they will take care that their families do not exceed their means; having an eye to poverty or war."

"But," said Glaucon, interposing, "you have not given them a relish to their meal."

"True," I replied, "I had forgotten; of course they must have a relish—salt and olives and cheese—and they will boil roots and herbs such as country people prepare; for a dessert we shall give them figs and peas and beans; and they will roast myrtle-berries and acorns at the fire, drinking in moderation. And with such a diet they may be expected to live in peace and health to a good old age, and bequeath a similar life to their children after them."

"Yes, Socrates," he said, "and if you were providing for a city of pigs, how else would you feed the beasts?"

"But what would you have, Glaucon?" I replied.

"Why," he said, "you should give them the ordinary conveniences of life. People who are to be comfortable are accustomed to lie on sofas, and dine off tables, and they should have sauces and sweets in the modern style."

"Yes," I said, "now I understand; the question which you would have me consider is, not only how a *polis*, but how a luxurious *polis* is created; and possibly there is no harm in this, for in such a *polis* we shall be more likely to see how justice and injustice originate. In my opinion the true and healthy constitution of the *polis* is the one which I have described. But if you wish also to see a *polis* at a more complex level, I have no objection. For I suspect that many will not be satisfied with the simpler way of life. They will be for adding sofas and tables and other furniture; also dainties and perfumes and incense and courtesans and cakes, all these not of one sort only, but in every variety. We must go beyond the necessities of which I was at first speaking, such as houses and clothes and shoes; the arts of the painter and the embroiderer will have to be set in motion, and gold and ivory and all sorts of materials must be procured."

"True," he said.

"Then we must enlarge our borders; for the original healthy *polis* is no longer sufficient. Now will the city have to fill and swell with a multitude of callings which are not required by any natural want; such as the whole tribe of hunters and actors, of whom one large class have to do with forms and colors; another will be the votaries of music—poets and their attendant train of rhapsodists, players, dancers, contractors; also makers of divers kinds of articles, including women's dresses. And we shall want more servants. Will not tutors be also in request, and nurses wet and dry, and barbers, as well as confectioners and cooks; and swineherds, too, who were not needed and therefore had no place in the former edition of our *polis*, but are needed now? They must not be forgotten; and there will be animals of many other kinds, if people eat them."

"Certainly."

"And living in this way we shall have much greater need of physicians than before?"

"Much greater."

"And the country which was enough to support the original inhabitants will be too small now, and not enough?"

"Quite true."

"Then a slice of our neighbors' land will be wanted by us for pasture and tillage, and they will want a slice of ours, if, like ourselves, they exceed the limit of necessity, and give themselves up to the unlimited accumulation of wealth?"

"That, Socrates, will be inevitable."

"And so we shall go to war, Glaucon. Shall we not?"

"Most certainly," he replied. "Then, without determining as yet whether war does good or harm, this much we may affirm, that now we have discovered war to be derived from causes which are also the causes of almost all the evils in states, private as well as public."

"Undoubtedly."

"And our *polis* must once more enlarge; and this time the enlargement will be nothing short of a whole army, which will have to go out and fight with the invaders for all that we have, as well as for the things and persons whom we were describing above."

"Why?" he said; "are they not capable of defending themselves?"

"No," I said; "not if we were right in the principle which was acknowledged by all of us when we were framing the *polis*. The principle, as you will remember, was that one man cannot practice many arts with success."

"Very true," he said.

"But is not war an art?

"Certainly."

"And an art requiring as much attention as shoemaking?"

"Quite true."

"And the shoemaker was not allowed by us to be a husbandman, or a weaver, or a builder—in order that we might have our shoes well made; but to him and to every other worker was assigned one work for which he was by nature fitted, and at that he was to continue working all his life long and at no other; he was not to let opportunities slip, and then he would become a good workman. Now nothing can be more important than that the work of a soldier should be well done. But is war an art so easily acquired that a man may be a warrior who is also a husbandman, or shoemaker, or other artisan; although no one in the world would be a good dice or checkers player who merely took up the game as a recreation, and had not from his earliest years devoted himself to this and nothing else?

"No tools will make a man a skilled workman or master of defense, nor be of any use to him who has not learned how to handle them, and has never bestowed any attention upon them. How, then, will he who takes up a shield or other implement of war become a good fighter all in a day, whether with heavy-armed or any other kind of troops?"

"Yes," he said, "the tools which would teach men their own use would be beyond price."

"And the higher the duties of the guardian," I said, "the more time and skill and art and application will be needed by him?"

"No doubt," he replied.

"Will he not also require natural aptitude for his calling?"

"Certainly."

"Then it will be our duty to select, if we can, natures which are fitted for the task of guarding the city?"

"It will."

"And the selection will be no easy matter, I said; but we must be brave and do our best."

"We must."

"Is not the noble youth very like a well-bred dog in respect of guarding and watching?"

"What do you mean?"

"I mean that both of them ought to be quick to see, and swift to overtake the enemy when they see him; and strong too if, when they have caught him, they have to fight with him."

"All these qualities," he replied, "will certainly be required by them."

"Well, and your guardian must be brave if he is to fight well?"

"Certainly."

"And is he likely to be brave who has no spirit, whether horse or dog or any other animal? Have you never observed how invincible and unconquerable is spirit and how the presence of it makes the soul of any creature to be absolutely fearless and indomitable?"

"I have."

"Then now we have a clear notion of the bodily qualities which are required in the guardian."

"True."

"And also of the mental ones; his soul is to be full of spirit?"

"Yes."

"But are not these spirited natures apt to be savage with one another, and with everybody else?"

"A difficulty by no means easy to overcome," he replied.

"Whereas," I said, "they ought to be dangerous to their enemies, and gentle to their friends; if not, they will destroy themselves without waiting for their enemies to destroy them."

"True," he said.

"What is to be done, then?" I said; "how shall we find a gentle nature which has also a great spirit, for the one is the contradiction of the other?"

"True."

"He will not be a good guardian who is wanting in either of these two qualities; and yet the combination of them appears to be impossible; and hence we must infer that to be a good guardian is impossible."

"I am afraid that what you say is true," he replied.

Here feeling perplexed I began to think over what had preceded. "My friend," I said, "no wonder that we are in a perplexity; for we have lost sight of the image which we had before us."

"What do you mean?" he said.

"I mean to say that there do exist natures gifted with those opposite qualities."

"And where do you find them?"

"Many animals," I replied, "furnish examples of them; our friend the dog is a very good one; you know that well-bred dogs are perfectly gentle to those with whom they are familiar, and the reverse to strangers."

"Yes, I know."

"Then there is nothing impossible or out of the order of nature in our finding a guardian who has a similar combination of qualities?"

"Certainly not."

"Would not he who is fitted to be a guardian, besides the spirited nature, need to have the qualities of a philosopher?"

"I do not apprehend your meaning."

"The trait of which I am speaking," I replied, "may be also seen in the dog, and is remarkable in the animal."

"What trait?"

"Why, a dog, whenever he sees a stranger, is angry; when an acquaintance, he welcomes him, although the one has never done him any harm, nor the other any good. Did this never strike you as curious?"

"The matter never struck me before; but I quite recognize the truth of your remark."

"And surely this instinct of the dog is very charming; your dog is a true philosopher."

"Why?"

"Why, because he distinguishes the face of a friend and of an enemy only by the criterion of knowing and not knowing. And must not an animal be a lover of learning who determines what he likes and dislikes by the test of knowledge and ignorance?"

"Most assuredly."

"And is not the love of learning the love of wisdom, which is philosophy?"

"They are the same," he replied.

"And may we not say confidently of man also, that he who is likely to be gentle to his friends and acquaintances, must by nature be a lover of wisdom and knowledge?"

"That we may safely affirm."

"Then he who is to be a really good and noble guardian of the *polis* will require to unite in himself philosophy and spirit and swiftness and strength?"

"Undoubtedly."

* * *

After describing an appropriate education for the guardians, the conversation turns to the class structure of the ideal society.

"Such, then, are our principles of nurture and education. Where would be the use of going into further details about the dances of our citizens, or about their hunting and coursing, their gymnastic and equestrian contests? For these all follow the general principle, and having found that, we shall have no difficulty in discovering them."

"I dare say that there will be no difficulty."

"Very good," I said; "then what is the next question? Must we not ask who are to be rulers and who subjects?"

"Certainly."

"There can be no doubt that the elder must rule the younger."

"Clearly."

"And that the best of these must rule."

"That is also clear."

"Now, are not the best husbandmen those who are most devoted to husbandry?"

"Yes."

"And as we are to have the best of guardians for our city, must they not be those who have most the character of guardians?"

"Yes."

"And to this end they ought to be wise and efficient, and to have a special care of the *polis*?"

"True."

"And a man will be most likely to care about that which he loves?"

"To be sure."

"And he will be most likely to love that which he regards as having the same interests with himself, and that of which the good or evil fortune is supposed by him at any time most to affect his own?"

"Very true," he replied.

"Then there must be a selection. Let us note among the guardians those who in their whole life show the greatest eagerness to do what is for the good of their country, and the greatest repugnance to do what is against her interests."

"Those are the right men."

"And they will have to be watched at every age, in order that we may see whether they preserve their resolution, and never, under the influence either of force or enchantment, forget or cast off their sense of duty to the *polis*."

"How cast off?" he said.

"I will explain to you," I replied. "A resolution may go out of a man's mind either with his will or against his will; with his will when he gets rid of a falsehood and learns better, against his will whenever he is deprived of a truth."

"I understand," he said, "the willing loss of a resolution; the meaning of the unwilling I have yet to learn."

"Why," I said, "do you not see that men are unwillingly deprived of good, and willingly of evil? Is not to have lost the truth an evil, and to possess the truth a good? And you would agree that to conceive things as they are is to possess the truth?"

"Yes," he replied; "I agree with you in thinking that mankind are deprived of truth against their will."

"And is not this involuntary deprivation caused either by theft, or force, or enchantment?"

"Still," he replied, "I do not understand you."

"I fear that I must have been talking darkly, like the tragedians. I only mean that some men are changed by persuasion and that others forget; argument steals away the hearts of one class, and time of the other; and this I call theft. Now you understand me?"

"Yes."

"Those again who are forced, are those whom the violence of some pain or grief compels to change their opinion."

"I understand," he said, "and you are quite right."

"And you would also acknowledge that the enchanted are those who change their minds either under the softer influence of pleasure, or the sterner influence of fear?"

"Yes," he said; "everything that deceives may be said to enchant."

"Therefore, as I was just now saying, we must inquire who are the best guardians of their own conviction that what they think the interest of the *polis* is to be the rule of their lives. We must watch them from their youth upward, and make them perform actions in which they are most likely to forget or to be deceived, and he who remembers and is not deceived is to be selected, and he who fails in the trial is to be rejected. That will be the way?"

"Yes."

"And there should also be toils and pains and conflicts prescribed for them, in which they will be made to give further proof of the same qualities."

"Very right," he replied.

"And then," I said, "we must try them with enchantments—that is the third sort of test—and see what will be their behavior: like those who take colts amid noise and tumult to see if they are of a timid nature, so must we take our youth amid terrors of some kind, and again pass them into pleasures, and prove them more thoroughly than gold is proved in the furnace, that we may discover whether they are armed against all enchantments, and of a noble bearing always, good guardians of themselves and of the music which they have learned, and retaining under all circumstances a rhythmical and harmonious nature, such as will be most service-able to the individual and to the *polis*. And he who at every age, as boy and youth and in mature life, has come out of the trial victorious and pure, shall be appointed a ruler and guardian of the *polis*; he shall be honored in life and death, and shall receive sepulchers and other memorials of honor, the greatest that we have to give. But him who fails, we must reject. I am inclined to think that this is the sort of way in which our rulers and guardians should be chosen and appointed. I speak generally, and not with any pretension to exactness."

"And, speaking generally, I agree with you," he said.

"And perhaps the word 'guardian' in the fullest sense ought to be applied to this higher class only who preserve us against foreign enemies and maintain peace among our citizens at home, that the one may not have the will, or the others the power, to harm us. The young men whom we before called guardians may be more properly designated auxiliaries and supporters of the principles of the rulers."

"I agree with you," he said.

"How then may we devise one of those needful falsehoods of which we lately spoke—just one royal lie which may deceive the rulers, if that be possible, and at any rate the rest of the city?

"What sort of lie?" he said.

"Nothing new," I replied; "only an old Phoenician tale of what has often occurred before now in other places (as the poets say, and have made the world believe), though not in our time, and I do not know whether such an event could ever happen again, or could now even be made probable, if it did."

"How your words seem to hesitate on your lips!"

"You will not wonder," I replied, "at my hesitation when you have heard."

"Speak," he said, "and fear not."

"Well, then, I will speak, although I really know not how to look you in the face, or in what words to utter the audacious fiction, which I propose to communicate gradually, first to the rulers, then to the soldiers, and lastly to the people. They are to be told that their youth was a dream, and the education and training which they received from us, an appearance only; in reality during all that time they were being formed and fed in the womb of the earth, where they themselves and their arms and appurtenances were manufactured; when they were completed, the earth, their mother, sent them up; and so, their country being their mother and also their nurse, they are bound to advise for her good, and to defend her against attacks, and her citizens they are to regard as children of the earth and their own brothers."

"You had good reason," he said, "to be ashamed of the lie which you were going to tell."

"True," I replied, "but there is more coming; I have only told you half. Citizens, we shall say to them in our tale, you are brothers, yet god has framed you differently. Some of you have the power of command, and in the composition of these he has mingled gold, wherefore also they have the greatest honor; others he has made of silver, to be auxiliaries; others again who are to be husbandmen and craftsmen he has composed of brass and iron; and the species will generally be preserved in the children. But as all are of the same original stock, a golden parent will sometimes have a silver son, or a silver parent a golden son. And god proclaims as a first principle to the rulers, and above all else, that there is nothing which they should so anxiously guard, or of which they are to be such good guardians, as of the purity of the race. They should observe what elements mingle in their offspring; for if the son of a golden or silver parent has an admixture of brass and iron, then nature orders a transposition of ranks, and the eye of the ruler must not be pitiful toward the child because he has to descend in the scale and become a husbandman or artisan, just as there may be sons of artisans who having an admixture of gold or silver in them are raised to honor, and become guardians or auxiliaries. For an oracle says that when a man of brass or iron guards the state, it will be destroyed. Such is the tale; is there any possibility of making our citizens believe in it?"

"Not in the present generation," he replied; "there is no way of accomplishing this; but their sons may be made to believe in the tale, and their sons' sons, and posterity after them."

"I see the difficulty," I replied; "yet the fostering of such a belief will make them care more for the city and for one another. Enough, however, of the fiction, which may now fly abroad upon the wings of rumor, while we arm our earth-born heroes, and lead them forth under the command of their rulers. Let them look round and select a spot whence they can best suppress insurrection, if any prove refractory within, and also defend themselves against enemies, who, like wolves, may come down on the fold from without; there let them encamp, and when they have encamped, let them sacrifice to the proper gods and prepare their dwellings."

"Just so," he said.

"And their dwellings must be such as will shield them against the cold of winter and the heat of summer."

"I suppose that you mean houses," he replied.

"Yes," I said; "but they must be the houses of soldiers, and not of shopkeepers."

"What is the difference?" he said.

"That I will endeavor to explain," I replied. "To keep watchdogs, who, from want of discipline or hunger, or some evil habit or other, would turn upon the sheep and worry them, and behave not like dogs, but wolves, would be a foul and monstrous thing in a shepherd?"

"Truly monstrous," he said.

"And therefore every care must be taken that our auxiliaries, being stronger than our citizens, may not grow to be too much for them and become savage tyrants instead of friends and allies?"

"Yes, great care should be taken."

"And would not a really good education furnish the best safeguard?"

"But they are well-educated already," he replied.

"I cannot be so confident, my dear Glaucon," I said; "I am much more certain that they ought to be, and that true education, whatever that may be, will have the greatest tendency to civilize and humanize them in their relations to one another, and to those who are under their protection."

"Very true," he replied.

"And not only their education, but their habitations, and all that belongs to them, should be such as will neither impair their virtue as guardians, nor tempt them to prey upon the other citizens. Any man of sense must acknowledge that."

"He must."

"Then now let us consider what will be their way of life, if they are to realize our idea of them. In the first place, none of them should have any property of his own beyond what is absolutely necessary; neither should they have a private house or store closed against anyone who has a mind to enter; their provisions should be only such as are required by trained warriors, who are men of temperance and courage; they should agree to receive from the citizens a fixed rate of pay, enough to meet the expenses of the year and no more; and they will go to mess and live together like soldiers in a camp. Gold and silver we will tell them that they have from god; the diviner metal is within them, and they have therefore no need of the dross which is current among men, and ought not to pollute the divine by any such earthly admixture; for that commoner metal has been the source of many unholy deeds, but their own is undefiled. And they alone of all the citizens may not touch or handle silver or gold, or be under the same roof with them, or wear them, or drink from them. And this will be their salvation, and they will be the saviors of the *polis*. But should they ever acquire homes or lands or moneys of their own, they will become good housekeepers and husbandmen instead of guardians, enemies and tyrants instead of allies of the other citizens; hating and being hated, plotting and being plotted against, they will pass their whole life in much greater terror of internal than of external enemies, and the hour of ruin, both to themselves and to the rest of the *polis*, will be at hand. For all which reasons may we not say that thus shall our *polis* be ordered, and that these shall be the regulations appointed by us for our guardians concerning their houses and all other matters?"

"Yes," said Glaucon.

Here Adeimantus interposed a question, "How would you answer, Socrates," said he, "if a person were to say that you are making these people miserable, and that they are the cause of their own unhappiness; the city in fact belongs to them, but they are none the better for it; whereas other men acquire lands, and build large and handsome houses, and have everything handsome about them, offering sacrifices to the gods on their own account, and practicing hospitality; moreover, as you were saying just now, they have gold and silver, and all that is usual among the favorites of fortune; but our poor citizens are no better than mercenaries who are quartered in the city and are always mounting guard?"

"Yes," I said; "and you may add that they are only fed, and not paid in addition to their food, like other men; and therefore they cannot, if they would, take a journey of pleasure; they have no money to spend on a mistress or any other luxurious fancy, which, as the world goes, is thought to be happiness; and many other accusations of the same nature might be added."

"But," said he, "let us suppose all this to be included in the charge."

"You mean to ask," I said, "what will be our answer?"

"Yes."

"If we proceed along the old path, my belief," I said, "is that we shall find the answer. And our answer will be that, even as they are, our guardians may very likely be the happiest of men; but that our aim in founding the *polis* was not the disproportionate happiness of any one class, but the greatest happiness of the whole; we thought that in a *polis* which is ordered with a view to the good of the whole we should be most likely to find justice, and in the ill-ordered *polis* injustice, and, having found them, we might then

decide which of the two is the happier. At present, I take it, we are
fashioning the happy *polis*, not piecemeal, or with a view of making
a few happy citizens, but as a whole; and by and by we will proceed
to view the opposite kind of *polis*. Suppose that we were painting
a statue, and someone came up to us and said, Why do you not
put the most beautiful colors on the most beautiful parts of the
body—the eyes ought to be purple, but you have made them
black—to him we might fairly answer, 'Sir, you would not surely
have us beautify the eyes to such a degree that they are no longer
eyes; consider rather whether, by giving this and the other features
their due proportion, we make the whole beautiful.' And so I say
to you, do not compel us to assign to the guardians a sort of
happiness which will make them anything but guardians; for we
too can clothe our husbandmen in royal apparel, and set crowns
of gold on their heads, and bid them till the ground as much as
they like, and no more. Our potters also might be allowed to repose
on couches, and feast by the fireside, passing round the wine-cup,
while their wheel is conveniently at hand, and working at pottery
only as much as they like; in this way we might make every class
happy—and then, as you imagine, the whole *polis* would be happy.
But do not put this idea into our heads; for, if we listen to you, the
husbandman will be no longer a husbandman, the potter will cease
to be a potter, and no one will have the character of any distinct
class in the *polis*. Now this is not of much consequence where the
corruption of society, and pretension to be what you are not, are
confined to cobblers; but when the guardians of the laws and of
the government are only seeming and not real guardians, then see
how they turn the *polis* upside down; and on the other hand they
alone have the power of giving order and happiness to the *polis*.
We mean our guardians to be true saviors and not the destroyers
of the *polis*, whereas our opponent is thinking of peasants at a
festival, who are enjoying a life of revelry, not of citizens who are
doing their duty to the *polis*. But, if so, we mean different things,
and he is speaking of something which is not a *polis*. And therefore
we must consider whether in appointing our guardians we would

look to their greatest happiness individually, or whether this principle of happiness does not rather reside in the *polis* as a whole. But
if the latter be the truth, then the guardians and auxiliaries, and all
others equally with them, must be compelled or induced to do
their own work in the best way. And thus the whole *polis* will grow
up in a noble order, and the several classes will receive the proportion of happiness which nature assigns to them."

"I think that you are quite right."

"I wonder whether you will agree with another remark which
occurs to me."

"What may that be?"

"There seem to be two causes of the deterioration of the arts."

"What are they?"

"Wealth," I said, "and poverty."

"How do they act?"

"The process is as follows: When a potter becomes rich, do you
think he will any longer take the same pains with his art?"

"Certainly not."

"He will grow more and more indolent and careless?"

"Very true."

"And the result will be that he becomes a worse potter?"

"Yes; he greatly deteriorates."

"But, on the other hand, if he has no money, and cannot provide
himself with tools or instruments, he will not work equally well
himself, nor will he teach his sons or apprentices to work equally
well."

"Certainly not."

"Then, under the influence either of poverty or of wealth,
workmen and their work are equally liable to degenerate?"

"That is evident."

"Here, then, is a discovery of new evils," I said, "against which
the guardians will have to watch, or they will creep into the city
unobserved."

"What evils?"

"Wealth," I said, "and poverty; the one is the parent of luxury and indolence, and the other of meanness and viciousness, and both of discontent."

"That is very true," he replied; "but still I should like to know, Socrates, how our city will be able to go to war, especially against an enemy who is rich and powerful, if deprived of the sinews of war."

"There would certainly be a difficulty," I replied, "in going to war with one such enemy; but there is no difficulty where there are two of them."

"How so?" he asked.

"In the first place," I said, "if we have to fight, our side will be trained warriors fighting against an army of rich men."

"That is true," he said.

"And do you not suppose, Adeimantus, that a single boxer who was perfect in his art would easily be a match for two stout and well-to-do gentlemen who were not boxers?"

"Hardly, if they came upon him at once."

"What, not," I said, "if he were able to run away and then turn and strike at the one who first came up? And supposing he were to do this several times under the heat of a scorching sun, might he not, being an expert, overturn more than one stout personage?"

"Certainly," he said, "there would be nothing wonderful in that."

"And yet rich men probably have a greater superiority in the science and practice of boxing than they have in military qualities."

"Likely enough."

"Then we may assume that our athletes will be able to fight with two or three times their own number?"

"I agree with you, for I think you right."

"And suppose that, before engaging, our citizens send an embassy to one of the two cities, telling them what is the truth: Silver and gold we neither have nor are permitted to have, but you may; do you therefore come and help us in war, and take the spoils of the other city. Who, on hearing these words, would choose to fight against lean wiry dogs, rather than, with the dogs on their side, against fat and tender sheep?"

"That is not likely; and yet there might be a danger to the poor *polis* if the wealth of many states were to be gathered into one."

"But how simple of you to use the term *polis* at all of any but our own!"

"Why so?"

"You ought to speak of other states in the plural number; not one of them is a city, but many cities, as they say in the game. For indeed any city, however small, is in fact divided into two, one the city of the poor, the other of the rich; these are at war with one another; and in either there are many smaller divisions, and you would be altogether beside the mark if you treated them all as a single *polis*. But if you deal with them as many, and give the wealth or power or persons of the one to the others, you will always have a great many friends and not many enemies. And your *polis*, while the wise order which has now been prescribed continues to prevail in her, will be the greatest of states, I do not mean to say in reputation or appearance, but in deed and truth, though she number not more than 1,000 defenders. A single *polis* which is her equal you will hardly find, either among Hellenes or barbarians, though many that appear to be as great and many times greater."

"That is most true," he said.

"And what," I said, "will be the best limit for our rulers to fix when they are considering the size of the *polis* and the amount of territory which they are to include, and beyond which they will not go?

"What limit would you propose?"

"I would allow the *polis* to increase so far as is consistent with unity; that, I think, is the proper limit."

"Very good," he said.

"Here then," I said, "is another order which will have to be conveyed to our guardians: Let our city be accounted neither large nor small, but one and self-sufficing."

"And surely," said he, "this is not a very severe order which we impose upon them."

"And the other," said I, "of which we were speaking before is lighter still—I mean the duty of degrading the offspring of the guardians when inferior, and of elevating into the rank of guardians the offspring of the lower classes, when naturally superior. The intention was, that, in the case of the citizens generally, each individual should be put to the use for which nature intended him, one to one work, and then every man would do his own business, and be one and not many; and so the whole city would be one and not many."

"Yes," he said; "that is not so difficult."

"The regulations which we are prescribing, my good Adeimantus, are not, as might be supposed, a number of great principles, but trifles all, if care be taken, as the saying is, of the one great thing—a thing, however, which I would rather call, not, great, but sufficient for our purpose."

"What may that be?" he asked.

"Education," I said, "and nurture. If our citizens are well educated, and grow into sensible men, they will easily see their way through all these, as well as other matters which I omit; such, for example, as marriage, the possession of women and the procreation of children, which will all follow the general principle that friends have all things in common, as the proverb says."

"That will be the best way of settling them."

"Also," I said, "the *polis*, if once started well, moves with accumulating force like a wheel. For good nurture and education implant good constitutions, and these good constitutions taking root in a good education improve more and more, and this improvement affects the breed in man as in other animals."

* * *

"Then on this view also justice will be admitted to be the having and doing what is a man's own, and belongs to him?"

"Very true."

"Think, now, and say whether you agree with me or not.

Suppose a carpenter to be doing the business of a cobbler, or a cobbler of a carpenter; and suppose them to exchange their implements or their duties, or the same person to be doing the work of both, or whatever be the change; do you think that any great harm would result to the *polis*?"

"Not much."

"But when the cobbler or any other man whom nature designed to be a trader, having his heart lifted up by wealth or strength or the number of his followers, or any like advantage, attempts to force his way into the class of warriors, or a warrior into that of legislators and guardians, for which he is unfitted, and either to take the implements or the duties of the other; or when one man is trader, legislator, and warrior all in one, then I think you will agree with me in saying that this interchange and this meddling of one with another is the ruin of the *polis*."

"Most true. Seeing, then, I said, that there are three distinct classes, any meddling of one with another, or the change of one into another, is the greatest harm to the *polis*, and may be most justly termed evil-doing?"

"Precisely."

"And the greatest degree of evil-doing to one's own city would be termed by you injustice?"

"Certainly. This, then, is injustice; and on the other hand when the trader, the auxiliary, and the guardian each do their own business, that is justice, and will make the city just."

"I agree with you."

"We will not," I said, "be over-positive as yet; but if, on trial, this conception of justice be verified in the individual as well as in the *polis*, there will be no longer any room for doubt; if it be not verified, we must have a fresh inquiry. First let us complete the old investigation, which we began, as you remember, under the impression that, if we could previously examine justice on the larger scale, there would be less difficulty in discerning her in the individual. That larger example appeared to be the *polis*, and accordingly we constructed as good a one as we could, knowing well that in the good *polis* justice would be found. Let the discovery which we made be now applied to the individual—if they agree, we shall be satisfied; or, if there be a difference in the individual, we will come back to the *polis* and have another trial of the theory. The friction of the two when rubbed together may possibly strike a light in which justice will shine forth, and the vision which is then revealed we will fix in our souls."

"That will be in regular course; let us do as you say."

I proceeded to ask, "When two things, a greater and less, are called by the same name, are they like or unlike in so far as they are called the same?"

"Like," he replied.

"The just man then, if we regard the idea of justice only, will be like the just *polis*?"

"He will."

"And a *polis* was thought by us to be just when the three classes in the *polis* severally did their own business; and also thought to be temperate and valiant and wise by reason of certain other affections and qualities of these same classes?"

"True," he said.

"And so of the individual; we may assume that he has the same three principles in his own soul which are found in the *polis*; and he may be rightly described in the same terms, because he is affected in the same manner?"

"Certainly," he said.

"Once more, then, O my friend, we have alighted upon an easy question—whether the soul has these three principles or not?"

"An easy question! Nay, rather, Socrates, the proverb holds that hard is the good."

"Very true," I said; "and I do not think that the method which we are employing is at all adequate to the accurate solution of this question; the true method is another and a longer one. Still we may arrive at a solution not below the level of the previous inquiry."

"May we not be satisfied with that?" he said; "under the circumstances, I am quite content."

"I, too," I replied, "shall be extremely well satisfied."

"Then faint not in pursuing the speculation," he said.

"Must we not acknowledge," I said, "that in each of us there are the same principles and habits which there are in the *polis*; and that from the individual they pass into the *polis?*—how else can they come there? Take the quality of passion or spirit; it would be ridiculous to imagine that this quality, when found in states, is not derived from the individuals who are supposed to possess it, e.g., the Thracians, Scythians, and in general the Northern nations; and the same may be said of the love of knowledge, which is the special characteristic of our part of the world, or of the love of money, which may, with equal truth, be attributed to the Phoenicians and Egyptians."

"Exactly so," he said.

"There is no difficulty in understanding this."

"None whatever."

"But the question is not quite so easy when we proceed to ask whether these principles are three or one; whether, that is to say, we learn with one part of our nature, are angry with another, and with a third part desire the satisfaction of our natural appetites; or whether the whole soul comes into play in each sort of action—to determine that is the difficulty."

"Yes," he said; "there lies the difficulty."

"Then let us now try and determine whether they are the same or different."

"How can we?" he asked.

I replied as follows, "The same thing clearly cannot act or be acted upon in the same part or in relation to the same thing at the same time, in contrary ways; and therefore whenever this contradiction occurs in things apparently the same, we know that they are really not the same, but different."

"Good."

"For example," I said, "can the same thing be at rest and in motion at the same time in the same part?"

"Impossible."

"Still," I said, "let us have a more precise statement of terms, lest we should hereafter fall out by the way. Imagine the case of a man who is standing and also moving his hands and his head, and suppose a person to say that one and the same person is in motion and at rest at the same moment—to such a mode of speech we should object, and should rather say that one part of him is in motion while another is at rest."

*   *   *

"And might a man be thirsty, and yet unwilling to drink?"

"Yes," he said, "it constantly happens."

"And in such a case what is one to say? Would you not say that there was something in the soul bidding a man to drink, and something else forbidding him, which is other and stronger than the principle which bids him?"

"I should say so."

"And the forbidding principle is derived from reason, and that which bids and attracts proceeds from passion and disease?"

"Clearly."

"Then we may fairly assume that they are two, and that they differ from one another; the one with which a man reasons, we may call the rational principle of the soul; the other, with which he loves, and hungers, and thirsts, and feels the fluttering of any other desire, may be termed the irrational or appetitive, the ally of sundry pleasures and satisfactions?"

"Yes," he said, "we may fairly assume them to be different."

"Then let us finally determine that there are two principles existing in the soul. And what of passion, or spirit? Is it a third, or akin to one of the preceding?"

"I should be inclined to say—akin to desire."

"Well," I said, "there is a story which I remember to have heard, and in which I put faith. The story is, that Leontius, the son of Aglaion, coming up one day from the Piraeus, under the north wall on the outside, observed some dead bodies lying on the ground at the place of execution. He felt a desire to see them, and also a dread and abhorrence of them; for a time he struggled and covered his

184

eyes, but at length the desire got the better of him; and forcing them open, he ran up to the dead bodies, saying, Look, ye wretches, take your fill of the fair sight."

"I have heard the story myself," he said.

"The moral of the tale is that anger at times goes to war with desire, as though they were two distinct things."

"Yes; that is the meaning," he said.

"And are there not many other cases in which we observe that when a man's desires violently prevail over his reason, he reviles himself, and is angry at the violence within him, and that in this struggle, which is like the struggle of factions in a *polis*, his spirit is on the side of his reason; but for the passionate or spirited element to take part with the desires when reason decides that she should not be opposed, is a sort of thing which I believe that you never observed occurring in yourself, nor, as I should imagine, in anyone else?"

"Certainly not."

"Suppose that a man thinks he has done a wrong to another, the nobler he is, the less able is he to feel indignant at any suffering, such as hunger, or cold, or any other pain which the injured person may inflict upon him—these he deems to be just, and, as I say, his anger refuses to be excited by them."

"True," he said.

"But when he thinks that he is the sufferer of the wrong, then he boils and chafes, and is on the side of what he believes to be justice; and because he suffers hunger or cold or other pain he is only the more determined to persevere and conquer. His noble spirit will not be quelled until he either slays or is slain; or until he hears the voice of the shepherd, that is, reason, bidding his dog bark no more."

"The illustration is perfect," he replied; "and in our *polis*, as we were saying, the auxiliaries were to be dogs, and to hear the voice of the rulers, who are their shepherds."

"I perceive," I said, "that you quite understand me; there is, however, a further point which I wish you to consider."

"What point?"

"You remember that passion or spirit appeared at first sight to be a kind of desire, but now we should say quite the contrary; for in the conflict of the soul spirit is arrayed on the side of the rational principle."

"Most assuredly."

"But a further question arises. Is passion different from reason also, or only a kind of reason; in which latter case, instead of three principles in the soul, there will only be two, the rational and the concupiscent; or rather, as the *polis* was composed of three classes, traders, auxiliaries, counselors, so may there not be in the individual soul a third element which is passion or spirit, and when not corrupted by bad education is the natural auxiliary of reason?"

"Yes," he said, "there must be a third."

"Yes," I replied, "if passion, which has already been shown to be different from desire, turn out also to be different from reason."

"But that is easily proved. We may observe even in young children that they are full of spirit almost as soon as they are born, whereas some of them never seem to attain to the use of reason, and most of them late enough."

"Excellent," I said, "and you may see passion equally in brute animals, which is a further proof of the truth of what you are saying. And we may once more appeal to the words of Homer, which have been already quoted by us, 'He smote his breast, and thus rebuked his soul'; for in this verse Homer has clearly supposed the power which reasons about the better and worse to be different from the unreasoning anger which is rebuked by it."

"Very true," he said.

"And so, after much tossing, we have reached land, and are fairly agreed that the same principles which exist in the *polis* exist also in the individual, and that they are three in number."

"Exactly."

"Must we not then infer that the individual is wise in the same way, and in virtue of the same quality which makes the *polis* wise?"

"Certainly."

"Also that the same quality which constitutes courage in the *polis* constitutes courage in the individual, and that both the *polis* and the individual bear the same relation to all the other virtues?"

"Assuredly."

"And the individual will be acknowledged by us to be just in the same way in which the *polis* is just?"

"That follows of course."

"We cannot but remember that the justice of the *polis* consisted in each of the three classes doing the work of its own class?"

"We are not very likely to have forgotten," he said.

"We must recollect that the individual in whom the several qualities of his nature do their own work will be just, and will do his own work?"

"Yes," he said, "we must remember that too."

"And ought not the rational principle, which is wise, and has the care of the whole soul, to rule, and the passionate or spirited principle to be the subject and ally?"

"Certainly."

"And, as we were saying, the united influence of music and gymnastics will bring them into accord, nerving and sustaining the reason with noble words and lessons, and moderating and soothing and civilizing the wildness of passion by harmony and rhythm?"

"Quite true," he said.

"And these two, thus nurtured and educated, and having learned truly to know their own functions, will rule over the concupiscent, which in each of us is the largest part of the soul and by nature most insatiable of gain; over this they will keep guard, lest, waxing great and strong with the fullness of bodily pleasures, as they are termed, the concupiscent soul, no longer confined to her own sphere, should attempt to enslave and rule those who are not her natural-born subjects, and overturn the whole life of man?"

"Very true," he said.

"Both together will they not be the best defenders of the whole soul and the whole body against attacks from without; the one counseling, and the other fighting under his leader, and coura-geously executing his commands and counsels?"

"True."

"And he is to be deemed courageous whose spirit retains in pleasure and in pain the commands of reason about what he ought or ought not to fear?"

"Right," he replied.

"And him we call wise who has in him that little part which rules, and which proclaims these commands; that part too being sup-posed to have a knowledge of what is for the interest of each of the three parts and of the whole?"

"Assuredly."

"And would you not say that he is temperate who has these same elements in friendly harmony, in whom the one ruling principle of reason, and the two subject ones of spirit and desire, are equally agreed that reason ought to rule, and do not rebel?"

"Certainly," he said, "that is the true account of temperance whether in the *polis* or individual."

"And surely," I said, "we have explained again and again how and by virtue of what quality a man will be just."

"That is very certain."

"And is justice dimmer in the individual, and is her form different, or is she the same which we found her to be in the *polis*?"

"There is no difference, in my opinion," he said.

"Because, if any doubt is still lingering in our minds, a few commonplace instances will satisfy us of the truth of what I am saying."

"What sort of instances do you mean?"

"If the case is put to us, must we not admit that the just *polis*, or the man who is trained in the principles of such a *polis*, will be less likely than the unjust to make away with a deposit of gold or silver? Would anyone deny this?"

"No one," he replied.

"Will the just man or citizen ever be guilty of sacrilege or theft, or treachery either to his friends or to his country?"

"Never."

"Neither will he ever break faith where there have been oaths or agreements."

"Impossible."

"No one will be less likely to commit adultery, or to dishonor his father and mother, or to fail in his religious duties?"

"No one."

"And the reason is that each part of him is doing its own business, whether in ruling or being ruled?"

"Exactly so."

"Are you satisfied, then, that the quality which makes such men and such states is justice, or do you hope to discover some other?"

"Not I, indeed."

"Then our dream has been realized; and the suspicion which we entertained at the beginning of our work of construction, that some divine power must have conducted us to a primary form of justice, has now been verified?"

"Yes, certainly."

"And the division of labor which required the carpenter and the shoemaker and the rest of the citizens to be doing each his own business, and not another's, was a shadow of justice, and for that reason it was of use?"

"Clearly."

"But in reality justice was such as we were describing, being concerned, however, not with the outward man, but with the inward, which is the true self and concernment of man; for the just man does not permit the several elements within him to interfere with one another, or any of them to do the work of others—he sets in order his own inner life, and is his own master and his own law, and at peace with himself; and when he has bound together the three principles within him, which may be compared to the higher, lower, and middle notes of the scale, and the intermediate intervals—when he has bound all these together, and is no longer many, but has become one entirely temperate and perfectly adjusted nature, then he proceeds to act, if he has to act, whether in a matter of property, or in the treatment of the body, or in some affair of politics or private business; always thinking and calling that which preserves and co-operates with this harmonious condition just and good action, and the knowledge which presides over it wisdom, and that which at any time impairs this condition he will call unjust action, and the opinion which presides over it ignorance."

"You have said the exact truth, Socrates."

"Very good; and if we were to affirm that we had discovered the just man and the just *polis*, and the nature of justice in each of them, we should not be telling a falsehood?"

"Most certainly not."

"May we say so, then?"

"Let us say so."

"And now," I said, "injustice has to be considered."

"Clearly."

"Must not an injustice be strife that arises from meddling and interfering in others' affairs, a rising up of a part of the soul against the whole, an assertion of unlawful authority, which is made by a rebellious subject against a true prince, of whom he is the natural vassal—what is all this confusion and delusion but injustice, and intemperance, and cowardice, and ignorance, and every form of vice?"

"Exactly so."

"And if the nature of justice and injustice be known, then the meaning of acting unjustly and being unjust, or, again, of acting justly, will also be perfectly clear?"

"What do you mean?" he said.

"Why," I said, "they are like disease and health; being in the soul just what disease and health are in the body."

"How so?" he said.

"Why," I said, "that which is healthy causes health, and that which is unhealthy causes disease."

"Yes."

"And just actions cause justice, and unjust actions cause injustice?"

"That is certain."

"And the creation of health is the institution of a natural order and government of one by another in the parts of the body; and the creation of disease is the production of a state of things at variance with this natural order?"

"True."

"And is not the creation of justice the institution of a natural order and government of one by another in the parts of the soul, and the creation of injustice the production of a state of things at variance with the natural order?"

"Exactly so," he said.

"Then virtue is the health, and beauty, and well-being of the soul, and vice the disease, and weakness, and deformity, of the same?"

"True."

"And do not good practices lead to virtue, and evil practices to vice?"

"Assuredly."

"Still our old question of the comparative advantage of justice and injustice has not been answered. Which is the more profitable, to be just and act justly and practice virtue, whether seen or unseen of gods and men, or to be unjust and act unjustly, if only unpunished and unreformed?"

"In my judgment, Socrates, the question has now become ridiculous. We know that, when the bodily constitution is gone, life is no longer endurable, though pampered with all kinds of meats and drinks, and having all wealth and all power; and shall we be told that when the very essence of the vital principle is undermined and corrupted, life is still worth having to a man, if only he be allowed to do whatever he likes with the single exception that he is not to acquire justice and virtue, or to escape from injustice and vice; assuming them both to be such as we have described?"

"Yes," I said, "the question is, as you say, ridiculous. Still, as we are near the spot at which we may see the truth in the clearest manner with our own eyes, let us not faint by the way."

"Certainly not," he replied.

"Come up hither," I said, "and behold the various forms of vice, those of them, I mean, which are worth looking at."

"I am following you," he replied, "proceed."

I said, "The argument seems to have reached a height from which, as from some tower of speculation, a man may look down and see that virtue is one, but that the forms of vice are innumerable; there being four special ones which are deserving of note."

"What do you mean?" he said.

"I mean," I replied, "that there appear to be as many forms of the soul as there are distinct forms of the *polis*."

"How many?"

"There are five of the *polis*, and five of the soul," I said.

"What are they?"

"The first," I said, "is that which we have been describing, and which may be said to have two names, monarchy and aristocracy, according as rule is exercised by one distinguished man or by many."

"True," he replied.

"But I regard the two names as describing one form only; for whether the government is in the hands of one or many, if the governors have been trained in the manner which we have supposed, the fundamental laws of the *polis* will be maintained."

"That is true," he replied.

* * *

Plato now addresses the role of women and families in his just society.

"Such is the good and true city or *polis*, and the good and true man is of the same pattern; and if this is right every other is wrong; and the evil is one which affects not only the ordering of the *polis*, but also the regulation of the individual soul, and is exhibited in four forms."

"What are they?" he said.

I was proceeding to tell the order in which the four evil forms appeared to me to succeed one another, when Polemarchus, who was sitting a little way off, just beyond Adeimantus, began to whisper to him; stretching forth his hand, he took hold of the upper part of his coat by the shoulder, and drew him toward him, leaning forward himself so as to be quite close and saying something in his ear, of which I only caught the words, "Shall we let him off, or what shall we do?"

"Certainly not," said Adeimantus, raising his voice.

"Who is it," I said, "whom you are refusing to let off?"

"You," he said.

I repeated, "Why am I especially not to be let off?"

"Why," he said, "we think that you are lazy, and mean to cheat us out of a whole chapter which is a very important part of the story; and you fancy that we shall not notice your airy way of proceeding; as if it were self-evident to everybody, that in the matter of women and children 'friends have all things in common.'"

"And was I not right, Adeimantus?"

"Yes," he said; "but what is right in this particular case, like everything else, requires to be explained; for community may be of many kinds. Please, therefore, say what sort of community you mean. We have been long expecting that you would tell us something about the family life of your citizens—how they will bring children into the world, and rear them when they have arrived, and, in general, what is the nature of this community of women and children—for we are of opinion that the right or wrong management of such matters will have a great and paramount influence on the *polis* for good or for evil. And now, since the question is still undetermined, and you are taking in hand another *polis*, we have resolved, as you heard, not to let you go until you give an account of all this."

"To that resolution," said Glaucon, "you may regard me in agreement"

"And without more ado," said Thrasymachus, "you may consider us all to be equally agreed."

I said, "You know not what you are doing in thus assailing me. What an argument are you raising about the *polis*! Just as I thought that I had finished, and was only too glad that I had laid this question to sleep, and was reflecting how fortunate I was in your acceptance of what I then said, you ask me to begin again at the very foundation, ignorant of what a hornet's nest of words you are stirring. Now I foresaw this gathering trouble, and avoided it."

"For what purpose do you conceive that we have come here," said Thrasymachus, "to look for gold, or to hear discourse?"

"Yes, but discourse should have a limit."

"Yes, Socrates," said Glaucon, "and the whole of life is the only limit which wise men assign to the hearing of such discourses. But never mind about us; take heart yourself and answer the question in your own way. What sort of community of women and children is this which is to prevail among our guardians? And how shall we manage the period between birth and education, which seems to require the greatest care? Tell us how these things will be."

"Yes, my simple friend, but the answer is the reverse of easy; many more doubts arise about this than about our previous conclusions. For the practicability of what is said may be doubted; and looked at in another point of view, whether the scheme, if ever so practicable, would be for the best, is also doubtful. Hence I feel a reluctance to approach the subject, lest our aspiration, my dear friend, should turn out to be a dream only."

"Fear not," he replied, "for your audience will not be hard upon you; they are not skeptical or hostile."

I said, "My good friend, I suppose that you mean to encourage me by these words."

"Yes," he said.

"Then let me tell you that you are doing just the reverse; the encouragement which you offer would have been all very well had I myself believed that I knew what I was talking about. To declare the truth about matters of high interest which a man honors and loves, among wise men who love him, need occasion no fear or faltering in his mind; but to carry on an argument when you are yourself only a hesitating inquirer, which is my condition, is a dangerous and slippery thing; and the danger is not that I shall be laughed at (of which the fear would be childish), but that I shall miss the truth where I have most need to be sure of my footing, and drag my friends after me in my fall. And I pray Nemesis not to visit upon me the words which I am going to utter. For I do indeed believe that to be an involuntary homicide is a less crime than to be a deceiver about beauty, or goodness, or justice, in the matter of laws. And that is a risk which I would rather run among enemies than among friends; and therefore you do well to encourage me."

Glaucon laughed and said, "Well, then, Socrates, in case you and your argument do us any serious injury you shall be acquitted beforehand of the homicide, and shall not be held to be a deceiver; take courage then and speak."

"Well," I said, "the law says that when a man is acquitted he is free from guilt, and what holds at law may hold in argument."

"Then why should you mind?"

"Well," I replied, "I suppose that I must retrace my steps and say what I perhaps ought to have said before in the proper place. The part of the men has been played out, and now properly enough comes the turn of the women. Of them I will proceed to speak, and the more readily since I am invited by you."

"For men born and educated like our citizens, the only way, in my opinion, of arriving at a right conclusion about the possession and use of women and children is to follow the path on which we originally started, when we said that the men were to be the guardians and watch-dogs of the herd."

"True."

"Let us further suppose the birth and education of our women to be subject to similar or nearly similar regulations; then we shall see whether the result accords with our design."

"What do you mean?"

"What I mean may be put into the form of a question," I said. "Are dogs divided into he's and she's, or do they both share equally in hunting and in keeping watch and in the other duties of dogs? or do we intrust to the males the entire and exclusive care of the flocks, while we leave the females at home, under the idea that the bearing and the suckling of their puppies are labor enough for them?"

"No," he said, "they share alike; the only difference between them is that the males are stronger and the females weaker."

"But can you use different animals for the same purpose, unless they are bred and fed in the same way?"

"You cannot."

"Then, if women are to have the same duties as men, they must have the same nurture and education?"

"Yes."

"The education which was assigned to the men was music and gymnastics. Yes."

"Then women must be taught music and gymnastics and also the art of war, which they must practice like the men?"

"That is the inference, I suppose."

"I should rather expect," I said, "that several of our proposals, if they are carried out, being unusual, may appear ridiculous."

"No doubt of it."

"Yes, and the most ridiculous thing of all will be the sight of women naked in the gymnasium, exercising with the men, especially when they are no longer young; they certainly will not be a vision of beauty, any more than the enthusiastic old men who, in spite of wrinkles and ugliness, continue to frequent the gymnasia."

"Yes, indeed," he said, "according to present notions the proposal would be thought ridiculous."

"But then," I said, "as we have determined to speak our minds, we must not fear the jests of the wits which will be directed against this sort of innovation; how they will talk of women's attainments, both in music and gymnastics, and above all about their wearing armor and riding upon horseback!"

"Very true," he replied. "Yet, having begun, we must go forward to the rough places of the law; at the same time begging of these gentlemen for once in their life to be serious. Not long ago, as we shall remind them, the Hellenes were of the opinion, which is still generally received among the barbarians, that the sight of a naked man was ridiculous and improper; and when first the Cretans, and then the Spartans, introduced the custom, the wits of that day might equally have ridiculed the innovation."

"No doubt."

"But when experience showed that to let all things be uncovered was far better than to cover them up, and the ludicrous effect to the outward eye had vanished before the better principle which reason asserted, then the man was perceived to be a fool who directs the shafts of his ridicule at any other sight but that of folly and vice, or seriously inclines to weigh the beautiful by any other standard but that of the good."

"Very true," he replied.

"First, then, whether the question is to be put in jest or in earnest, let us come to an understanding about the nature of woman. Is she capable of sharing either wholly or partially in the actions of men, or not at all? And is the art of war one of those arts in which she can or cannot share? That will be the best way of commencing the inquiry, and will probably lead to the fairest conclusion."

"That will be much the best way."

"Shall we take the other side first and begin by arguing against ourselves? in this manner the adversary's position will not be undefended."

"Why not?" he said.

"Then let us put a speech into the mouths of our opponents. They will say, 'Socrates and Glaucon, no adversary need convict you, for you yourselves, at the first foundation of the *polis*, admitted the principle that everybody was to do the one work suited to his own nature.' And certainly, if I am not mistaken, such an admission was made by us. 'And do not the natures of men and women differ very much indeed?' And we shall reply, Of course they do. Then we shall be asked, 'Whether the tasks assigned to men and to women should not be different, and such as are agreeable to their different natures?' Certainly they should. 'But if so, have you not fallen into a serious inconsistency in saying that men and women, whose natures are so entirely different, ought to perform the same actions?' What defense will you make for us, my good sir, against anyone who offers these objections?"

"That is not an easy question to answer when asked suddenly; and I shall and I do beg of you to draw out the case on our side."

"These are the objections, Glaucon, and there are many others of a like kind, which I foresaw long ago; they made me afraid and reluctant to take in hand any law about the possession and nurture of women and children."

"By Zeus," he said, "the problem to be solved is anything but easy."

"Why, yes," I said, "but the fact is that when a man is out of his depth, whether he has fallen into a little swimming-bath or into mid-ocean, he has to swim all the same."

"Very true."

"And must not we swim and try to reach the shore—we will hope that Arion's dolphin or some other miraculous help may save us?"

"I suppose so," he said. "Well, then, let us see if any way of escape can be found. We acknowledged—did we not?—that different natures ought to have different pursuits, and that men's and women's natures are different. And now what are we saying?—that different natures ought to have the same pursuits—this is the inconsistency which is charged upon us."

"Precisely."

"Verily, Glaucon," I said, "glorious is the power of the art of contradiction!"

"Why do you say so?"

"Because I think that many a man falls into the practice against his will. When he thinks that he is reasoning he is really disputing, just because he cannot define and divide, and so know that of which he is speaking; and he will pursue a merely verbal opposition in the spirit of contention and not of fair discussion."

"Yes," he replied, "such is very often the case; but what has that to do with us and our argument?"

"A great deal; for there is certainly a danger of our getting unintentionally into a verbal opposition."

"In what way? Why we valiantly and pugnaciously insist upon the verbal truth, that different natures ought to have different pursuits, but we never considered at all what was the meaning of sameness or difference of nature, or why we distinguished them when we assigned different pursuits to different natures and the same to the same natures."

"Why, no," he said, "that was never considered by us."

I said, "Suppose that by way of illustration we were to ask the question whether there is not an opposition in nature between bald men and hairy men; and if this is admitted by us, then, if bald men are cobblers, we should forbid the hairy men to be cobblers, and conversely?"

"That would be a jest," he said.

"Yes," I said, "a jest; and why? because we never meant when we constructed the *polis*, that the opposition of natures should extend to every difference, but only to those differences which affected the pursuit in which the individual is engaged; we should have argued, for example, that a physician and one who is in mind a physician may be said to have the same nature."

"True."

"Whereas the physician and the carpenter have different natures?"

"Certainly."

"And if," I said, "the male and female sex appear to differ in their fitness for any art or pursuit, we should say that such pursuit or art ought to be assigned to one or the other of them; but if the difference consists only in women bearing and men begetting children, this does not amount to a proof that a woman differs from a man in respect of the sort of education she should receive; and we shall therefore continue to maintain that our guardians and their wives ought to have the same pursuits."

"Very true," he said.

"Next, we shall ask our opponent how, in reference to any of the pursuits or arts of civic life, the nature of a woman differs from that of a man?"

"That will be quite fair."

"And perhaps he, like yourself, will reply that to give a sufficient answer on the instant is not easy; but after a little reflection there is no difficulty."

"Yes, perhaps."

"Suppose then that we invite him to accompany us in the argument, and then we may hope to show him that there is nothing peculiar in the constitution of women which would affect them in the administration of the *polis*."

"By all means."

"Let us say to him, Come now, and we will ask you a question. 'When you spoke of a nature gifted or not gifted in any respect, did you mean to say that one man will acquire a thing easily, another with difficulty; a little learning will lead the one to discover a great deal, whereas the other, after much study and application, no sooner learns than he forgets; or again, did you mean that the one has a body which is a good servant to his mind, while the body of the other is a hindrance to him? —would not these be the sort of differences which distinguish the man gifted by nature from the one who is ungifted?'"

"No one will deny that."

"And can you mention any pursuit of mankind in which the male sex has not all these gifts and qualities in a higher degree than the female? Need I waste time in speaking of the art of weaving, and the management of pancakes and preserves, in which woman-kind does really appear to be great, and in which for her to be beaten by a man is of all things the most absurd?"

"You are quite right," he replied, "in maintaining the general inferiority of the female sex; although many women are in many things superior to many men, yet on the whole what you say is true."

"And if so, my friend," I said, "there is no special faculty of administration in a *polis* which a woman has because she is a woman, or which a man has by virtue of his sex, but the gifts of nature are alike diffused in both; all the pursuits of men are the pursuits of women also, but in all of them a woman is inferior to a man."

"Very true."

"Then are we to impose all our enactments on men and none of them on women?"

"That will never do."

"One woman has a gift of healing, another not; one is a musician, and another has no music in her nature?"

"Very true."

"And one woman has a turn for gymnastic and military exercises, and another is unwarlike and hates gymnastics?"

"Certainly."

"And one woman is a philosopher, and another is an enemy of philosophy; one has spirit, and another is without spirit?"

"That is also true."

"Then one woman will have the temper of a guardian, and another not. Was not the selection of the male guardians determined by differences of this sort?"

"Yes."

"Men and women alike possess the qualities which make a guardian; they differ only in their comparative strength or weakness."

"Obviously."

"And those women who have such qualities are to be selected as the companions and colleagues of men who have similar qualities and whom they resemble in capacity and in character?"

"Very true."

"And ought not the same natures to have the same pursuits?"

"They ought."

"Then, as we were saying before, there is nothing unnatural in assigning music and gymnastics to the wives of the guardians—to that point we come round again."

"Certainly not."

"The law which we then enacted was agreeable to nature, and therefore not an impossibility or mere aspiration; and the contrary practice, which prevails at present, is in reality a violation of nature."

"That appears to be true."

"We had to consider, first, whether our proposals were possible, and secondly whether they were the most beneficial?"

"Yes."

"And the possibility has been acknowledged?"

"Yes."

"The very great benefit has next to be established?"

"Quite so."

"You will admit that the same education which makes a man a good guardian will make a woman a good guardian; for their original nature is the same?"

"Yes."

"I should like to ask you a question."

"What is it?"

"Would you say that all men are equal in excellence, or is one man better than another?"

"The latter."

"And in the commonwealth which we were founding do you conceive the guardians who have been brought up on our model system to be more perfect men, or the cobblers whose education has been cobbling?"

"What a ridiculous question!"

"You have answered me," I replied. "Well, and may we not further say that our guardians are the best of our citizens?"

"By far the best."

"And will not their wives be the best women?"

"Yes, by far the best."

"And can there be anything better for the interests of the *polis* than that the men and women of a *polis* should be as good as possible?"

"There can be nothing better."

"And this is what the arts of music and gymnastics, when present in such a manner as we have described, will accomplish?"

"Certainly."

"Then we have made an enactment not only possible but in the highest degree beneficial to the *polis*?"

"True."

"Then let the wives of our guardians strip, for their virtue will be their robe, and let them share in the toils of war and the defense of their country; only in the distribution of labors the lighter are to be assigned to the women, who are the weaker natures, but in other respects their duties are to be the same."

"Very true."

"Here, then, is one difficulty in our law about women, which we may say that we have now escaped; the wave has not swallowed us up alive for enacting that the guardians of either sex should have all their pursuits in common; to the utility and also to the possibility of this arrangement the consistency of the argument with itself bears witness."

"Yes, that was a mighty wave which you have escaped."

"Yes," I said, "but a greater is coming; you will not think much of this when you see the next."

"Go on; let me see."

"The law," I said, "which is the sequel of this and of all that has preceded, is to the following effect, 'that the wives of our guardians are to be common, and their children are to be common, and no parent is to know his own child, nor any child his parent.'"

"Yes," he said, "that is a much greater wave than the other; and the possibility as well as the utility of such a law are far more questionable."

"I do not think," I said, "that there can be any dispute about the very great utility of having wives and children in common; the possibility is quite another matter, and will be very much disputed."

"I think that a good many doubts may be raised about both."

"You imply that the two questions must be combined," I replied. "Now I meant that you should admit the utility; and in this way, as I thought, I should escape from one of them, and then there would remain only the possibility."

"But that little attempt is detected, and therefore you will please to give a defense of both."

"Well," I said, "I submit to my fate. Yet grant me a little favor; let me feast my mind with the dream as day-dreamers are in the habit of feasting themselves when they are walking alone; for before they have discovered any means of effecting their wishes—that is a matter which never troubles them—they would rather not tire themselves by thinking about possibilities; but assuming that what they desire is already granted to them, they proceed with their plan, and delight in detailing what they mean to do when their wish has come true—that is a way which they have of not doing much good to a capacity which was never good for much. Now I myself am beginning to lose heart, and I should like, with your permission, to pass over the question of possibility at present. Assuming therefore the possibility of the proposal, I shall now proceed to inquire how the rulers will carry out these arrangements, and I shall demonstrate that our plan, if executed, will be of the greatest benefit to the *polis* and to the guardians. First of all, then, if you have no objection, I will endeavor with your help to consider the advantages of the measure; and hereafter the question of possibility."

"I have no objection; proceed."

"First, I think that if our rulers and their auxiliaries are to be worthy of the name which they bear, there must be willingness to obey in the one and the power of command in the other; the guardians themselves must obey the laws, and they must also imitate the spirit of them in any details which are intrusted to their care."

"That is right," he said.

"You," I said, "who are their legislator, having selected the men, will now select the women and to give to them; they must be as far as possible of like natures with them; and they must live in common houses and meet at common meals. None of them will have anything specially his or her own; they will be together, and will be brought up together, and will associate at gymnastic exercises. And so they will be drawn by a necessity of their natures to have intercourse with each other—necessity is not too strong a word, I think?"

"Yes," he said; "necessity, not geometrical, but another sort of necessity which lovers know, and which is far more convincing and constraining to the mass of mankind."

"True," I said; "and this, Glaucon, like all the rest, must proceed after an orderly fashion; in a city of the blessed, licentiousness is an unholy thing which the rulers will forbid."

"Yes," he said, "and it ought not to be permitted."

"Then clearly the next thing will be to make matrimony sacred in the highest degree, and what is most beneficial will be deemed sacred?"

"Exactly."

"And how can marriages be made most beneficial? That is a question which I put to you, because I see in your house dogs for hunting, and of the nobler sort of birds not a few. Now, I beseech you, do tell me, have you ever attended to their pairing and breeding?"

"In what particulars?"

"Why, in the first place, although they are all of a good sort, are not some better than others?"

"True."

"And do you breed from them all indifferently, or do you take care to breed from the best only?"

"From the best."

"And do you take the oldest or the youngest, or only those of ripe age?"

"I choose only those of ripe age."

"And if care was not taken in the breeding, your dogs and birds would greatly deteriorate?"

"Certainly."

"And the same of horses and of animals in general?"

"Undoubtedly."

"Good heavens! my dear friend," I said, "what consummate skill will our rulers need if the same principle holds of the human species!"

"Certainly, the same principle holds; but why does this involve any particular skill?"

"Because," I said, "our rulers will often have to practice upon the body corporate with medicines. Now you know that when patients do not require medicines, but have only to be put under a regimen, the inferior sort of practitioner is deemed to be good enough; but when medicine has to be given, then the doctor should be more of a man."

"That is quite true," he said; "but to what are you alluding?"

"I mean," I replied, "that our rulers will find a considerable dose of falsehood and deceit necessary for the good of their subjects; we were saying that the use of all these things regarded as medicines might be of advantage."

"And we were very right."

"And this lawful use of them seems likely to be often needed in the regulations of marriages and births."

"How so?"

"Why," I said, "the principle has been already laid down that the best of either sex should be united with the best as often, and the inferior with the inferior as seldom, as possible; and that they should rear the offspring of the one sort of union, but not of the other, if the flock is to be maintained in first-rate condition. Now these goings on must be a secret which the rulers only know, or there will be a further danger of our herd, as the guardians may be termed, breaking out into rebellion."

"Very true."

"Had we better not appoint certain festivals at which we will bring together the brides and bridegrooms, and sacrifices will be offered and suitable hymeneal songs composed by our poets; the number of weddings is a matter which must be left to the discretion of the rulers, whose aim will be to preserve the average of population? There are many other things which they will have to consider, such as the effects of wars and diseases and any similar agencies, in order as far as this is possible to prevent the *polis* from becoming either too large or too small."

"Certainly," he replied.

"We shall have to invent some ingenious kind of lots which the less worthy may draw on each occasion of our bringing them together, and then they will accuse their own ill-luck and not the rulers."

"To be sure," he said.

"And I think that our braver and better youth, besides their other honors and rewards, might have greater facilities of intercourse with women given them; their bravery will be a reason, and such fathers ought to have as many sons as possible."

"True."

"And the proper officers, whether male or female or both, for offices are to be held by women as well as by men?"

"The proper officers will take the offspring of the good parents to the pen or fold, and there they will deposit them with certain nurses who dwell in a separate quarter; but the offspring of the inferior, or of the better when they chance to be deformed, will be put away in some mysterious, unknown place, as they should be."

"Yes," he said, "that must be done if the breed of the guardians is to be kept pure."

"They will provide for their nurture, and will bring the mothers to the fold when they are full of milk, taking the greatest possible care that no mother recognizes her own child; and other wet-nurses may be engaged if more are required. Care will also be taken that the process of suckling shall not be protracted too long; and the mothers will have no getting up at night or other trouble, but will hand over all this sort of thing to the nurses and attendants."

"You suppose the wives of our guardians to have a fine easy time of it when they are having children."

"Why," said I, "and so they ought. Let us, however, proceed with our scheme. We were saying that the parents should be in the prime of life?"

"Very true."

"And what is the prime of life? May it not be defined as a period of about twenty years in a woman's life, and thirty years in a man's?"

"Which years do you mean to include?"

"A woman," I said, "at twenty years of age may begin to bear children to the *polis*, and continue to bear them until forty; a man may begin at five-and-twenty, when he has passed the point at which the pulse of life beats quickest, and continue to beget children until he be fifty-five."

"Certainly," he said, "both in men and women those years are the prime of physical as well as of intellectual vigor. Anyone above or below the prescribed ages who takes part in the public religious rituals shall be said to have done an unholy and unrighteous thing; the child of which he is the father, if it steals into life, will have been conceived under auspices very unlike the sacrifices and prayers, which at each hymeneal priestesses and priests and the whole city will offer, that the new generation may be better and more useful than their good and useful parents, whereas his child will be the offspring of darkness and strange lust."

"Very true," he replied.

"And the same law will apply to any one of those within the prescribed age who forms a connection with any woman in the prime of life without the sanction of the rulers; for we shall say that he is raising up a bastard to the *polis*, uncertified and uncon-secrated."

"Very true," he replied.

"This applies, however, only to those who are within the specified age; after that we will allow them to range at will, except that a man may not marry his daughter or his daughter's daughter, or his mother or his mother's mother; and women, on the other hand, are prohibited from marrying their sons or fathers, or son's son or father's father, and so on in either direction. And we grant all this, accompanying the permission with strict orders to prevent any embryo which may come into being from seeing the light; and if any force a way to the birth, the parents must understand that the offspring of such a union cannot be maintained, and arrange accordingly."

"That also," he said, "is a reasonable proposition. But how will they know who are fathers and daughters, and so on?"

"They will never know. The way will be this: dating from the day of the hymeneal, the bridegroom who was then married will call all the male children who are born in the seventh and the tenth month afterward his sons, and the female children his daughters, and they will call him father, and he will call their children his grandchildren, and they will call the elder generation grandfathers and grandmothers. All who were begotten at the time when their fathers and mothers came together will be called their brothers and sisters, and these, as I was saying, will be forbidden to intermarry. This, however, is not to be understood as an absolute prohibition of the marriage of brothers and sisters; if the lot favors them, and they receive the sanction of the Delphic oracle, the law will allow them."

"Quite right," he replied.

"Such is the scheme, Glaucon, according to which the guardians of our *polis* are to have their wives and families in common. And now you would have the argument show that this community is consistent with the rest of our polity, and also that nothing can be better—would you not?"

"Yes, certainly."

"Shall we try to find a common basis by asking of ourselves what ought to be the chief aim of the legislator in making laws and in the organization of a *polis*—what is the greatest good, and what is the greatest evil, and then consider whether our previous description has the stamp of the good or of the evil?"

"By all means."

"Can there be any greater evil than discord and distraction and plurality where unity ought to reign? or any greater good than the bond of unity?"

"There cannot."

"And there is unity where there is community of pleasures and pains—where all the citizens are glad or grieved on the same occasions of joy and sorrow?"

"No doubt."

"Yes; and where there is no common but only private feeling a *polis* is disorganized—when you have one-half of the world triumphing and the other plunged in grief at the same events happening to the city or the citizens?"

"Certainly."

"Such differences commonly originate in a disagreement about the use of the terms 'mine' and 'not mine,' 'his' and 'not his.'"

"Exactly so."

"And is not that the best-ordered *polis* in which the greatest number of persons apply the terms 'mine' and 'not mine' in the same way to the same thing?"

"Quite true."

"Or that again which most nearly approaches to the condition of the individual—as in the body, when but a finger of one of us is hurt, the whole frame, drawn toward the soul as a center and forming one kingdom under the ruling power therein, feels the hurt and sympathizes all together with the part affected, and we say that the man has a pain in his finger; and the same expression is used about any other part of the body, which has a sensation of pain at suffering or of pleasure at the alleviation of suffering."

"Very true," he replied; "and I agree with you that in the best ordered *polis* there is the nearest approach to this common feeling which you describe."

"Then when any one of the citizens experiences any good or evil, the whole *polis* will make his case their own, and will either rejoice or sorrow with him?"

"Yes," he said, "that is what will happen in a well-ordered *polis*."

"It will now be time," I said, "for us to return to our *polis* and see whether this or some other form is most in accordance with these fundamental principles."

"Very good."

"Our *polis*, like every other, has rulers and subjects?"

"True."

"All of whom will call one another citizens?"

"Of course."

"But is there not another name which people give to their rulers in other states?"

"Generally they call them masters, but in democratic states they simply call them rulers."

"And in our *polis* what other name besides that of citizens do the people give the rulers?"

"They are called saviors and helpers," he replied.

"And what do the rulers call the people?"

"Their maintainers and foster-fathers."

"And what do they call them in other states?"

"Slaves."

"And what do the rulers call one another in other states?"

"Fellow-rulers."

"And what in ours?"

"Fellow-guardians."

"Did you ever know an example in any other *polis* of a ruler who would speak of one of his colleagues as his friend and of another as not being his friend?"

"Yes, very often."

"And the friend he regards and describes as one in whom he has an interest, and the other as a stranger in whom he has no interest?"

"Exactly."

"But would any of your guardians think or speak of any other guardian as a stranger?"

"Certainly he would not; for everyone whom they meet will be regarded by them either as a brother or sister, or father or mother, or son or daughter, or as the child or parent of those who are thus connected with him."

"Excellent," I said; "but let me ask you once more, Shall they be a family in name only; or shall they in all their actions be true to the name? For example, in the use of the word 'father,' would the care of a father be implied and the filial reverence and duty and obedience to him which the law commands; and is the violator of these duties to be regarded as an impious and unrighteous person who is not likely to receive much good either at the hands of god or of man? Are these to be or not to be the strains which the children will hear repeated in their ears by all the citizens about those who are intimated to them to be their parents and the rest of their kinsfolk?"

"These," he said, "and none other; for what can be more ridiculous than for them to utter the names of family ties with the lips only and not to act in the spirit of them?"

"Then in our city the language of harmony and concord will be more often heard than in any other. As I was describing before, when anyone is well or ill, the universal word will be 'with me it is well' or 'it is ill.'"

"Most true."

"And agreeably to this mode of thinking and speaking, were we not saying that they will have their pleasures and pains in common?"

"Yes, and so they will."

"And they will have a common interest in the same thing which they will alike call 'my own,' and having this common interest they will have a common feeling of pleasure and pain?"

"Yes, far more so than in other states."

"And the reason of this, over and above the general constitution of the *polis*, will be that the guardians will have a community of women and children?"

"That will be the chief reason."

"And this unity of feeling we admitted to be the greatest good, as was implied in our comparison of a well-ordered *polis* to the relation of the body and the members, when affected by pleasure or pain?"

That we acknowledged, and very rightly.

"Then the community of wives and children among our citizens is clearly the source of the greatest good to the *polis*?"

"Certainly."

"And this agrees with the other principle which we were affirm-ing—that the guardians were not to have houses or lands or any other property; their pay was to be their food, which they were to receive from the other citizens, and they were to have no private expenses; for we intended them to preserve their true character of guardians."

"Right," he replied.

"Both the community of property and the community of fami-lies, as I am saying, tend to make them more truly guardians; they will not tear the city in pieces by differing about 'mine' and 'not mine'; each man dragging any acquisition which he has made into a separate house of his own, where he has a separate wife and children and private pleasures and pains; but all will be affected as far as may be by the same pleasures and pains because they are all of one opinion about what is near and dear to them, and therefore they all tend toward a common end."

"Certainly," he replied.

"And as they have nothing but their persons which they can call their own, suits and complaints will have no existence among them; they will be delivered from all those quarrels of which money or children or relations are the occasion."

"Of course they will."

"Neither will trials for assault or insult ever be likely to occur among them. For that equals should defend themselves against equals we shall maintain to be honorable and right; we shall make the protection of the person a matter of necessity."

"That is good," he said.

"Yes; and there is a further good in the law, namely, that if a man has a quarrel with another he will satisfy his resentment then and there, and not proceed to more dangerous lengths."

"Certainly."

"To the elder shall be assigned the duty of ruling and chastising the younger."

"Clearly."

"Nor can there be a doubt that the younger will not strike or do any other violence to an elder, unless the magistrates command him; nor will he slight him in any way. For there are two guardians, shame and fear, mighty to prevent him: shame, which makes men refrain from laying hands on those who are to them in the relation of parents; fear, that the injured one will be succored by the others who are his brothers, sons, fathers."

"That is true," he replied.

"Then in every way the laws will help the citizens to keep the peace with one another?"

"Yes, there will be no want of peace."

"And as the guardians will never quarrel among themselves there will be no danger of the rest of the city being divided either against them or against one another."

"None whatever."

"I hardly like even to mention the little meanness of which they will be rid, for they are beneath notice; such, for example, as the flattery of the rich by the poor, and all the pains and pangs which men experience in bringing up a family, and in finding money to buy necessaries for their household, borrowing and then repudiating, getting how they can, and giving the money into the hands of women and slaves to keep—the many evils of so many kinds which people suffer in this way are mean enough and obvious enough, and not worth speaking of."

"Yes," he said, "a man has no need of eyes in order to perceive that."

"And from all these evils they will be delivered, and their life will be blessed as the life of Olympic victors and yet more blessed."

"How so?"

"The Olympic victor," I said, "is deemed happy in receiving a part only of the blessedness which is secured to our citizens, who have won a more glorious victory and have a more complete maintenance at the public cost. For the victory which they have won is the salvation of the whole *polis*; and the crown with which they and their children are crowned is the fullness of all that life needs; they receive rewards from the hands of their country while living, and after death have an honorable burial."

"Do you remember," I said, "how in the course of the previous discussion someone who shall be nameless accused us of making our guardians unhappy—they had nothing and might have possessed all things—to whom we replied that, if an occasion offered, we might perhaps hereafter consider this question, but that, as at present divided, we would make our guardians truly guardians, and that we were fashioning the *polis* with a view to the greatest happiness, not of any particular class, but of the whole?"

"Yes, I remember."

"And what do you say, now that the life of our protectors is made out to be far better and nobler than that of Olympic victors—is the life of shoemakers, or any other artisans, or of husbandmen, to be compared with it?"

"Certainly not."

"At the same time I ought here to repeat what I have said elsewhere, that if any of our guardians shall try to be happy in such a manner that he will cease to be a guardian, and is not content with this safe and harmonious life, which, in our judgment, is of all lives the best, but, infatuated by some youthful conceit of happiness which gets up into his head shall seek to appropriate the whole *polis* to himself, then he will have to learn how wisely Hesiod spoke, when he said, 'half is more than the whole.'"

"If he were to consult me, I should say to him, 'Stay where you are, when you have the offer of such a life.'"

"You agree then," I said, "that men and women are to have a common way of life such as we have described—common education, common children; and they are to watch over the citizens in common whether abiding in the city or going out to war; they are to keep watch together, and to hunt together like dogs; and always and in all things, as far as they are able, women are to share with the men? And in so doing they will do what is best, and will not violate, but preserve, the natural relation of the sexes."

*   *   *

Socrates argues that the ideal polis should be ruled by philosophers, those who grasp true knowledge. He then outlines his concept of true knowledge with his cave analogy.

"And now, I said, let me show in a figure how far our nature is enlightened or unenlightened. Consider human beings living in an underground den, which has a mouth open toward the light and reaching all along the den; here they have been from their childhood, and have their legs and necks chained so that they cannot move, and can only see before them, being prevented by the chains from turning round their heads. Above and behind them a fire is blazing at a distance, and between the fire and the prisoners there is a raised way; and you will see, if you look, a low wall built along the way, like the screen which marionette-players have in front of them, over which they show the puppets."

"I see."

"And do you see," I said, "men passing along the wall carrying all sorts of vessels, and statues and figures of animals made of wood and stone and various materials, which appear over the wall? Some of them are talking, others silent."

"You have shown me a strange image, and they are strange prisoners."

"Like ourselves," I replied; "and they see only their own shadows, or the shadows of one another, which the fire throws on the opposite wall of the cave?"

"True," he said; "how could they see anything but the shadows if they were never allowed to move their heads?"

"And of the objects which are being carried in like manner they would only see the shadows?"

"Yes," he said.

"And if they were able to converse with one another, would they not suppose that they were naming what was actually before them?"

"Very true."

"And suppose further that the prison had an echo which came from the other side, would they not be sure to fancy when one of the passers-by spoke that the voice which they heard came from the passing shadow?"

"No question," he replied.

"To them," I said, "the truth would be literally nothing but the shadows of the images."

"That is certain."

"And now look again, and see what will naturally follow if the prisoners are released and disabused of their error. At first, when any of them is liberated and compelled suddenly to stand up and turn his neck round and walk and look toward the light, he will suffer sharp pains; the glare will distress him, and he will be unable to see the realities of which in his former state he had seen the shadows; and then conceive someone saying to him, that what he saw before was an illusion, but that now, when he is approaching nearer to being and his eye is turned toward more real existence, he has a clearer vision—what will be his reply? And you may further imagine that his instructor is pointing to the objects as they pass and requiring him to name them—will he not be perplexed? Will he not fancy that the shadows which he formerly saw are truer than the objects which are now shown to him?"

"Far truer."

"And if he is compelled to look straight at the light, will he not have a pain in his eyes which will make him turn away to take refuge in the objects of vision which he can see, and which he will conceive to be in reality clearer than the things which are now being shown to him?"

"True," he said.

"And suppose once more, that he is reluctantly dragged up a steep and rugged ascent, and held fast until he is forced into the presence of the sun himself, is he not likely to be pained and irritated? When he approaches the light his eyes will be dazzled, and he will not be able to see anything at all of what are now called realities."

"Not all in a moment," he said.

"He will require to grow accustomed to the sight of the upper world. And first he will see the shadows best, next the reflections of men and other objects in the water, and then the objects themselves; then he will gaze upon the light of the moon and the stars and the spangled heaven; and he will see the sky and the stars by night better than the sun or the light of the sun by day?"

"Certainly."

"Last of all he will be able to see the sun, and not mere reflections of him in the water, but he will see himself in his own proper place, and not in another; and he will contemplate himself as he is."

"Certainly."

"He will then proceed to argue that this is he who gives the season and the years, and is the guardian of all that is in the visible world, and in a certain way the cause of all things which he and his fellows have been accustomed to behold?"

"Clearly," he said, "he would first see the sun and then reason about him."

"And when he remembered his old habitation, and the wisdom of the den and his fellow-prisoners, do you not suppose that he would felicitate himself on the change, and pity him?"

"Certainly, he would."

"And if they were in the habit of conferring honors among themselves on those who were quickest to observe the passing shadows and to remark which of them went before, and which followed after, and which were together; and who were therefore best able to draw conclusions as to the future, do you think that he would care for such honors and glories, or envy the possessors of them?"

"Yes," he said, "I think that he would rather suffer anything than entertain these false notions and live in this miserable manner."

"Imagine once more," I said, "such a one coming suddenly out of the sun to be replaced in his old situation; would he not be certain to have his eyes full of darkness?"

"To be sure," he said.

"And if there were a contest, and he had to compete in measuring the shadows with the prisoners who had never moved out of the den, while his sight was still weak, and before his eyes had become steady (and the time which would be needed to acquire this new habit of sight might be very considerable), would he not be ridiculous? Men would say of him that up he went and down he came without his eyes; and that it was better not even to think of ascending; and if anyone tried to free another and lead him up to the light, let them only catch the offender, and they would put him to death."

"No question," he said.

"This entire allegory," I said, "you may now append, dear Glaucon, to the previous argument; the prison-house is the world of sight, the light of the fire is the sun, and you will not misapprehend me if you interpret the journey upward to be the ascent of the soul into the intellectual world according to my poor belief, which, at your desire, I have expressed—whether rightly or wrongly, god knows. But, whether true or false, my opinion is that in the world of knowledge the idea of good appears last of all, and is seen only with an effort; and, when seen, is also inferred to be the universal author of all things beautiful and right, parent of light and of the lord of light in this visible world, and the immediate source of reason and truth in the intellectual; and that this is the power upon which he who would act rationally either in public or private life must have his eye fixed."

"I agree," he said, "as far as I am able to understand you."

"Moreover," I said, "you must not wonder that those who attain to this beatific vision are unwilling to descend to human affairs; for their souls are ever hastening into the upper world where they desire to dwell; which desire of theirs is very natural, if our allegory may be trusted."

"Yes, very natural."

"And is there anything surprising in one who passes from divine contemplations to the evil state of man, misbehaving himself in a ridiculous manner; if, while his eyes are blinking and before he has become accustomed to the surrounding darkness, he is compelled to fight in courts of law, or in other places, about the images or the shadows of images of justice, and is endeavoring to meet the conceptions of those who have never yet seen absolute justice?"

"Anything but surprising," he replied.

"Anyone who has common-sense will remember that the bewilderment of the eyes are of two kinds, and arise from two causes, either from coming out of the light or from going into the light, which is true of the mind's eye, quite as much as of the bodily eye; and he who remembers this when he sees anyone whose vision is perplexed and weak, will not be too ready to laugh; he will first ask whether that soul of man has come out of the brighter life, and is unable to see because unaccustomed to the dark, or having turned from darkness to the day is dazzled by excess of light. And he will count the one happy in his condition and state of being, and he will pity the other; or, if he have a mind to laugh at the soul which comes from below into the light, there will be more reason in this than in the laugh which greets him who returns from above out of the light into the den."

"That," he said, "is a very just distinction."

"But then, if I am right, certain professors of education must be wrong when they say that they can put a knowledge into the soul which was not there before, like sight into blind eyes."

"They undoubtedly say this," he replied.

"Whereas, our argument shows that the power and capacity of learning exists in the soul already; and that just as the eye was unable to turn from darkness to light without the whole body, so too the instrument of knowledge can only by the movement of the whole soul be turned from the world of becoming into that of being, and learn by degrees to endure the sight of being, and of the brightest and best of being, or, in other words, of the good."

"Very true."

"And must there not be some art which will effect conversion in the easiest and quickest manner; not implanting the faculty of sight, for that exists already, but has been turned in the wrong direction, and is looking away from the truth?"

"Yes," he said, "such an art may be presumed."

"And whereas the other so-called virtues of the soul seem to be akin to bodily qualities, for even when they are not originally innate they can be implanted later by habit and exercise, the virtue of wisdom more than anything else contains a divine element which always remains, and by this conversion is rendered useful and profitable; or, on the other hand, hurtful and useless. Did you never observe the narrow intelligence flashing from the keen eye of a clever rogue—how eager he is, how clearly his paltry soul sees the way to his end; he is the reverse of blind, but his keen eyesight is forced into the service of evil, and he is mischievous in proportion to his cleverness?"

"Very true," he said.

"But what if there had been a circumcision of such natures in the days of their youth; and they had been severed from those sensual pleasures, such as eating and drinking, which, like leaden weights, were attached to them at their birth, and which drag them down and turn the vision of their souls upon the things that are below—if, I say, they had been released from these impediments and turned in the opposite direction, the very same faculty in them would have seen the truth as keenly as they see what their eyes are turned to now."

"Very likely."

"Yes," I said; "and there is another thing which is likely, or rather a necessary inference from what has preceded, that neither the uneducated and uninformed of the truth, nor yet those who never make an end of their education, will be able ministers of the *polis*; not the former, because they have no single aim of duty which is the rule of all their actions, private as well as public; nor the latter, because they will not act at all except upon compulsion, fancying that they are already dwelling apart in the islands of the blessed."

"Very true," he replied.

"Then," I said, "the business of us who are the founders of the *polis* will be to compel the best minds to attain that knowledge which we have already shown to be the greatest of all—they must continue to ascend until they arrive at the good; but when they have ascended and seen enough we must not allow them to do as they do now."

"What do you mean?"

"I mean that they remain in the upper world; but this must not be allowed; they must be made to descend again among the prisoners in the den, and partake of their labors and honors, whether they are worth having or not."

"But is this not unjust?" he said; "ought we to give them a worse life, when they might have a better?"

"You have again forgotten, my friend," I said, "the intention of the legislator, who did not aim at making any one class in the *polis* happy above the rest; the happiness was to be in the whole *polis*, and he held the citizens together by persuasion and necessity, making them benefactors of the *polis*, and therefore benefactors of one another; to this end he created them, not to please themselves, but to be his instruments in binding up the *polis*."

"True," he said, "I had forgotten."

"Observe, Glaucon, that there will be no injustice in compelling our philosophers to have a care and providence of others; we shall explain to them that in other states, men of their class are not obliged to share in the toils of politics; and this is reasonable, for they grow up at their own sweet will, and the government would rather not have them. Being self-taught, they cannot be expected to show any gratitude for a culture which they have never received. But we have brought you into the world to be rulers of the hive, kings of yourselves and of the other citizens, and have educated you far better and more perfectly than they have been educated, and you are better able to share in the double duty. Wherefore each of you, when his turn comes, must go down to the general underground abode, and get the habit of seeing in the dark. When you have acquired the habit, you will see ten thousand times better than the inhabitants of the den, and you will know what the several images are, and what they represent, because you have seen the beautiful and just and good in their truth. And thus our *polis*, which is also yours, will be a reality, and not a dream only, and will be administered in a spirit unlike that of other states, in which men fight with one another about shadows only and are distracted in the struggle for power, which in their eyes is a great good. Whereas the truth is that the *polis* in which the rulers are most reluctant to govern is always the best and most quietly governed, and the *polis* in which they are most eager, the worst."

"Quite true," he replied.

"And will our pupils, when they hear this, refuse to take their turn at the toils of *polis*, when they are allowed to spend the greater part of their time with one another in the heavenly light?"

"Impossible," he answered; "for they are just men, and the commands which we impose upon them are just; there can be no doubt that every one of them will take office as a stern necessity, and not after the fashion of our present rulers of *polis*."

"Yes, my friend, I said; and there lies the point. You must contrive for your future rulers another and a better life than that of a ruler, and then you may have a well-ordered *polis*; for only in the *polis* which offers this, will they rule who are truly rich, not in silver and gold, but in virtue and wisdom, which are the true blessings of life. Whereas, if they go to the administration of public affairs, poor and hungering after their own private advantage, thinking that hence they are to snatch the chief good, order there can never be; for they will be fighting about office, and the civil and domestic broils which thus arise will be the ruin of the rulers themselves and of the whole *polis*."

"Most true," he replied.

"And the only life which looks down upon the life of political ambition is that of true philosophy. Do you know of any other?"

"Indeed, I do not," he said.

"And those who govern ought not to be lovers of the task? For, if they are, there will be rival lovers, and they will fight."

"No question. Who, then, are those whom we shall compel to be guardians? Surely they will be the men who are wisest about affairs of *polis*, and by whom the *polis* is best administered, and who at the same time have other honors and another and a better life than that of politics?"

"They are the men, and I will choose them," he replied.

9. Aristotle, *Politics*

Aristotle (384-322 B.C.E.*) was probably the most prolific and undoubtedly one of the most influential of Greek philosophers. A student of Plato, he became a tutor to the young Alexander the Great, and later opened a rival school of philosophy in Athens, the Lyceum. His works later influenced Muslim thought in the Near East, and became the basis of medieval and early modern thought after they were rediscovered by the West in the twelfth century.*

His closely-reasoned treatises encompass the full range of human knowledge: metaphysics, ethics, government, aesthetics, rhetoric, the natural sciences. He argued that true wisdom comes from understanding the purpose of things (telos); his treatises include rigorous definitions and classifications of reality. He was also a thorough scholar, and collected enormous amounts of data before composing his works.

The Politics *is Aristotle's major work on political theory. Based on extensive study and reflection, it summarizes his thought on the social characteristics of human nature and the purposes of government and social organization. With the* Republic, *it has become the basis for much Western political thought.*

BOOK ONE

I

Every state is a community of some kind, and every community is established with a view to some good; for mankind always acts in order to obtain that which they think good. But, if all communities aim at some good, the state or political community, which is the highest of all, and which embraces all the rest, aims at good in a greater degree than any other, and at the highest good.'

Some people think that the qualifications of a statesman, king, householder, and master are the same, and that they differ, not in kind, but only in the number of their subjects. For example, the ruler over a few is called a master; over more, the manager of a household; over a still larger number, a statesman or king, as if there were no difference between a great household and a small state. The distinction which is made between the king and the statesman is as follows: When the government is personal, the ruler is a king; when, according to the rules of the political science, the citizens rule and are ruled in turn, then he is called a statesman.

But all this is a mistake; for governments differ in kind, as will be evident to any one who considers the matter according to the method which has hitherto guided us. As in other departments of science, so in politics, the compound should always be resolved into the simple elements or least parts of the whole.' We must therefore look at the elements of which the state is composed, in order that we may see in what the different kinds of rule differ from one another, and whether any scientific result can be attained about each one of them.

II

He who thus considers things in their first growth and origin, whether a state or anything else, will obtain the clearest view of them. In the first place there must be a union of those who cannot exist without each other; namely, of male and female, that the race may continue (and this is a union which is formed, not of deliberate purpose, but because, in common with other animals and with plants, mankind has a natural desire to leave behind them an image of themselves), and of natural ruler and subject, that both may be preserved.' For that which can foresee by the exercise of mind is by nature intended to be lord and master, and that which can with its body give effect to such foresight is a subject, and by nature a slave; hence master and slave have the same interest. Now nature has distinguished between the female and the slave. For she is not miserly, like the smith who fashions the Delphian knife for many uses; she makes each thing for a single use, and every instrument is best made when intended for one and not for many uses. But among barbarians no distinction is made between women and slaves, because there is no natural ruler among them: they are a community of slaves, male and female. Wherefore the poets say, "It is just that Hellenes should rule over barbarians," as if they thought that the barbarian and the slave were by nature one.

Out of these two relationships between man and woman, master and slave, the first thing to arise is the family, and Hesiod is right when he says, "First house and wife and an ox for the plough," for the ox is the poor man's slave. The family is the association established by nature for the supply of men's everyday wants, and the members of it are called by Charondas "companions of the cupboard," and by Epimenides the Cretan, "companions of the manger." But when several families are united, and the association aims at something more than the supply of daily needs, the first society to be formed is the village. And the most natural form of the village appears to be that of a colony from the family, composed of the children and grandchildren, who are said to be suckled "with the same milk." And this is the reason why Hellenic states were originally governed by kings; because the Hellenes were under royal rule before they came together, as the barbarians still are. Every family is ruled by the eldest, and therefore in the colonies of the family the kingly form of government prevailed because they were of the same blood....

When several villages are united in a single complete community, large enough to be nearly or quite self-sufficing, the state comes into existence, originating in the bare needs of life, and continuing in existence for the sake of a good life. And therefore, if the earlier forms of society are natural, so is the state, for it is the end of them, and the nature of a thing is its end. For what each thing is when fully developed, we call its nature, whether we are speaking of a man, a horse, or a family. Besides, the final cause and end of a thing is the best, and to be self-sufficient is the end and the best.

Hence it is evident that the state is a creation of nature, and that man is by nature a political animal [literally, *man is by nature an animal intended to live in a polis*]. And he who by nature and not by mere accident is without a state, is either a bad man or above humanity; he is like the "tribeless, lawless, hearthless one," whom Homer denounces.

Now, that man is more of a political animal than bees or any other gregarious animals is evident. Nature, as we often say, makes nothing in vain; and man is the only animal whom she has endowed with the gift of speech. And whereas mere voice is but an indication of pleasure or pain, and is therefore found in other animals (for their nature attains to the perception of pleasure and pain and the intimation of them to one another, and no further), the power of speech is intended to set forth the expedient and inexpedient, and therefore likewise the just and the unjust. And it is a characteristic of man that he alone has any sense of good and evil, of just and unjust, and the like, and the association of living beings who have this sense makes a family and a state.

Further, the state is by nature clearly prior to the family and to the individual, since the whole is of necessity prior to the part; for example, if the whole body be destroyed, there will be no foot or hand, except in an equivocal sense, as we might speak of a stone hand; for when destroyed the hand will be no better than that. But things are defined by their working and power; and we ought not to say that they are the same when they no longer have their proper quality, but only that they have the same name. The proof that the state is a creation of nature and prior to the individual is that the individual, when isolated, is not self-sufficing; and therefore he is like a part in relation to the whole. But he who is unable to live in society, or who has no need because he is sufficient for himself, must be either a beast or a god: he is no part of a state. A social instinct is implanted in all men by nature, and yet he who first founded the state was the greatest of benefactors. For man, when perfected, is the best of animals, but, when separated from law and justice, he is the worst of all; since armed injustice is the more dangerous, and he is equipped at birth with arms, meant to be used by intelligence and virtue, which he may use for the worst ends. Wherefore, if he have not virtue, he is the most unholy and the most savage of animals, and the most full of lust and gluttony. But justice is the bond of men in states, for the administration of justice, which is the determination of what is just, is the principle of order in political society.

III

Seeing then that the state is made up of households, before speaking of the state we must speak of the management of the household. The parts of household management correspond to the persons who compose the household, and a complete household consists of slaves and freemen. Now we should begin by examining everything in its fewest possible elements; and the first and fewest possible parts of a family are master and slave, husband and wife, father and children. We have therefore to consider what each of these three relations is and ought to be: I mean the relation of master and servant, the marriage relation (the conjunction of man and wife has no name of its own), and thirdly, the procreative relation (this also has no proper name). And there is another element of a household, the so-called art of getting wealth, which, according to some, is identical with household management, according to others, a principal part of it; the nature of this art will also have to be considered by us.

Let us first speak of master and slave, looking to the needs of practical life and also seeking to attain some better theory of their relation than exists at present. For some are of opinion that the rule of a master is a science, and that the management of a household, and the mastership of slaves, and the political and royal rule, as I was saying at the outset, are all the same. Others affirm that the rule of a master over slaves is contrary to nature, and that the distinction between slave and freeman exists by law only, and not by nature; and being an interference with nature is therefore unjust.

IV

Property is a part of the household, and the art of acquiring property is a part of the art of managing the household; for no man can live well, or indeed live at all, unless he be provided with necessaries. And as in the arts which have a definite sphere the workers must have their own proper instruments for the accomplishment of their work, so it is in the management of a household. Now instruments are of various sorts; some are living, others lifeless; in the rudder, the pilot of a ship has a lifeless, in the look-out man, a living instrument; for in the arts the servant is a kind of instrument. Thus, too, a possession is an instrument for maintaining life. And so, in the arrangement of the family, a slave is a living possession, and property a number of such instruments; and the servant is himself an instrument which takes precedence of all other instruments. For if every instrument could accomplish its own work, obeying or anticipating the will of others, like the statues of Daedalus, or the tripods of Hephaestus, which, says the poet, "of their own accord entered the assembly of the gods"; if, in like manner, the shuttle would weave and the plectrum touch the lyre without a hand to guide them, chief workmen would not want servants, nor masters slaves....

V

But is there any one thus intended by nature to be a slave, and for whom such a condition is expedient and right, or rather is not all slavery a violation of nature?

There is no difficulty in answering this question, on grounds both of reason and of fact. For that some should rule and others be ruled is a thing not only necessary, but expedient; from the hour of their birth, some are marked out for subjection, others for rule.

And there are many kinds both of rulers and subjects (and that rule is the better which is exercised over better subjects—for example, to rule over men is better than to rule over wild beasts;

230

for the work is better which is executed by better workmen, and where one man rules and another is ruled, they may be said to have a work); for in all things which form a composite whole and which are made up of parts, whether continuous or discrete, a distinction between the ruling and the subject element comes to fight. Such a duality exists in living creatures, but not in them only; it originates in the constitution of the universe; even in things which have no life there is a ruling principle, as in a musical mode. But we are wandering from the subject. We will therefore restrict ourselves to the living creature, which, in the first place, consists of soul and body: and of these two, the one is by nature the ruler, and the other the subject. But then we must look for the intentions of nature in things which retain their nature, and not in things which are corrupted. And therefore we must study the man who is in the most perfect state both of body and soul, for in him we shall see the true relation of the two; although in bad or corrupted natures the body will often appear to rule over the soul, because they are in an evil and unnatural condition. At all events we may firstly observe in living creatures both a despotic and a constitutional rule; for the soul rules the body with a despotic rule, whereas the intellect rules the appetites with a constitutional and royal rule. And it is clear that the rule of the soul over the body, and of the mind and the rational element over the passionate, is natural and expedient; whereas the equality of the two or the rule of the inferior is always hurtful. The same holds good of animals in relation to men; for tame animals have a better nature than wild, and all tame animals are better off when they are ruled by man; for then they are preserved. Again, the male is by nature superior, and the female inferior; and the one rules, and the other is ruled; this principle, of necessity, extends to all mankind.

Where then there is such a difference as that between soul and body, or between men and animals (as in the case of those whose business is to use their body, and who can do nothing better), the lower sort are by nature slaves, and it is better for them as for all inferiors that they should be under the rule of a master. For he who can be, and therefore is, another's and he who participates in rational principle enough to apprehend, but not to have, such a principle, is a slave by nature. Whereas the lower animals cannot even apprehend a principle; they obey their instincts. And indeed the use made of slaves and of tame animals is not very different; for both with their bodies minister to the needs of life. Nature would like to distinguish between the bodies of freemen and slaves, making the one strong for servile labor, the other upright, and although useless for such services, useful for political life in the arts both of war and peace. But the opposite often happens—that some have the souls and others have the bodies of freemen. And doubtless if men differed from one another in the mere forms of their bodies as much as the statues of the gods do from men, all would acknowledge that the inferior class should be slaves of the superior. And if this is true of the body, how much more just that a similar distinction should exist in the soul? but the beauty of the body is seen, whereas the beauty of the soul is not seen. It is clear, then, that some men are by nature free, and others slaves, and that for these latter slavery is both expedient and right....

VII

The previous remarks are quite enough to show that the rule of a master is not a constitutional rule, and that all the different kinds of rule are not, as some affirm, the same with each other. For there is one rule exercised over subjects who are by nature free, another over subjects who are by nature slaves. The rule of a household is a monarchy, for every house is under one head: whereas constitutional rule is a government of freemen and equals. The master is not called a master because he has science, but because he is of a certain character, and the same remark applies to the slave and the freeman. Still there may be a science for the master and science for the slave. The science of the slave would be such as the man of Syracuse taught, who made money by instructing slaves in their ordinary duties. And such a knowledge may be carried further, so as to include cookery and similar menial arts. For some duties are of the more necessary, others of the more honorable sort; as the proverb says, "slave before slave, master before master." But all such branches of knowledge are servile. There is likewise a science of the master, which teaches the use of slaves; for the master as such is concerned, not with the acquisition, but with the use of them. Yet this so-called science is not anything great or wonderful; for the master need only know how to order that which the slave must know how to execute. Hence those who are in a position which places them above toil have stewards who attend to their households while they occupy themselves with philosophy or with politics. But the art of acquiring slaves, I mean of justly acquiring them, differs both from the art of the master and the art of the slave, being a species of hunting or war. Enough of the distinction between master and slave.

BOOK THREE

I

He who would inquire into the essence and attributes of various kinds of governments must first of all determine "What is a state?" At present this is a disputed question. Some say that the state has done a certain act; others, no, not the state, but the oligarchy or the tyrant. And the legislator or statesman is concerned entirely with the state; a constitution or government being an arrangement of the inhabitants of a state. But a state is composite, like any other whole made up of many parts; these are the citizens, who compose it. It is evident, therefore, that we must begin by asking, Who is the citizen, and what is the meaning of the term? For here again there may be a difference of opinion. He who is a citizen in a democracy will often not be a citizen in an oligarchy. Leaving out of consideration those who have been made citizens, or who have obtained the name of citizen any other accidental manner, we may say, first, that a citizen is not a citizen because he lives in a certain place, for resident aliens and slaves share in the place; nor is he a citizen who has no legal right except that of suing and being sued; for this right may be enjoyed under the provisions of a treaty. Nay, resident aliens in many places do not possess even such rights completely, for they are obliged to have a patron, so that they do but imperfectly participate in citizenship, and we call them citizens only in a qualified sense, as we might apply the term to children who are too young to be on the register, or to old men who have been relieved from state duties. Of these we do not say quite simply that they are citizens, but add in the one case that they are not of age, and in the other, that they are past the age, or something of that sort; the precise expression is immaterial, for our meaning is clear. Similar difficulties to those which I have mentioned may be raised and answered about deprived citizens and about exiles. But the citizen whom we are seeking to define is a citizen in the strictest sense, against whom no such exception can be taken, and his special characteristic is that he shares in the administration of justice, and in offices. Now some offices are discontinuous so that the same persons are not allowed to hold them twice, or can only hold them after a fixed interval; others have no limit of time—for example, the office of a dicast or ecclesiast. It may, indeed, be argued that these are not magistrates at all, and that their functions give them no share in the government. But surely it is ridiculous to say that those who have the power do not govern. Let us not dwell further upon this, which is a purely verbal question; what we want is a common term including both dicast and ecclesiast. Let us, for the sake of distinction, call it "indefinite office," and we will assume that those who share in such office are citizens. This is the most comprehensive definition of a citizen, and best suits all those who are generally so called.

But we must not forget that things of which the underlying principles differ in kind, one of them being first, another second, another third, have, when regarded in this relation, nothing, or hardly anything, worth mentioning in common. Now we see that governments differ in kind, and that some of them are prior and that others are posterior; those which are faulty or perverted are necessarily posterior to those which are perfect. (What we mean by perversion will be hereafter explained.) The citizen then of necessity differs under each form of government; and our definition is best adapted to the citizen of a democracy; but not necessarily to other states. For in some states the people are not acknowledged, nor have they any regular assembly, but only extraordinary ones; and suits are distributed by sections among the magistrates. At Lacedaemon, for instance, the Ephors determine suits about contracts, which they distribute among themselves, while the elders are judges of homicide, and other causes are decided by other magistrates. A similar principle prevails at Carthage; there certain magistrates decide all causes. We may, indeed, modify our definition of the citizen so as to include these states. In them it is the holder of a definite, not of an indefinite office, who legislates and judges, and to some or all such holders of definite offices is reserved the right of deliberating or judging about some things or about all things. The conception of the citizen now begins to clear up.

He who has the power to take part in the deliberative or judicial administration of any state is said by us to be a citizens of that state; and, speaking generally, a state is a body of citizens sufficing for the purposes of life....

VI

Having determined these questions, we have next to consider whether there is only one form of government or many, and if many, what they are, and how many, and what are the differences between them.

A constitution is the arrangement of magistracies in a state, especially of the highest of all. The government is everywhere sovereign in the state, and the constitution is in fact the government. For example, in democracies the people are supreme, but in oligarchies, the few; and, therefore, we say that these two forms of government also are different: and so in other cases.

First, let us consider what is the purpose of a state, and how many forms of government there are by which human society is regulated. We have already said, in the first part of this treatise, when discussing household management and the rule of a master, that man is by nature a political animal. And therefore, men, even when they do not require one another's help, desire to live together;

for they are brought together by their common interests even as they individually seek to any measure of well-being. This is certainly the chief end, both of individuals and of states. And also for the sake of mere life (in which there is possibly some noble element so long as the evils of existence do not greatly overbalance the good) men meet together and maintain a political community. And we all see that men cling to life even at the cost of enduring great misfortune, seeming to find in life a natural sweetness and happiness.

There is no difficulty in distinguishing the various kinds of authority; they have been often defined already in discussions outside the school. The rule of a master, although the slave by nature and the master by nature have in reality the same interests, is nevertheless exercised primarily with a view to the interest of the master, but accidentally considers the slave, since, if the slave perish, the rule of the master perishes with him. On the other hand, the government of a wife and children and of a household, which we have called household management, is exercised in the first instance for the good of the governed or for the common good of both parties, but essentially for the good of the governed, as we see to be the case in medicine, gymnastics, and the arts in general, which are only accidentally concerned with the good of the artists themselves. For there is no reason why the trainer may not sometimes practice gymnastics, and the helmsman is always one of the crew. The trainer or the helmsman considers the good of those committed to his care. But, when he is one of the persons taken care of, he accidentally participates in the advantage, for the helmsman is also a sailor, and the trainer becomes one of those in training. And so in politics: when the state is framed upon the principle of equality and likeness, the citizens think that they ought to hold office by turns. Formerly, as is natural, every one would take his turn of service; and then again, somebody else would look after his interest, just as he, while in office, had looked after theirs. But nowadays, for the sake of the advantage which is to be gained from the public revenues and from office, men want to be always in office. One might imagine that the rulers, being sickly, were only kept in health while they continued in office; in that case we may be sure that they would be hunting after places. The conclusion is evident: that governments that have a regard for the common interest are constituted in accordance with strict principles of justice and are therefore true forms; but those which regard only the interest of the rulers are all defective and perverted forms, for they are despotic, whereas a state is a community of freemen.

VII

Having determined these points, we have next to consider how many forms of government [or constitutions] there are, and what they are; and in the first place what are the true forms, for when they are determined, the perversions of them will at once be apparent. The words constitution and government should have the same meaning, and the government, which is the supreme authority in states, will be in the hands of one, or of a few, or of the many. The true forms of government, therefore, are those in which the one, or the few, or the many, govern with a view to the common interest; but governments which rule with a view to the private interest, whether of the one or of the few, or of the many, are perversions. For the members of a state, if they are truly citizens, ought to participate in its advantages. Of forms of government in which one rules, we call that which regards the common interests, kingship or royalty; that in which more than one, but not many, rule, aristocracy; and it is so called, either because the rulers are the best men, or because they have at heart the best interests of the state and of the citizens. But when the citizens at large administer the state for the common interest, the government is an ideal constitutional *polis.* And there is a reason for this use of language. One man or a few may excel in virtue; but as the number increases it becomes more difficult for them to attain perfection in every kind of virtue, though they may in military virtue, for this is found in the masses. Hence in a constitutional government the fighting-men have the supreme power, and those who possess arms are the citizens.

Of the above-mentioned forms, the perversions are as follows: of royalty, tyranny; of aristocracy, oligarchy; of constitutional government, democracy. For tyranny is a kind of monarchy which has in view the interest of the monarch only; oligarchy has in view the interest of the wealthy; democracy, of the needy: none of them the common good of all.

BOOK FOUR

XI

We have now to inquire what is the best constitution for most states, and the best life for most men, neither assuming a standard of virtue which is above ordinary persons, nor an education which is exceptionally favored by nature and circumstances, nor yet an ideal state which is an aspiration only, but having regard to the life in which the majority are able to share, and to the form of government which states in general can attain. As to those aristocracies, as they are called, of which we were just now speaking, they either lie beyond the possibilities of the greater number of states, or they approximate to the so-called constitutional government, and therefore need no separate discussion. And in fact the conclusion at which we arrive respecting all these forms rests upon the same grounds. For if what was said in the Ethics is true, that the happy life is the life according to virtue lived without impediment, and that virtue is a mean, then the life which is in a mean, and in a mean attainable by every one, must be the best. And the same principles of virtue and vice are characteristic of cities and of constitutions; for the constitution is in a figure the life of the city.

Now in all states there are three elements: one class is very rich, another very poor, and a third in a mean. It is admitted that moderation and the mean are best, and therefore it will clearly be best to possess the gifts of fortune in moderation; for in that condition of life men are most ready to follow rational principle. But he who greatly excels in beauty, strength, birth, or wealth, or on the other hand who is very poor, or very weak, or very much disgraced, finds it difficult to follow rational principle. Of these two the one sort grows into violent and great criminals, the others into rogues and petty rascals. And two sorts of offenses correspond to them, the one committed from violence, the other from roguery. Again, the middle class is least likely to shrink from rule, or to be over-ambitious for it; both of which are injuries to the state. Again, those who have too much of the goods of fortune, strength, wealth, friends, and the like, are neither willing nor able to submit to authority. The evil begins at home; for when they are boys, by reason of the luxury in which they are brought up, they never learn, even at school, the habit of obedience. On the other hand, the very poor, who are in the opposite extreme, are too degraded. So that the one class cannot obey, and can only rule despotically; the other knows not how to command and must be ruled like slaves. Thus arises a city, not of freemen, but of masters and slaves, the one despising, the other envying; and nothing can be more fatal to friendship and good fellowship in states than this: for good fellowship springs from friendship; when men are at enmity with one another, they would rather not even share the same path. But a city ought to be composed, as far as possible, of those who are equal and similar; and these are generally the middle classes. Wherefore the city which is composed of middle-class citizens is necessarily best constituted in respect of the elements of which we say the fabric of the state naturally consists. And this is the class of citizens which is most secure in a state, for they do not, like the poor, covet their neighbors' goods; nor do others covet theirs, as the poor covet the goods of the rich; and as they neither plot against others, nor are themselves plotted against, they pass through life safely. Wisely then did Phocylides pray—"Many things are best in the mean; I desire to be of a middle condition in my city."

Thus it is manifest that the best political community is formed by citizens of the middle class, and that those states are likely to be well-administered in which the middle class is large, and stronger if possible than both the other classes, or at any rate than either singly; for the addition of the middle class turns the scale, and prevents either of the extremes from being dominant. Great then is the good fortune of a state in which the citizens have a moderate and sufficient property; for where some possess much, and the others nothing, there may arise an extreme democracy, or a pure oligarchy; or a tyranny may grow out of either extreme—either out of the most rampant democracy, or out of an oligarchy; but it is not so likely to arise out of the middle constitutions and those akin to them. I will explain the reason of this hereafter, when I speak of the revolutions of states. The mean condition of states is clearly best, for no other is free from faction; and where the middle class is large, there are least likely to be factions and dissensions. For a similar reason large states are less liable to faction than small ones, because in them the middle class is large; whereas in small states it is easy to divide all the citizens into two classes who are either rich or poor, and to leave nothing in the middle. And democracies are safer and more permanent than oligarchies, because they have a middle class which is more numerous and has a greater share in the government; for when there is no middle class, and the poor greatly exceed in number, troubles arise, and the state soon comes to an end. A proof of the superiority of the middle class is that the best legislators have been of a middle condition; for example, Solon, as his own verses testify; and Lycurgus, for he was not a king; and Charondas, and almost all legislators.

These considerations will help us to understand why most governments are either democratical or oligarchical. The reason is that the middle class is seldom numerous in them, and whichever party, whether the rich or the common people, transgresses the mean and predominates, draws the constitution its own way, and thus arises either oligarchy or democracy. There is another reason—the poor and the rich quarrel with one another, and whichever side gets the better, instead of establishing a just or popular government, regards political supremacy as the prize of victory, and the one party sets up a democracy and the other an oligarchy. Further, both the parties which had the supremacy in Hellas looked only to the interest of their own form of government, and established in states, the one, democracies, and the other, oligarchies;

they thought of their own advantage, of the public not at all. For these reasons the middle form of government has rarely, if ever, existed, and among a very few only. One man alone of those who ruled in Hellas was induced to give this middle constitution to states. But it has now become a habit among the citizens of states, not even to care about equality; all men are seeking for dominion, or, if conquered, are willing to submit.

What then is the best form of government, and what makes it the best, is evident; and of other constitutions, since we say that there are many kinds of democracy and many of oligarchy, it is not difficult to see which has the first and which the second or any other place in the order of excellence, now that we have determined which is the best. For that which is nearest to the best must of necessity be better, and that which is furthest from it worse, if we are judging absolutely and not relatively to given conditions: I say "relatively to given conditions," since a particular government may be preferable, but another form may be better for some people.

10. Cicero, *On Law*

Marcus Tullius Cicero (106-43 B.C.E.*) was a prominent statesman and orator at the height of the Roman Republic. An active
participant in public affairs, his deep sense of civic duty influenced
all of his writing, much of which was designed to remind his fellow
citizens, who were becoming increasingly preoccupied with accumulating wealth, of the traditional values that had made Rome great.
Cicero's philosophical perspectives are considered an example of Stoi-
cism.*

In his treatise On Law, *Cicero expands notions of justice to
encompass all humankind.*

MARCUS: The whole subject of universal law and jurisprudence
must be comprehended in this discussion, in order that this which
we call civil law, may be confined in some one small and narrow
space of nature. For we shall have to explain the true nature of
moral justice, which must be traced back from the nature of man.
And laws will have to be considered by which all political states
should be governed. And last of all, we shall have to speak of those
laws and customs of nations which are framed for the use and
convenience of particular countries (in which even our own people
will not be omitted), which are known by the title of civil laws.

QUINTUS: You take a noble view of the subject, my brother, and
go to the fountainhead, in order to throw light on the subject of
our consideration; and those who treat civil law in any other

243

manner, are not so much pointing out the paths of justice as those of litigation.

MARCUS: That is not quite the case, my Quintus. It is not so much the science of law that produces litigation, as the ignorance of it. But more of this by-and-by. At present let us examine the first principles of Right.

Now, many learned men have maintained that it springs from law. I hardly know if their opinion be not correct, at least according to their own definition; for "law," they say, "is the highest reason implanted in nature, which prescribes those things which ought to be done, and forbids the contrary." And when this same reason is confirmed and established in men's minds, it is then law.

They therefore conceive that prudence is a law, whose operation is to urge us to good actions, and restrain us from evil ones. And they think, too, that the Greek name for law, which is derived from the word, to distribute, implies the very nature of the thing, that is, to give every man his due. The Latin name, *lex*, conveys the idea of selections, a *legendo*. According to the Greeks, therefore, the name of law implies an equitable distribution: according to the Romans, an equitable selection. And, indeed, both characteristics belong peculiarly to law.

And if this be a correct statement, which it seems to me for the most part to be, then the origin of right is to be sought in the law. For this is the true energy of nature, this is the very soul and reason of a wise man, and the test of virtue and vice. But since all this discussion of ours relates to a subject, the terms of which are of frequent occurrence in the popular language of the citizens, we shall be sometimes obliged to use the same terms as the vulgar, and to call that law, which in its written enactments sanctions what it thinks fit by special commands or prohibitions.

Let us begin, then, to establish the principles of justice on that supreme law, which has existed from all ages before any legislative enactments were drawn up in writing, or any political governments constituted.

QUINTUS: That will be more convenient, and more sensible with

reference to the subject of the discussion which we have determined on.

MARCUS: Shall we, then, seek for the origin of justice at its
fountainhead? When we have discovered which, we shall be in no
doubt to what these questions which we are examining ought to
be referred.

QUINTUS: Such is the course I would advise.

ATTICUS: I also subscribe to your brother's opinion.

MARCUS: Since, then, we wish to maintain and preserve the
constitution of that republic which Scipio, in those six books
which I have written under that title, has proved to be the best,
and since all our laws are to be accommodated to the kind of
political government there described, we must also treat of the
general principles of morals and manners, and not limit ourselves
on all occasions to written laws; but I purpose to trace back the
origin of right from nature itself, who will be our best guide in
conducting the whole discussion.

ATTICUS: You will do right, and when she is our guide it is
absolutely impossible for us to err.

MARCUS: Do you then grant, my Atticus (for I know my brother's
opinion already), that the entire universe is regulated by the power
of the immortal gods, that by their nature, reason, energy, mind,
divinity, or some other word of clearer signification, if there be
such, all things are governed and directed? For if you will not grant
me this, that is what I must begin by establishing.

ATTICUS: I grant you all you can desire. But owing to this singing
of birds and babbling of water, I fear my fellow-learners can
scarcely hear me.

MARCUS: You are quite right to be on your guard; for even the
best men occasionally fall into a passion, and they will be very
indignant if they hear you denying the first article of this notable
book, entitled "The Chief Doctrines of Epicurus," in which he
says "that god takes care of nothing, neither of himself nor of any
other being!"

ATTICUS: Pray proceed, for I am waiting to know what advantage you mean to take of the concession I have made you.

MARCUS: I will not detain you long. This is the bearing which they have on our subject. This animal—prescient, sagacious, complex, acute, full of memory, reason, and counsel, which we call man—has been generated by the supreme god in a most transcendent condition. For he is the only creature among all the races and descriptions of animated beings who is endowed with superior reason and thought, in which the rest are deficient. And what is there, I do not say in man alone, but in all heaven and earth, more divine than reason, which, when it becomes right and perfect, is justly termed wisdom?

There exists, therefore, since nothing is better than reason, and since this is the common property of god and man, a certain primal rational intercourse between divine and human natures. But where reason is common, there right reason must also be common to the same parties; and since this right reason is what we call law, god and men must be considered as associated by law. Again, there must also be a communion of right where there is communion of law. And those who have law and right thus in common, must be considered members of the same commonwealth.

And if they are obedient to the same rule and the same authority, they are even much more so to this one celestial regency, this divine mind and omnipotent deity. So that the entire universe may be looked upon as forming one vast commonwealth of gods and men. And, as in earthly states certain ranks are distinguished with reference to the relationships of families, according to a certain principle which will be discussed in its proper place, that principle, in the nature of things, is far more magnificent and splendid by which men are connected with the gods, as belonging to their kindred and nation.

For when we are reasoning on universal nature, we are accustomed to argue (and indeed the truth is just as it is stated in that argument) that in the long course of ages, and the uninterrupted succession of celestial revolutions, there arrived a certain ripe time for the sowing of the human race; and when it was sown and scattered over the earth, it was animated by the divine gift of souls. And as men retained from their terrestrial origin those other particulars by which they cohere together, which are frail and perishable, their immortal spirits were generated by the deity. From which circumstance it may be truly said, that we possess a certain consanguinity, and kindred, and fellowship with the heavenly powers. And among all the varieties of animals, there is not one except man which retains any idea of the divinity. And among men themselves, there is no nation so savage and ferocious as not to admit the necessity of believing in a god, however ignorant they may be what sort of god they ought to believe in. From whence we conclude that every man who has any recollection and knowledge of his own origin must recognize a deity.

Now, the law of virtue is the same in god and man, and in no other disposition besides them. This virtue is nothing else than a nature perfect in itself, and wrought up to the most consummate excellence. There exists, therefore, a similitude between god and man. And as this is the case, what connection can there be which concerns us more nearly, and is more certain?

Since, then, the deity has been pleased to create and adorn man to be the chief and president of all terrestrial creatures, so it is evident, without further argument, that human nature has also made very great advances by its own intrinsic energy; that nature, which without any other instruction than her own, has developed the first rude principles of the understanding, and strengthened and perfected reason to all the appliances of science and art.

ATTICUS: Oh ye immortal gods! To what a distance back are you tracing the principles of justice! However, you are discoursing in such a style that I will not show any impatience to hear what I expect you to say on the civil law. But I will listen patiently, even if you spend the whole day in this kind of discourse; for assuredly these, which perhaps you are embracing in your argument for the sake of others, are grander topics than even the subject itself for which they prepare the way.

MARCUS: You may well describe these topics as grand, which we are now briefly discussing. But of all the questions which are ever the subject of discussion among learned men, there is none which it is more important thoroughly to understand than this, that man is born for justice, and that law and equity have not been established by opinion, but by nature. This truth will become still more apparent if we investigate the nature of human association and society.

For there is no one thing so like or so equal to another, as in every instance man is to man. And if the corruption of customs, and the variation of opinions, did not induce an imbecility of minds, and turn them aside from the course of nature, no one would more nearly resemble than all men would resemble all men. Therefore, whatever definition we give of man, will be applicable to the whole human race. And this is a good argument that there is no dissimilarity of kind among men; because if this were the case, one definition could not include all men.

In fact, reason, which alone gives us so many advantages over beasts, by means of which we conjecture, argue, refute, discourse, and accomplish and conclude our designs, is assuredly common to all men; for the faculty of acquiring knowledge is similar in all human minds, though the knowledge itself may be endlessly diversified. By the same senses we all perceive the same objects, and those things which move the senses at all, do move in the same way the senses of all men. And those first rude elements of intelligence which, as I before observed, are the earliest developments of thought, are similarly impressed upon all men; and that faculty of speech which is the interpreter of the mind, agrees in the ideas which it conveys, though it may differ in the words by which it expresses them. And therefore there exists not a man in any nation, who, if he adopts nature for his guide, may not arrive at virtue.

Nor is this resemblance which all men bear to each other remarkable in those things only which are in accordance with right reason, but also in errors. For all men alike are captivated by pleasure, which, although it is a temptation to what is disgraceful, nevertheless bears some resemblance to natural good; for, as by its delicacy and sweetness it is delightful, it is through a mistake of the intellect adopted as something salutary.

And by error scarcely less universal, we shun death as if it were a dissolution of nature, and cling to life because it keeps us in that existence in which we were born. Thus, likewise, we consider pain as one of the greatest evils, not only on account of its present asperity, but also because it seems the precursor of mortality. Again, on account of the apparent resemblance between renown with honor, those men appear to us happy who are honored, and miserable who happen to be inglorious. In like manner our minds are all similarly susceptible of inquietude, joys, desires, and fears; nor if different men have different opinions, does it follow that those who deify dogs and cats, do not labor under superstition equally with other nations, though they may differ from them in the forms of its manifestation.

Again, what nation is there which has not a regard for kindness, benignity, gratitude, and mindfulness of benefits? What nation is there in which arrogance, malice, cruelty, and ingratitude are not reprobated and detested? And while this uniformity of opinions proves that the whole race of mankind is united together, the last point is that a system of living properly makes men better. If what I have said meets your approbation, I will proceed; or if any doubts occur to you, we had better clear them up first.

ATTICUS: There is nothing which strikes us, if I may reply for both of us.

MARCUS: It follows, then, that nature made us just that we might share our goods with each other, and supply each other's wants. You observe in this discussion, whenever I speak of nature, I mean nature in its genuine purity, but that there is, in fact, such corruption engendered by evil customs, that the sparks, as it were, of virtue which have been given by nature are extinguished, and that antagonist vices arise around it and become strengthened.

But if, as nature prompts them to, men would with deliberate judgments, in the words of the poet, "being men, think nothing that concerns mankind indifferent to them," then would justice be cultivated equally by all. For to those to whom nature he is given reason, she has also given right reason, and therefore also law, which is nothing else than right reason enjoining what is good, and forbidding what is evil. And if nature has given us law, she has also given us right. But she has bestowed reason on all, therefore right has been bestowed on all. And therefore did Socrates deservedly execrate the man who first drew a distinction between utility and nature, for he used to complain that this error was the source of all human vices, to which this sentence of Pythagoras refers, "The things belonging to friends are common," and that other, "Friendly equality." From whence it appears, that when a wise man has displayed this benevolence which is so extensively and widely diffused towards one who is endowed with equal virtue, then that phenomenon takes place which is altogether incredible to some people, but which is a necessary consequence, that he loves himself not more dearly than he loves his friends. For how can a difference of interests arise where all interests are similar? If there could be ever so minute a difference of interests, then there would be an end of even the nature of friendship, the real meaning of which is such, that there is no friendship at all the moment that a person prefers anything happening to himself rather than to his friend.

Now, these preliminary remarks have been put forward as a preparation for the rest of our discourse and argument, in order that you may more easily understand that nature herself is the foundation of justice. And when I have explained this a little more at large, then I will proceed to the consideration of that civil law from which all these arguments of mine are derived.

QUINTUS: Then you have not much to add, my brother, for the arguments you have already used have sufficiently proved to Atticus, or at all events to me, that nature is the fountain of justice....

MARCUS: It is therefore an absurd extravagance in some philosophers to assert, that all things are necessarily just which are established by the civil laws and the institutions of nations. Are then the laws of tyrants just, simply because they are laws? Suppose the thirty tyrants of Athens had imposed certain laws on the Athenians? or suppose again that these Athenians were delighted with these tyrannical laws, would these laws on that account have been considered just? For my own part, I do not think such laws deserve any greater estimation than that passed during our own interregnum, which ordained that the dictator should be empowered to put to death with impunity whatever citizens he pleased, without hearing them in their own defense.

For there is but one essential justice which cements society, and one law which establishes this justice. This law is right reason, which is the true rule of all commandments and prohibitions. Whoever neglects this law, whether written or unwritten, is necessarily unjust and wicked.

But if justice consists in submission to written laws and national customs, and if, as the same school affirms, everything must be measured by utility alone, he who thinks that such conduct will be advantageous to him will neglect the laws, and break them if it is in his power. And the consequence is, that real justice has really no existence if it have not one by nature, and if that which is established as such on account of utility is overturned by some other utility.

But if nature does not ratify law, then all the virtues may lose their sway. For what becomes of generosity, patriotism, or friendship? Where will the desire of benefitting our neighbors, or the gratitude that acknowledges kindness, be able to exist at all? For all these virtues proceed from our natural inclination to love mankind. And this is the true basis of justice, and without this not only the mutual charities of men, but the religious services of the gods, would be at an end; for these are preserved, as I imagine, rather by the natural sympathy which subsists between divine and human beings, than by mere fear and timidity.

But if the will of the people, the decrees of the senate, the adjudications of magistrates, were sufficient to establish rights, then it might become right to rob, right to commit adultery, right to substitute forged wills, if such conduct were sanctioned by the votes or decrees of the multitude. But if the opinions and suffrages of foolish men had sufficient weight to out-balance the nature of things, when why should they not determine among them, that what is essentially bad and pernicious should henceforth pass for good and beneficial? Or why, since law can make right out of injustice, should it not also be able to change evil into good?

But we have no other rule by which we may be capable of distinguishing between a good or a bad law than that of nature. Nor is it only right and wrong which are discriminated by nature, but generally all that is honorable is by this means distinguished from all that is shameful; for common sense has impressed in our minds the first principles of things, and has given us a general acquaintance with them; by which we connect with virtue every honorable quality, and with vice all that is disgraceful.

But to think that these differences exist only in opinion, and not in nature, is the part of an idiot. For even the virtue of a tree or a horse, in which expression there is an abuse of terms, does not exist in our opinion only, but in nature; and if that is the case, then what is honorable and disgraceful must also be discriminated by nature.

For if opinion could determine respecting the character of universal virtue, it might also decide respecting particular or partial virtues. But who will dare to determine that a man is prudent and cautious, not from his general conduct, but from some external appearances? For virtue evidently consists in perfect reason, and this certainly resides in nature. Therefore so does all honor and honesty in the same way.

For as what is true and false, creditable and discreditable, is judged of rather by their essential qualities than their external relations, so the consistent and perpetual course of life, which is virtue, and the inconsistency of life, which is vice, are judged of according to their own nature-and that inconstancy must necessarily be vicious.

We form an estimate of the opinions of youths, but not by their opinions. Those virtues and vices which reside in their moral natures must not be measured by opinions. And so of all moral qualities, we must discriminate between honorable and dishonorable by reference to the essential nature of the things themselves.

The good we commend must contain in itself something commendable; for as I before stated, goodness is not a mode of opinion, but of nature. For if it were otherwise, opinion alone might constitute virtue and happiness, which is the most absurd of suppositions. And since we judge of good and evil by their nature, and since good and evil are the first principles of nature, certainly we should judge in the same manner of all honorable and all shameful things, referring them all to the law of nature.

But we are often too much disturbed by the dissensions of men and the variation of opinions. And because the same thing does not happen with reference to our senses, we look upon them as certain by nature. Those objects indeed, which sometimes present to us one appearance, sometimes another, and which do not always appear to the same people in the same way, we term fictions of the senses; but it is far otherwise. For neither parent, nor nurse, nor master, nor poet, nor drama, deceive our senses; nor do popular prejudices seduce them from the truth. But all kinds of snares are laid for the mind, either by those errors which I have just enumerated, which, taking possession of the young and uneducated, imbue them deeply, and bend them any way they please; or by that pleasure which is the imitator of goodness, being thoroughly and closely implicated with all our senses—the prolific mother of all evils. For she so corrupts us by her blandishments, that we no longer perceive some things which are essentially excellent because they have none of this deliciousness and prurience.

It follows that I may now sum up the whole of this argument by asserting, as is plain to every one from these positions which have been already laid down, that all right and all that is honorable is to be sought for its own sake. In truth, all virtuous men love justice and equity for what they are in themselves; nor is it like a good man to make a mistake, and love that which does not deserve their affection. Right, therefore, is desirable and deserving to be cultivated for its own sake; and if this be true of right, it must be true also of justice. What then shall we say of liberality? Is it exercised gratuitously, or does it covet some reward and recompense? If a man does good without expecting any recompense for his kindness, then it is gratuitous: if he does expect compensation, it is a mere matter of traffic. Nor is there any doubt that he who truly deserves the reputation of a generous and kindhearted man, is thinking of his duty, not of his interest. In the same way the virtue of justice demands neither emolument nor salary, and therefore we desire it for its own sake. And the case of all the moral virtues is the same, and so is the opinion of them.

Besides this, if we weigh virtue by the mere utility and profit that attend it, and not by its own merit, the one virtue which results from such an estimate will be in fact a species of vice. For the more a man refers all his actions especially to his own advantage, the further he recedes from probity; so that they who measure virtue by profit, acknowledge no other virtue than this, which is a kind of vice. For who can be called benevolent, if no one ever acts kindly for the sake of another? And where are we to find a grateful person, if those who are disposed to be so can find no benefactor to whom they can show gratitude? What will become of sacred friendship, if we are not to love our friend for his own sake with all our heart and soul, as people say? If we are even to desert and discard him, as soon as we despair of deriving any further assistance or advantage from him. What can be imagined more inhuman than this conduct? But if friendship ought rather to be cultivated on its own account, so also for the same reason are society, equality, and justice desirable for their own sakes. If this be not so, then there can be no such thing as justice at all; for the most unjust thing of all is to seek a reward for one's just conduct.

What then shall we say of temperance, sobriety, continence, modesty, bashfulness, and chastity? Is it the fear of infamy, or the dread of judgments and penalties, which prevent men from being intemperate and dissolute? Do men then live in innocence and moderation, only to be well spoken of, and to acquire a certain fair reputation? Modest men blush even to speak of indelicacy. And I am greatly ashamed of those philosophers, who assert that there are no vices to be avoided other than those which the laws have branded with infamy. For what shall I say? Can we call those persons truly chaste, who abstain from adultery merely for the fear of public exposure, and that disgrace which is only one of its many evil consequences? For what can be either praised or blamed with reason, if you depart from that great law and rule of nature, which makes the difference between right and wrong? Shall corporal defects, if they are remarkable, shock our sensibilities, and shall those of the soul make no impression on us?—of the soul, I say, whose turpitude is so evidently proved by its vices. For what is there more hideous than avarice, more brutal than lust, more contemptible than cowardice, more base than stupidity and folly? Well, then, are we to call those persons unhappy, who are conspicuous for one or more of these, on account of some injuries, or disgraces, or sufferings to which they are exposed, or on account of the moral baseness of their sins? And we may apply the same test in the opposite way to those who are distinguished for their virtue.

Lastly, if virtue be sought for on account of some other things, it necessarily follows that there is something better than virtue. Is it money, then? Is it fame, or beauty, or health? All of which appear of little value to us when we possess them; nor can it be by any possibility certainly known how long they will last. Or is it (what it is shameful even to utter) that basest of all, pleasure? Surely not; for it is in the contempt and disdain of pleasure that virtue is most conspicuous.... But the real state of the case is that since law ought to be both a correctness of vice and a recommender of virtue, the principles on which we direct our conduct ought to be drawn from her. And, thus it comes to pass wisdom is the mother of all the virtuous arts, from the love of which the Greeks have composed the word Philosophy; and which is beyond all contradiction the richest, the brightest, and the most excellent of the gifts which the gods have bestowed on the life of mankind. For wisdom alone has taught us, among other things, the most difficult of all lessons, namely, *to know ourselves*, a precept so forcible and so comprehensive, that it has been attributed not to a man, but to the god of Delphi himself.

For he who knows himself must in the first place be conscious that he is inspired by a divine principle. And he will look upon his rational part as a resemblance to some divinity consecrated within him, and will always be careful that his sentiments as well as his external behavior be worthy of so inestimable a gift of god. And after he has thoroughly examined himself and tested himself in every way, he will become aware what signal advantages he has received from nature at his entrance into life, and with what infinite means and appliances he is furnished for the attainment and acquisition of wisdom, since in the very beginning of all things, he has, as it were, the intelligible principles of things delineated, as it were, on his mind and soul, by the enlightening assistance of which, and the guidance of wisdom, he sees that he shall become a good and consequently a happy man.

For what can be described or conceived more truly happy than the state of that man, whose mind having attained to an exact knowledge and perception of virtue, has entirely discarded all obedience to and indulgence of the body, and has trampled on voluptuousness as a thing unbecoming the dignity of his nature, and has raised himself above all fear of death or pain; who maintains a benevolent intercourse with his friends, and has learnt to look upon all who are united to him by nature as his kindred; who has learnt to preserve piety and reverence towards the gods and pure religion; and who has sharpened and improved the perceptions of his mind, as well as of his eyesight, to choose the good and reject the evil, which virtue from its foreseeing things is called Prudence?

When this man shall have surveyed the heavens, the earth, and the seas, and studied the nature of all things, and informed himself from whence they have been generated, to what state they will return, and of the time and manner of their dissolution, and has learnt to distinguish what parts of them are mortal and perishable, and what divine and eternal—when we shall have almost attained to a knowledge of that Being who superintends and governs these things, and shall look on himself as not confined within the walls of one city, or as the member of any particular community, but as a citizen of the whole universe, considered as a single common-wealth: amid such a grand magnificence of things as this, and such a prospect and knowledge of nature, what a knowledge of himself, O ye immortal gods, will a man arrive at!

11. Cicero, *On Duties*

On Duties *is a less formal, more practical treatise, written by Cicero in the form of a letter to his son, Marcus, who was studying at Athens. In this work, written in 44* B.C.E., *Cicero discusses the apparent difference between what is advantageous and what is right, and argues that a Roman citizen must always choose what is right.*

My son: every part of philosophy is fruitful and rewarding, none barren or desolate. But the most luxuriantly fertile field of all is that of our moral obligations—since, if we clearly understand these, we have mastered the rules for leading a good and consistent life. No doubt you are conscientiously attending and absorbing the lectures on this subject by my friend Cratippus, and he is our leading contemporary philosopher. Nevertheless, I hope to make your ears ring with this kind of moralizing from every quarter! Indeed, if it were only possible, I should like them to hear nothing else.

To everyone who proposes to have a good career, moral philosophy is indispensable. And I am inclined to think that this applies particularly to yourself. For upon your shoulders rests a special responsibility. People have high expectations that you will work hard, as I have. They also trust that you will have a career like mine; and perhaps they look to you to win the same sort of reputation. Athens and Cratippus add to your responsibilities. You went to them in order to take on board, if one may put it in this way, a cargo of education. It would be discreditable, then, if you came back empty; for in that case you would not have lived up either to the city or to your professor. So make every effort you can. Work as hard as possible (if study comes under the heading of work and not of pleasure!) and do your very best. I have supplied you with all you need, so do not let people say that the failure is on your side.

But enough of this! I have sent you similar exhortations times without number. Let us now return to the subject we proposed for discussion, and deal with its outstanding subdivision.

A Practical Code

The most thorough analysis of moral obligations is unquestionably that of Panaetius, and on the whole, with certain modifications, I have followed him. The questions relating to this topic which arouse most discussion and inquiry are classified by Panaetius under three headings:

1. Is a thing morally right or wrong?
2. Is it advantageous or disadvantageous?
3. If apparent right and apparent advantage clash, what is to be the basis for our choice between them?

Panaetius wrote a three-part treatise about the first two of these questions; the third question he said he would deal with in its proper turn. But he never fulfilled his promise. This seems to me all the more surprising because he was still alive thirty years after the publication of the first three parts of his work—his pupil Posidonius records this.

Posidonius himself briefly refers to the subject in certain notes, but it seems to me strange that he, too, did not deal with it at greater length. For he expressed the opinion that there is no more vital theme in the whole range of philosophy.

Now one theory is that Panaetius did not overlook this problem but that his omission was deliberate—indeed that no discussion on the subject was required, since the possibility of a clash between right and advantage does not exist. Personally I cannot agree with such a view. Or rather, this last point could raise legitimate doubts—had Panaetius been right to include this third heading in his classification—should he not instead have omitted it altogether? But the other fact is incontrovertible; the subject was included in his classification, and yet he never dealt with it. If someone draws up a triple classification and completes two parts of his threefold task, he obviously still has the third ahead of him. Besides, at the end of his third part Panaetius actually promises that he will deal with this third topic at the proper time.

On this point Posidonius is a reliable witness. In one of his letters he quotes a favorite remark of Publius Rutilius Rufus, himself a pupil of Panaetius, about the painting of the Venus of Cos. No painter, said Rutilius, had ever been able to complete that part of the picture which Apelles had left unfinished, since the beauty of Venus's face made the adequate representation of the rest of her a hopeless task. Similarly, the quality of what Panaetius had written was so outstanding that nobody was able to supply his omissions.

What Panaetius intended, then, is not in doubt. But whether he had been justified when, at the outset, he included this third heading in his program for the study of moral obligations may well be, as I have said, a matter for discussion. The Stoics believe that right is the only good. Your Peripatetics, on the other hand, hold that right is the highest good—to the degree that all other things collected together scarcely begin to weigh down the balance on the other side. Now, according to either doctrine, there can be no doubt whatever about one point: advantage can never conflict with right. That is why Socrates, as the tradition goes, used to curse the men who had first begun to differentiate between these things which nature had made inseparable. The Stoics agreed with him; for their view is that everything which is morally right is advantageous, and there can be no advantage in anything which is not right.

Those, on the other hand, whose yardstick of desirability is pleasure or absence of pain say that right is only worth cultivating as a source of advantage. If Panaetius were the kind of man to hold the same opinion he might argue that clashes between right and advantage are conceivable. However, he is not that sort of thinker at all. On the contrary, he interprets right as the only good and judges that things which conflict with this, however advantageous they may look, can in fact make life neither better by their presence nor worse by their absence. So we reach the conclusion, after all, that there was no need for Panaetius to deal with the comparison between what is right and what appears (falsely) to be advantageous.

Besides, the Stoics' ideal is to live consistently with nature. I suppose what they mean is this: throughout our lives we ought invariably to aim at morally right courses of action, and, in so far as we have other aims also, we must select only those which do not clash with such courses. That is another reason why, according to the school of thought that I have mentioned, there ought never to have been any question of weighing advantage against right, and the whole topic ought to have been excluded from any philosophical discussion.

*　　*　　*

However, there is more to the matter than that. For moral goodness, in the truest and fullest sense of the word—goodness and right being wholly synonymous—could only be found among those hypothetical people who are endowed with ideal wisdom. Nobody who falls short of this perfect wisdom can possibly claim perfect goodness: its semblance is the most he can acquire. And these are the men, the ordinary men falling short of the ideal, whose moral obligations form the subject of my present work. The Stoics call these 'second-class' obligations. They are incumbent upon everybody in the world—so their application could not be wider! And what is more, natural decency and progress in understanding enable many people to live up to these obligations.

On the one hand, then, there is that ideal, unlimited obligation—the perfect obligation, as the Stoics put it, 'satisfying all the numbers'—which none but the ideally wise man can fulfill. And then there are also these other actions in which we see the working of a 'second-class' obligation. When the latter situation arises, there is often a very general impression that here, too, an ideal action has been performed; most people fail to understand that, in fact, the deed falls short of the ideal—their intelligence is insufficient to appreciate what is lacking. Judgements of poems, paintings, and much else reveal the same fault: uninformed readers and viewers admire and praise things that do not deserve to be praised. For evidently ignorant people can grasp such merits as these poems and pictures and so one may possess without being capable of detecting their deficiencies. What they need is expert instruction, and then they quickly revise their opinions.

The obligations, then, which I am discussing in this book are those related by the Stoics to this 'second-class' kind of goodness, which is not the exclusive possession of the hypothetical man of ideal wisdom, but is relevant to the whole of mankind. That is to say, everyone who is not devoid of good is prompted by obligations of this sort. Take for example the two Deciuses, or the two Scipios. We call them 'brave men' and we describe Gaius Fabricias Luscinus as 'just'. But this does not mean that they are perfect models of bravery or justice as the truly wise man would be. For none of them were 'wise' in the ideal sense we are here attributing to that word. Nor was Cato the Censor, nor was Gaius Laelius, although they received names indicating that they were so regarded. Even the Seven Wise Men were not wise in this sense—they merely bore a certain resemblance to wise men, because of their consistent per-formance of 'second-class' obligations.

Now it is mistaken, we know, to weigh what is ideally right against apparent advantage when the two things are in conflict. And apparent advantage should equally not be weighed against this 'second-class' sort of right which is cultivated by everyone who aspires to a reputation for goodness. For we are morally bound to cherish and observe the degree of right which comes within our comprehension just as carefully as the ideally wise man is obliged to cherish what is right in the full and ideal sense of the word. Because that is the only way in which we can maintain whatever progress we have made towards achieving goodness.

So much then for people who fulfill their moral obligations sufficiently well to be regarded as good. But those who habitually weigh the right course against what they regard as advantageous are in quite a different category. Unlike good men, they judge everything by profits and gains, which seem to them just as valuable as what is right. Panaetius observed that people often doubtingly weigh those two things against one another. I am sure he meant just what he said: that they often do this, not that they ought to. For preferring advantage to right is not the only crime. It is also sinful even to attempt a comparison between the two things—even to hesitate between them.

But can there be any sort of contingency warranting doubts and special consideration? I believe that there can; certain situations are perplexingly difficult to assess. On occasion, a course of action generally regarded as wrong turns out not to be wrong after all. Let me quote a particular instance, which admits of a wider application. There could be no more terrible crime than to kill someone who is not merely a fellow human being but a close friend. Yet surely someone who kills a tyrant, however close friends the two men have been, has not committed a crime. At any rate the people of Rome do not think so, since they regard that deed which was done as the most splendid of all noble actions. Has advantage then, in this case, prevailed over right? No; advantage has come from right.

All the same, there are occasions on which advantage, as we understand the term, will give the impression of clashing with what we interpret as right. In order to avoid mistaken conclusions when this happens, we must establish some rule to guide us in comparing the two things, and to keep us true to our obligations. That rule will be in accordance with the teaching and system of the Stoics. They are my models in this work; and I will tell you why. It is true that the earlier members of the Academy and your Peripatetics (who were once indistinguishable from them) regard right as preferable to apparent advantage. But the Stoics go further, and actually identify advantage with right, insisting that a thing must be right before it can be advantageous. This treatment of the subject is more impressive than the Peripatetic and earlier Academic belief that some particular good actions may not be advantageous and some advantageous actions may not be good. I, however, belong to the New Academy, which allows wide latitude to adopt any theory supported by probability.

The Unnaturalness of Doing Wrong

But to return to my rule. To take something away from someone else—to profit by another's loss—is more unnatural than death, or destitution, or pain, or any other physical or external blow. To begin with, this strikes at the roots of human society and fellowship. For if we each of us propose to rob or injure one another for our personal gain, then we are dearly going to demolish what is more emphatically nature's creation than anything else in the whole world: namely, the link that unites every human being with every other. Just imagine if each of our limbs had its own consciousness and saw advantage for itself in appropriating the nearest limb's strength! Of course the whole body would inevitably collapse and die. In precisely the same way, a general seizure and appropriation of other people's property would cause the collapse of the human community, the brotherhood of man. Granted that there is nothing unnatural in a man preferring to earn a living for himself rather than for someone else, what nature forbids is that we should increase our own means, property, and resources by plundering others.

Indeed this idea—that one must not injure anybody else for one's own profit—is not only natural law, an international valid principle: the same idea is also incorporated in the statutes which individual communities have framed for their national purposes. The whole point and intention of these statutes is that one citizen shall live safely with another; anyone who attempts to undermine that association is punished with fines, imprisonment, exile, or death.

The same conclusion follows even more forcibly from nature's rational principle, the law that governs gods and men alike. Whoever obeys this principle—and everyone who wants to live according to nature's laws must obey it—will never be guilty of coveting another man's goods or taking things from someone else and appropriating them for himself. For great-heartedness and heroism, and courtesy, and justice, and generosity, are far more in conformity with nature than self-indulgence, or wealth, or even life itself. But to despise this latter category of things, to attach no importance to them in comparison with the common good, really does need a heroic and lofty heart.

In the same way, it is more truly natural to model oneself on Hercules and undergo the most terrible labors and troubles in order to help and save all the nations of the earth than (however superior you are in looks or strength) to live a secluded, untroubled life with plenty of money and pleasures. And mankind was grateful to Hercules, for his services; popular belief gave him a place among the gods. That is to say, the finest and noblest characters prefer a life of dedication to a life of self-indulgence: and one may conclude that such men conform with nature and are therefore incapable of doing harm to their fellow-men.

A man who wrongs another for his own benefit can be explained in two different ways. Either he does not see that what he is doing is unnatural, or he refuses to agree that death, destitution, pain, the loss of children, relations, and friends are less deplorable than doing wrong to another person. But if he sees nothing unnatural in wronging a fellow-man, is he not beyond the reach of argument?—he is taking away from human beings all that makes them human. If, however, he concedes that this ought to be avoided, yet still regards death, destitution, and pain as even more undesirable, he is mistaken. He ought not to concede that any damage, either to his person or to his property, is worse than a moral failure.

So everyone ought to have the same purpose: to identify the interest of each with the interest of all. Once men grab for themselves, human society will completely collapse. But if nature prescribes (as she does) that every human being must help every other human being, whoever he is, just precisely because they are all human beings, then—by the same authority—all men have identical interests. Having identical interests means that we are all subject to one and the same law of nature: and, that being so, the very least that such a law enjoins is that we must not wrong one another. This conclusion follows inevitably from the truth of the initial assumption.

If people claim (as they sometimes do) that they have no intention of robbing their parents or brothers for their own gain, but that robbing their other compatriots is a different matter, they are not talking sense. For that is the same as denying their common interest with their fellow-countrymen, and all the legal or social obligations that follow therefrom: a denial which shatters the whole fabric of national life. Another objection urges that one ought to take account of compatriots but not of foreigners. But people who put forward these arguments subvert the whole foundation of the human community—and its removal means the annihilation of all kindness, generosity, goodness, and justice: which is a sin against the immortal gods, since they were the creators of the society which such men are seeking to undermine. And the tightest of the bonds uniting that society is the belief that robbery from another man for the sake of one's personal gain is more unnatural than the endurance of any loss whatever to one's person or property—or even to one's very soul. That is, provided that no violation of justice is involved...

Difficult Moral Decisions

Let us consider possible objections.

1. Suppose a man of great wisdom were starving to death: would he not be justified in taking food belonging to someone who was completely useless?

2. Suppose an honest man had the chance to steal the clothes of a cruel and inhuman tyrant like Phalaris, and needed them to avoid freezing to death; should he not do so?

These questions are very easy to answer. For to rob even a

completely useless man for your own advantage is an unnatural, inhuman action. If, however, your qualities were such that, provided you stayed alive, you could render great services to your country and to mankind, then there would be nothing blameworthy in taking something from another person for that reason. But, apart from such cases, every man must bear his own misfortunes rather than remedy them by damaging someone else. The possible exception I have quoted does not mean that stealing and covetousness in general are any less unnatural than illness, want, and the rest. The point is rather that neglect of the common interest is unnatural, because it is unjust; that nature's law promotes and coincides with the common interest; and therefore that this law must surely ordain that the means of subsistence may, if necessary, be transferred from the feeble, useless person to the wise, honest, brave man, whose death would be a grave loss to society? But in that case the wise man must guard against any excessive self-regard and conceit, since that could only lead to a wrongful course of action. If he avoids these pitfalls, he will be doing his duty—working for the interests of his fellow-men, and, I repeat yet again, of the human community.

An answer to the query about Phalaris can very easily be given. With autocrats we have nothing in common; in fact we and they are totally at variance. There is nothing unnatural about robbing—if you can—a man whom it is morally right even to kill. Indeed, the whole sinful and pestilential gang of dictatorial rulers ought to be cast out from human society. For when limbs have lost their life-blood and vital energy, their amputation may well follow. That is precisely how these ferocious, bestial monsters in human form ought to be severed from the body of mankind.

Such are the problems which beset our efforts to define obligations which may arise in particular circumstances. And this is the sort of theme which I believe Panaetius would have dealt with if some accident or distraction had not altered his plan. Indeed, plenty of rules bearing on precisely this sort of question had emerged from the earlier parts of his work. Those rules already suggest which courses of action have to be shunned as wrong, and which can be tolerated as right.

* * *

Well, the structure of my book is still not complete, but completion is not far off: now for the topmost stone. Mathematicians often simplify their arguments by leaving out the proofs of certain propositions and requiring that a number of conclusions should be taken for granted; and I shall adopt the same procedure. I shall invite you, my son, to concede to me (if you feel you can) that we must aim at nothing other that what is right. And even if Cratippus forbids such a concession, at least you will grant me this: that right is more worth aiming at, for its own sake, than anything else. Either of these assumptions is enough for my purpose. Sometimes the one alternative may seem more convincing, sometimes the other; and no solution apart from these two has any probability at all.

Before going on, I must refute a charge against Panaetius. He never made the improper assertion that advantage could in certain circumstances conflict with right. What he said was that apparent advantage could do so. But he frequently asserted that nothing can be advantageous unless it is right and nothing right unless it is advantageous; and he comments that no greater plague has ever visited mankind than the attitude of mind which has regarded the two things as separable. So the conflicts that he postulated were not real but only apparent ones. Far from permitting us ever to allow advantage priority over right, he was thinking of occasions when we should have to distinguish whether advantage or right were truly present, or whether their apparent presence was illusory; and his intention was to help us to reach such decisions correctly. However, as I have pointed out, Panaetius did not after all discuss this subject of apparent clashes. Accordingly in my treatment of the matter—which is now to follow—I shall be unsupported and fighting my own battle. True, I have seen studies on this theme by writers subsequent to Panaetius, but personally I have not found them satisfactory.

When we encounter advantage in some plausible form, we

cannot help being impressed. But close examination may reveal something morally wrong with this apparently advantageous action. In such a case the question of abandoning advantage does not arise, since it is axiomatic that where there is wrong there can be no true advantage. For nature demands that all things should be right and harmonious and consistent with itself and therefore with each other. But nothing is less harmonious with nature than wrong-doing: and equally, nothing is more in harmony with nature than what is truly advantageous. So advantage cannot possibly coexist with wrong. Take it for granted, then, that we are born—that our nature impels us—to seek what is morally right. In that case, whether we adopt Zeno's view that this is the only thing worth trying for, or Aristotle's opinion that it is at any rate infinitely more worth trying for than anything else, then one must conclude that right is either the only good or at least the highest of all goods. Being identified, therefore, with good—which is certainly advantageous—right is advantageous too.

A man who has in mind an apparent advantage and promptly proceeds to dissociate this from the question of what is right shows himself to be mistaken and immoral. Such a standpoint is the parent of assassinations, poisonings, forged wills, thefts, diversion of public money, and the ruinous exploitation of provincials and Roman citizens alike. Another result is passionate desire—desire for excessive wealth, for unendurable tyranny, and ultimately for the despotic seizure of free states. These desires are the most horrible and repulsive things imaginable. The perverted intelligences of men who are animated by such feelings are competent to understand the material rewards, but not the penalties. I do not mean penalties established by law, for these they often escape. I mean the most terrible of all punishments: their own degradation.

Away, then, with the whole wicked, godless crowd of people who hesitate which course to follow—the course they know to be right, or deliberate immersion and self-pollution in sin and crime! For the mere fact of their indecision is an offense: some courses of action are wrong even to consider—merely to pause over them is evil. Nor will it help the vacillator to expect or hope for his offense to be covered by secrecy or privacy. For if we have learnt any philosophy at all, this at least we ought to appreciate: all the secrets we may be able to keep from any and every god and human being do not in the least absolve us from the obligation to refrain from whatever actions are greedy, unjust, sensual, or otherwise immoderate.

12. *Gospel of Matthew*

*M*atthew, one of Jesus' disciples, wrote his Gospel primarily for
a Jewish audience in order to demonstrate that Jesus was the promised Messiah.

*The following selection is from the Sermon on the Mount, a
beautiful summary of his teachings. In it he contrasts his own
teachings with the conventional wisdom of the time, and
emphasizes how his teachings fulfill the promise of Mosaic law
rather than change it.*

Chapters 4 - 7

And seeing the crowd, he went up onto the mountain; and when
he was seated, his disciples came to him. And he began to teach
them, saying,

Blessed are the poor in spirit; for theirs is the kingdom of heaven.

Blessed are they who mourn; for they shall be comforted.

Blessed are the meek; for they shall inherit the earth.

Blessed are they who hunger and thirst after righteousness; for
they shall be satisfied.

Blessed are the merciful; for they shall obtain mercy.

Blessed are the pure in heart; for they shall see God.

Blessed are the peacemakers; for they shall be called the children
of God.

Blessed are they who are persecuted for righteousness' sake; for
theirs is the kingdom of heaven.

Blessed are you, when men shall revile you, and persecute you, and shall say all manner of evil against you falsely, for my sake. Rejoice, and be exceedingly glad; for great is your reward in heaven; for so did they persecute the prophets who were before you.

You are the salt of the earth; but if the salt has lost his taste, with what shall it be salted? It is then good for nothing but to be cast out, and to be trodden under foot.

You are the light of the world. A city that is set on a hill cannot be hidden. Neither do men light a candle, and put it under a bushel, but on a candlestick; and it gives light to all that are in the house. Let your light shine before men, that they may see your good works, and glorify your Father who is in heaven.

Do not think that I have come to destroy the law, or the prophets. I have not come to destroy, but to fulfill. For verily I say to you, Until heaven and earth pass, not one jot or one tittle shall pass from the law, until all be fulfilled. Therefore, whoever shall break one of these least commandments, and so teaches other men, shall be called least in the kingdom of heaven; but whoever shall follow and teach them shall be called great in the kingdom of heaven. For I say to you, That unless your righteousness shall exceed the righteousness of the scribes and Pharisees, you shall not enter the kingdom of heaven.

You have heard that it was said in ancient times, You shall not kill; and whoever shall kill shall be liable to judgment. But I say to you, That whoever is angry with his brother without a cause shall be in danger of the judgment; and whoever shall say to his brother, Raca, shall be in danger of the council; and whoever shall say, You fool, shall be in danger of hell fire. Therefore if you bring your gift to the altar and there remember that your brother has anything against you, Leave there your gift before the altar, and go your way; first be reconciled to your brother, and then come and offer your gift. Reconcile with your adversary quickly, while you are with him; lest your adversary deliver you to the judge, and the judge deliver you to the officer, and you be cast into prison. I say to you, You shall not come out until you have paid the last penny.

You have heard that it was said in ancient times, You shall not commit adultery. But I say to you, whoever looks with lust at a woman has committed adultery with her already in his heart. So if your right eye is a source of temptation to you, pluck it out, and cast it from you; for it is better for you that one of your members should perish than your whole body be cast into hell. And if your right hand is a source of temptation to you, cut it off, and cast it from you; for it is better for you that one of your members should perish than your whole body be cast into hell.

It has been said, Whoever shall put away his wife, let him give her a written divorce. But I say to you, That whoever shall put away his wife, except in the case of adultery, causes her to commit adultery; and whoever shall marry a divorced woman commits adultery.

You have heard that it has been said, An eye for an eye, and a tooth for a tooth. But I say to you, Do not resist evil; but if someone strike you on your right cheek, turn to him the other also. And if any man sue you at court and take away your tunic, let him have your cloak also. And if anyone compel you to go one mile, go with him two miles. Give to him that asks something of you, and do not turn away from him that would borrow from you.

You have heard that it has been said, Love your neighbor, and hate your enemy. But I say to you, Love your enemies, bless those who curse you, do good to those who hate you, and pray for those who spitefully use you, and persecute you; so that you may be children of your Father in heaven; for he makes his sun rise on the evil and on the good, and sends rain on the just and on the unjust. For if you love those who love you, what reward have you earned? Do not even the publicans do the same? And if you salute your brethren only, what more do you merit than any others? Do not even the publicans do the same? You must therefore be perfect, even as your Father in heaven is perfect.

Take heed not to do good before men, to be seen of them; otherwise you have no reward from your Father in heaven. When you give alms, do not sound a trumpet before you, as the hypocrites do in the synagogues and in the streets, so that they may have glory of men. Verily I say to you, They have their reward. But when you give alms, let not your left hand know what your right hand is doing so that your alms may be in secret. Then your Father who sees in secret shall reward you openly.

When you pray, do not be like the hypocrites, who love to pray standing in the synagogues and in the corners of the streets, where they can be seen by others. I say to you, They have their reward. But you, when you pray, enter into your closet, and when you have shut your door, pray to your Father in secret; and your Father who sees in secret shall reward you openly.

After this manner therefore pray you:

Our Father who is in heaven, Hallowed be your name.

Your kingdom come, Your will be done in earth, as it is in heaven.

Give us this day our daily bread.

And forgive us our debts, as we forgive our debtors.

And lead us not into temptation, but deliver us from evil. For yours is the kingdom, and the power, and the glory, forever. Amen.

For if you forgive men their offenses, your heavenly Father will also forgive you. But if you do not forgive men their offenses, neither will your Father forgive your offenses.

Do not lay up for yourselves treasures on earth, where moth and rust corrupt, and thieves break through and steal. Lay up for yourself treasures in heaven, where neither moth nor rust corrupts, and thieves do not break through nor steal. For where your treasure is, there will your heart be also.

No man can serve two masters; for either he will hate the one, and love the other; or else he will stand by the one, and despise the other. You cannot serve God and man.

Therefore I say to you, Take no thought for your life, what you shall eat, or what you shall drink; nor yet for your body, what you shall put on. Is not the life more than meat, and the body than clothing? Behold the birds of the air; for they neither sow nor reap, nor gather into barns; yet your heavenly Father feeds them. Are you not much better than they?....

Do not judge, so that you not be judged. For you shall be judged according to whatever judgment you judge; whatever measure you use shall be used against you. And why do you worry about the mote in your brother's eye, when you do not consider the beam in your own eye? Or how will you say to your brother, Let me pull the mote out of your eye; and, behold, a beam is in your own eye? You hypocrite! First cast out the beam from your own eye; and then shall you see clearly to cast out the mote from your brother's eye. Ask, and it shall be given you; seek, and you shall find; knock, and it shall be opened to you. For every one that asks receives; and he that seeks finds; and to him that knocks it shall be opened. Or what man is there of you, who if his son asks for bread will give him a stone? Or if he asks for a fish will give him a serpent? If you then, being evil, know how to give good gifts to your children, how much more shall your Father in heaven give good things to them that ask him? Therefore all things whatever you would have men do to you, do also to them; for this is the law and the prophets.

Enter by the narrow gate, for wide is the gate, and broad is the way, that leads to destruction; many enter that way. Because straight is the gate, and narrow the way, that leads to life; few are they who find it.

Beware of false prophets, who come to you in sheep's clothing, but inwardly are ravening wolves. You shall know them by their fruits. Do men gather grapes of thorns, or figs of thistles? Every good tree bears good fruit; but a bad tree bears bad fruit. A good tree cannot bear bad fruit, and a bad tree cannot bear good fruit. Every tree that bears bad fruit is cut down, and cast into the fire. Thus by their fruits you shall know them.

Not every one that says to me, Lord, Lord, shall enter into the kingdom of heaven; but he who follows the will of my Father in heaven. Many will say to me in that day, Lord, Lord, have we not prophesied in your name? And in your name have cast out devils? And in your name done many wonderful works? And then I will declare to them, I never knew you; depart from me, you who work iniquity.

Whoever hears my sayings and follows them is like a wise man who built his house upon a rock. And the rain descended, and the floods came, and the winds blew, and beat upon that house; and it fell not; for it was founded upon a rock. And every one that hears my words but does not follow them is like a foolish man who built his house upon the sand. And the rain descended, and the floods came, and the winds blew, and beat upon that house; and it fell, and great was its fall.

13. *Paul's Letter to the Romans*

Paul's letter to the Romans is the classic statement of Pauline Christian theology. In it, Paul deals with the purpose of law. He not only distinguishes between the old law of Judaism and the new law of Christianity, but goes significantly further to emphasize the primacy of faith through God's grace in the achievement of salvation. Paul's letter to the Romans was to be a significant influence on Augustine and Martin Luther.

Paul, a servant of Jesus Christ, called to be an apostle, set apart for the gospel of God, which he promised beforehand through his prophets in the holy scriptures, the gospel concerning his Son Jesus Christ our Lord, who was made of the seed of David according to the flesh; and declared to be the Son of God with power, according to the spirit of holiness, by the resurrection from the dead; from whom we have received grace and apostleship, for obedience to the faith among all nations for his name.

To all beloved of God in Rome, called to be saints: Grace to you and peace from God our Father, and the Lord Jesus Christ.

First, I thank my God through Jesus Christ for all of you, because your faith is proclaimed in all the world. For God is my witness, whom I serve with my spirit in the gospel of his Son, that without ceasing I mention you always in my prayers, asking that somehow by God's will I may now at last succeed in coming to you. For I long to see you, that I may impart to you some spiritual gift to strengthen you, that is, that we may be mutually encouraged by each other's faith, both yours and mine. I want you to know, brethren, that I have often intended to come to you but thus far have been prevented, in order that I may reap some harvest among you as well as among the rest of the Gentiles. I am under obligation both to Greeks and to barbarians, both to the wise and to the foolish. So I am eager to preach the gospel to you also who are in Rome.

For I am not ashamed of the gospel: it is the power of God for salvation to everyone who has faith, to the Jew first and also to the Greek. For in it the righteousness of God is revealed through faith for faith; as it is written, "He who through faith is righteous shall live..."

All who have sinned without the law will also perish without the law, and all who have sinned under the law will be judged by the law. For it is not the hearers of the law who are righteous before God, but the doers of the law who will be justified. When Gentiles who have not the law do by nature what the law requires, they are a law unto themselves, even though they do not have the law. They show that what the law requires is written on their hearts while their conscience also bears witness and their conflicting thoughts accuse or perhaps excuse them on that day when, according to my gospel, God judges the secrets of men by Christ Jesus.

But if you call yourself a Jew and rely upon the law and boast of your relation to God and know his will and approve what is excellent, because you are instructed in the law, and if you are sure that you are a guide to the blind, a light to those who are in darkness, a corrector of the foolish, a teacher of children, having in the law the embodiment of knowledge and truth—you then who teach others, will you not teach yourself? While you preach against stealing, do you steal? You who say that one must not commit adultery, do you commit adultery? You who abhor idols, do you rob temples? You who boast in the law, do you dishonor

God by breaking the law? For, as it is written, "The name of God is blasphemed among the Gentiles because of you."

Circumcision indeed is of value if you obey the law; but if you break the law, your circumcision becomes uncircumcision. So, if a man who is uncircumcised keeps the precepts of the law, will not his uncircumcision be regarded as circumcision? Then those who are physically uncircumcised but keep the law will condemn you who have the written code and circumcision but break the law. For he is not a real Jew who is one outwardly, nor is true circumcision something external and physical. He is a Jew who is one inwardly, and real circumcision is a matter of the heart, spiritual and not literal. His praise is not from men but from God.

Then what advantage has the Jew? Or what is the value of circumcision? Much in every way. To begin with, the Jews are entrusted with the oracles of God. What if some were unfaithful? Does their faithlessness nullify the faithfulness of God? By no means! Let God be true though every man be false, as it is written, "That you may be justified in your words, and prevail when you are judged." But if our wickedness serves to show the justice of God, what shall we say? That God is unjust to inflict wrath on us? (I speak in a human way.) By no means! For then how could God judge the world? But if through my falsehood God's truthfulness abounds to his glory, why am I still being condemned as a sinner? And why not do evil that good may come?—as some people slanderously charge us with saying. Their condemnation is just.

What then? Are we Jews any better off? No, not at all; for I have already charged that all men, both Jews and Greeks, are under the power of sin, as it is written: "None is righteous, no, not one; no one understands, no one seeks for God. All have turned aside, together they have gone wrong; no one does good, not even one..."

Now we know that whatever the law says it speaks to those who are under the law, so that every mouth may be stopped, and the whole world may be held accountable to God. For no human being will be justified in his sight by works of the law, since through the law comes knowledge of sin.

But now the righteousness of God has been manifested apart from law, although the law and the prophets bear witness to it, the righteousness of God comes through faith in Jesus Christ for all who believe. For there is no distinction, since all have sinned and fall short of the glory of God, they are justified by his grace as a gift, through the redemption which is in Christ Jesus, whom God put forward as an expiation by his blood, to be received by faith. This was to show God's righteousness, because in his divine forbearance he had passed over former sins; it was to prove at the present time that he himself is righteous and that he justifies him who has faith in Jesus. *Jew's*

Then what becomes of our boasting? It is excluded. On what principle? On the principle of works? No, but on the principle of faith. For we hold that a man is justified by faith apart from works of law. Or is God the God of Jews only? Is he not the God of Gentiles also? Yes, of Gentiles also, since God is one; and he will justify the circumcised on the ground of their faith and the uncircumcised through their faith. Do we then overthrow the law by this faith? By no means! On the contrary, we uphold the law.

What then shall we say about Abraham, our forefather according to the flesh? For if Abraham was justified by works, he has something to boast about, but not before God. For what does the scripture say? "Abraham believed God, and it was reckoned to him as righteousness." Now to one who works, his wages are not reckoned as a gift but as his due. And to one who does not work but trusts him who justifies the ungodly, his faith is reckoned as righteousness. So also David pronounces a blessing upon the man to whom God reckons righteousness apart from works: "Blessed are those whose iniquities are forgiven, and whose sins are covered; blessed is the man against whom the Lord will not reckon his sin."

Is this blessing pronounced only upon the circumcised, or also upon the uncircumcised? We say that faith was reckoned to Abraham as righteousness. How then was it reckoned to him? Was it before or after he had been circumcised? It was not after, but before he was circumcised. He received circumcision as a sign or seal of the righteousness which he had by faith while he was still uncircumcised. The purpose was to make him the father of all who believe without being circumcised and who thus have righteousness reckoned to them, and likewise the father of the circumcised who are not merely circumcised but also follow the example of the faith which our father Abraham had before he was circumcised.

The promise to Abraham and his descendants, that they should inherit the world, did not come through the law but through the righteousness of faith. If it is the adherents of the law who are to be the heirs, faith is null and the promise is void. For the law brings wrath, but where there is no law there is no transgression.

That is why it depends on faith, in order that the promise may rest on grace and be guaranteed to all his descendants—not only to the adherents of the law but also to those who share the faith of Abraham, for he is the father of us all, as it is written, "I have made you the father of many nations"—in the presence of the God in whom he believed, who gives life to the dead and calls into existence the things that do not exist...

Therefore, since we are justified by faith, we have peace with God through our Lord Jesus Christ. Through him we have obtained access to this grace in which we stand, and we rejoice in our hope of sharing the glory of God...

Let not sin, therefore, reign in your mortal bodies, to make you obey their passions. Do not yield your members to sin as instruments of wickedness, but yield yourself to God as men who have been brought from death to life, and your members to God as instruments of righteousness. For sin will have no dominion over you, since you are not under the law, but grace.

What then? Are we to sin because we are not under the law but under grace? By no means! Do you not know that if you yield yourselves to any one as obedient as slaves, you are slaves of the one whom you obey, either of sin, which leads to death, or of obedience, which leads to righteousness....

But now that you have been set free from sin and have become slaves of God, the return you get is sanctification and its end, eternal life. For the wages of sin is death, but the free gift of God is eternal life in Christ Jesus our Lord....

Do you not know, brethren—for I am speaking to those who know the law—that the law is binding on a person only during his life? Thus a married woman is bound by law to her husband as long as he lives; but if her husband dies she is discharged from the law concerning the husband. Accordingly, she will be called an adulteress if she lives with another while her husband is alive. But if her husband dies she is free from that law, and if she marries another man she is not an adulteress.

Likewise, my brethren, you have died to the law through the body of Christ, so that you may belong to another, to him who has been raised from the dead in order that we may bear fruit for God. While we were living in the flesh, our sinful passions, aroused by the law, were at work in our members to bear fruit for death. But now we are discharged from the law, dead to that which held us captive, so that we serve not under the old written code but in the new life of the Spirit....

For they that live according to the flesh pursue the things of the flesh; but they that live according to the Spirit pursue the things of the Spirit. For to be carnally minded is death; but to be spiritually minded is life and peace. The carnal mind is against God, so then they that live by the flesh cannot please God.

But you are not in the flesh, rather you live in the Spirit, if the Spirit of God dwells in you. But if any man does not have the Spirit of Christ, he does not belong to Christ. If Christ is in you, the body is dead because of sin; but the Spirit is life because of your righteousness....

Brethren, my heart's desire and prayer to God for Israel is, that they might be saved. For I bear witness about them that they have a zeal for God, but not according to knowledge. For they being ignorant of God's righteousness, and going about establishing their own righteousness, have not submitted themselves to the righteousness of God. For Christ is the end of the law of righteousness for every one that believes....

If you confess with your mouth to the Lord Jesus, and believe in your heart that God has raised him from the dead, you shall be saved. For with the heart man believes in righteousness; and with the mouth confession is made for salvation. There is no difference between the Jew and the Greek; for the same Lord over all is rich to all who call upon him....

I ask, then, has God rejected his people? By no means! I myself am an Israelite, a descendant of Abraham, a member of the tribe of Benjamin. God has not rejected his people whom he once knew.... So too at the present time there is a faithful remnant chosen by grace. But it is by grace, it is no longer on the basis of works; otherwise grace would no longer be grace.

* * *

I beseech you therefore, brethren, by the mercy of God, to present your bodies as a living sacrifice, holy, acceptable to God, which is your reasonable service. And do not conform to this world: but be transformed by the renewing of your mind, so that you may discern what is the good and acceptable and perfect will of God. I say, through the grace given unto me, to each of you that you should not think of yourself more highly than you ought; rather think of yourself in moderate terms since God hath dealt to every man the measure of faith. For just as we have many members in one body, and all members have not the same office, so we, being many, are one body in Christ, and every one members one of another. But each of us has different gifts according to the grace that is given to us.

* * *

Let everyone be subject to higher authorities, for there is no authority except from God, the authorities that have been ordained by God. Whoever therefore resists authority resists the ordinance of God; and they that resist shall receive to themselves damnation. For rulers are not a terror to good works, but to evil. Do you wish then not be afraid of the power? Do that which is good, and you shall have its praise. For that power is the minister of God to you for good. But if you do what is evil, be afraid; for the power does not bear the sword in vain, for it is the minister of God, a revenger to execute wrath upon him who does evil. Indeed, you must subject yourself, not only from fear, but also for your conscience' sake. For this is the reason you pay tribute: for they are God's ministers...Render therefore to all their due: tribute to whom tribute is due; taxes to whom taxes are due; fear to whom fear is due; honor to whom honor is due.

14. Augustine, *Confessions*

Augustine (354-430) was the most influential of the Western Church Fathers. Strongly influenced by both neo-Platonism and Paul, his articulation of Christian teaching became synonymous with orthodox Christianity. Augustine is also important for the powerful philosophical foundation he provides for Christian faith.

The Confessions *is ostensibly Augustine's autobiography, the compelling story of his search for meaning in life that culminates in his conversion to Christianity. But it is much more: a theological treatise, a study of human nature, an exploration into the nature of good and evil. Augustine wrote the* Confessions *in 401, years after his conversion.*

BOOK II

...Theft is punished by your law, O Lord, and the law written in the hearts of all people, which cannot be erased no matter how sinful they are. For what thief will tolerate another thief? Even a rich thief will not tolerate a poor thief stealing by necessity. Yet I longed to thieve, and did it, not compelled by hunger or poverty, but because of an appearance of doing well and a tolerance of evil. For I stole that of which I had plenty. Nor did I enjoy what I stole, but took joy in the theft and the sin itself.

There was a pear tree near our vineyard, laden with fruit, tempting neither for color nor taste. Some wild young friends and I went out to shake and rob this tree late one night (having, according to our evil custom, prolonged our sports in the streets until then), and took huge loads, not for our eating, but to fling to the hogs. And this we did only because we wanted to do that which was disliked. Behold my heart, O God, behold my heart, which you had pity upon in the bottom of the bottomless pit. Now, behold, let my heart tell you what it sought there, that I should be so gratuitously evil, having no temptation to profit from the evil, but to do the evil itself. It was foul, and I loved it; I loved to perish, I loved my own evil, not the act which was evil, but my evil itself. Foul soul, falling from your firmament to utter destruction; not seeking anything through the shame, but the shame itself!...

When we ask why a crime was done, we can't believe the reason, unless it appears that there might have been some desire of obtaining something from the lower order, or a fear of losing something from the lower order. For these things often appear beautiful and comely; although compared with those higher and beatific goods, they are vile and low. A man has murdered another; why? He loved his wife or his estate; or would rob for his own livelihood; or feared to lose some such things by him; or, wronged, was on fire to be revenged. Would anyone commit murder with no cause, delighted simply in murdering? Who would believe it?...

What then was so wretched about me that I did so love the theft—you theft of mine, you deed of darkness—in that sixteenth year of my age? Lovely you were not, because you were theft. But are you anything, that thus I speak to you? The pears we stole were beautiful, because they were your creation, you most beautiful of all, creator of all, you good God; God, the sovereign good and my true good. Beautiful were those pears, although my wretched soul did not desire them, since I had a store of better pears. Those I did gather, I gathered only so that I might steal, for as soon as I gathered them, I flung them away. My only feast was my own sin, in which I took great pleasure. For even if any part of those pears had come within my mouth, what sweetened it was the sin. And now, O Lord my God, I enquire what in that theft delighted me? And behold it has no loveliness; I mean not such loveliness as in justice and wisdom; nor such as is in the mind and memory, and senses, and animal life of man; nor yet as the stars are glorious and beautiful in their orbs; or the earth, or sea, full of life, replacing by its birth that which decays; nay, nor even that false and shadowy beauty which belongs to deceiving vices....

What then did I love in that theft? And did I even try corruptly and pervertedly to imitate my Lord? Did I wish even by stealth to do contrary to your law? By my own power I could not, but being a prisoner, I might mimic a maimed liberty by doing with impunity things not permitted, a darkened likeness of your omnipotence....

What shall I render to the Lord, that, while my memory recalls these things, my soul is not frightened at them? I will love you, O Lord, and thank you, and confess to your name; because you have forgiven me these great and heinous deeds of mine. To your grace I ascribe it, and to your mercy, that you have melted away my sins as it were ice. To your grace I ascribe also whatever I have not done of evil;... Yea, all I confess has been forgiven: both what evils I committed by my own willfulness, and what by your guidance I did not commit.

BOOK VII

*...And still I sought "the origin of evil," and sought in an evil way; and saw not the evil in my very search. I set before me the sight of the whole creation, whatever we can see (as sea, earth, air, stars, trees, mortal creatures); yea, and whatever in it we do not see (as the firmament of heaven, all angels, and all the spiritual inhabitants).... You, O Lord, I imagined on every part of creation, living in it and penetrating it, though in every way infinite: as if there were a sea every where, and on every side, through unmeasured space, one boundless sea, and it contained within it some sponge, huge, but bounded; that sponge must, in all its parts, be filled from that unmeasurable sea. So I conceived of your creation, itself finite, full of you, the infinite; and I said, "Behold God, and

behold what God has created; and God is good, most mightily and incomparably better than all of his creation: but yet he, the good, created them good; and see how he lives in them and fulfills them. Where is evil then, and how did it creep into creation?... How is it then? God, the good, has created all these things good. He indeed, the greater and chief good, has created these lesser goods; still both creator and created, all are good. Where does evil come from? Or, was there some evil matter of which he made, and formed, and ordered it, yet left something in it which he did not convert into good? Why so then? Had he no power to turn and change the whole, so that no evil should remain in it, seeing he is all-mighty? Lastly, why would he make any thing at all...?" These thoughts I revolved in my miserable heart, overcharged with gnawing uncertainty, lest I should die before I had found the truth. Yet the faith of your Christ, our Lord and Savior, professed in the Church Catholic, was firmly fixed in my heart, indeed, as yet unformed, and fluctuating from the rule of doctrine; yet my mind did not leave the question, but rather daily took in more and more of it....

And it was finally made clear to me that those things are good even though they are corrupted;... for if they were completely good, they would be incorruptible; and if they were completely not good, there would be nothing in them to be corrupted. For corruption injures; there must be goodness that is diminished, otherwise there could be no injury. Either then corruption does not injure, which cannot be; or all which is corrupted is deprived of some good. But if they were deprived of all good, they would cease to exist.... So long therefore as they are, they are good: therefore whatever is, is good. That evil then which I sought, therefore, is not a substance, for if it were a substance, it would be good. For either the substance would be an incorruptible substance, and so the highest good; or a corruptible substance.... I perceived therefore, and it was manifested to me, that you made all things good, and there is no substance at all that you did not make....

And I perceived and did not find it strange that bread which is pleasant to a healthy palate is loathsome to one distempered; and to sore eyes light is offensive...and so it is that your righteousness displeases the wicked... And I enquired what iniquity was, and found it not to be a substance, but the perversion of the will, turned aside from you, O God, the supreme, towards these lower things....

Most eagerly then did I seize that venerable writing of your gospel, and chiefly the apostle Paul. Whereupon reading him, the difficulties vanished away;... And the face of that pure word appeared to me one and the same; and I learned to rejoice with trembling. So I began; and whatever truth I had read in earlier books, I also found here amid the praise of your grace;...

For, though a person be delighted with the law of God within, what shall one do with that other law which abides in the body and which makes war against the law of the mind, and brings one into captivity under the law of sin which is in the body? For, you are righteous, O Lord, but we have sinned and committed iniquity, and have done wickedly, and your hand is grown heavy upon us, and we are justly delivered over to that ancient sinner, the king of death; because our will was persuaded to be like his will, and he abides not in your truth. What shall wretched people do? Who shall deliver us from the body of his death? Only your grace, through Jesus Christ our Lord, whom you have begotten co-eternal.... "Shall not my soul be submitted to God? For from him comes my salvation. For he is my God and my salvation, my guardian, I shall no more be moved"... These things did wonderfully sink into my bowels, when I read that least of your apostles, and had meditated upon your works, and trembled exceedingly....

BOOK VIII

...Then in this great struggle of my inner being, which I had strongly raised against my soul in the chamber of my heart, and troubled in mind and body, I turned to my friend Alypius. "What ails us?" I exclaimed: "What is it? What have you heard? The uneducated take heaven by force, and we with our learning, and without heart, we wallow in flesh and blood! Are we ashamed to follow, because others have gone before?" Some such words I spoke and my fever of mind tore me away from him, while he stared at me in astonishment and kept silent. For it wasn't my anguished words; rather my forehead, cheeks, eyes, color, tone of voice—all these spoke my mind more than the words I uttered.

There was a little garden there in our lodging, which we had the use of, as of the whole house, for the master of the house, our host, was not living there. There to the garden did the tumult in my breast hurry me, where no one might hinder the hot contention that had engaged me (until it should end as you know how, but I knew not). Only I was distracted and dying, knowing what evil thing I was, and not knowing what good thing I was shortly to become. I retired then into the garden, and Alypius followed on my steps. For his presence did not lessen my privacy, and how could he forsake me so disturbed? We sat down as far as possible from the house. I was troubled in spirit, and was most vehemently indignant that I could not understand your will and covenant, O my God, which all my bones cried out to know and praise.... There was nothing else to do but to will to know, and to will resolutely and thoroughly; not to turn and toss, this way and that, as a maimed and half-divided will, struggling with one part sinking as another rose.

Finally, in the very fever of my irresoluteness, my body made many such motions that men sometimes make; but they cannot make these motions if either they have not the limbs or if they are bound with bands, weakened with infirmity, or in any other way hindered. Thus, when I tore my hair, beat my forehead, or locked my fingers around my knee; I willed to do it and I did it. But I might have willed to do it, and not done it if the power of motion in my limbs had not obeyed. Many things then I did, when "to will" was not the same as "to be able." At times, I did not do what both I longed to do and what I was be able to do.... For in these things the ability is one with the will, and to will was to do; and yet it was not done. My body obeyed more easily the weakest willing of my soul in moving its limbs at its nod, than the soul obeyed its own self to do what it wills to do.

Why do we suffer this monstrousness? and to what end? Let your mercy answer what I ask. Is it the secret penalty of mankind, those darkest pangs of the sons of Adam? What is the source of this monstrousness? and to what end? The mind commands the body, and it obeys instantly; the mind commands itself, and is resisted. The mind commands the hand to be moved and the readiness is there so much so that the command is hardly distinct from obedience. Yet the mind is mind, the hand is body. The mind commands the mind, its own self, to will, and yet it does not obey itself. Whence this monstrousness? and to what end? It commands itself, or as I say, to will itself, and it would not command so unless it willed so; and, yet, what it commands is not done. But it does not will entirely: therefore it does not command entirely. Only in so far as it commands, does it will: and only in so far as a thing is commanded and not done, is it not willed. For the will commands that there be a will; not another, but itself. But it does not command entirely, therefore what it commands is not done. For if the will was complete, it would not even command it to be, because it would already be. It is therefore not monstrousness to will partly, but a disease of the mind that causes it to rise only partially, rising by truth, falling down by custom. And therefore there are two wills: one of them is not entire, and what that one lacks, the other has completely.

Let them perish from your presence, O God, those who observing that in deliberating there are two wills and affirm that there are two minds in us, one good, the other evil. They are truly evil when they believe these evil things; and they shall become good when they hold and assent to the truth, that your apostle may say to them, "You were sometimes darkness, but now light in the Lord."... Even myself, when I was deliberating upon serving the Lord my God, it was I who willed partially, I myself. I neither willed entirely, nor did not will entirely. Therefore I was at strife with myself and rent asunder by myself. This indicated, not the presence of another mind, but my punishment. Therefore it was not I that caused it, but the sin that dwelt in me; the punishment of a sin more freely committed, in that I was a son of Adam.

Now if there are as many contrary natures as there be conflicting wills, there will be not two only, but many. If someone deliberates whether to go to a Manichaean service or meeting or go to the theater, the Manichees cry out, "Behold, here are two natures: one good, draws this way; another bad, draws back that way. For how else to account for this hesitation between conflicting wills?" But I say that both are bad: that which draws to their service, as that which draws back to the theater. But they believe that will is either good or bad. What then if one of us should deliberate, and amid the strife of our two wills be in a quandary whether to go to the theater or to our church? Would not these Manichees also be in a quandary as to what to answer? For either they must confess (which they happily would not) that the will which leads to our church is good, as well as theirs; or they must suppose two evil natures, and two evil souls conflicting in one person. So... they must be converted to the truth, and no more deny that when one deliberates, one soul fluctuates between contrary wills.

Let them no longer say then that when they perceive two conflicting wills in one man, that the conflict is between two contrary souls, of two contrary substances, from two contrary principles, one good, and the other bad. For you, O true God, do disprove, as when, both wills being bad, one deliberates whether to kill someone by poison or by the sword; whether to seize this or that estate of another's; whether to purchase pleasure by luxury or keep money by covetousness; whether to go to the circus or the theater, if both be open on one day; or to rob another's house, if he have the opportunity, or to commit adultery... For they all rend the mind amid the vast variety of things desired... So also in wills which are good.... Thus when eternity delights us, but the pleasure of temporal good holds us down below, it is the same soul which wills not this or that with an entire will; and therefore it is rent asunder with grievous perplexities, while out of truth it sets one thing first, but out of habit it sets it aside.

Thus soul-sick was I, and tormented, accusing myself much more severely than was my custom, rolling and turning me in my chains... And you, O Lord, pressed upon me in my inward parts a powerful mercy, redoubling the lashes of fear and shame, lest I should again give way... For I said with myself, "Be it done now, be it done now." And as I spoke, I all but made it happen; I all but did it. Yet I did it not and sunk not back to my former state, but kept my stand hard by, and took breath. And I endeavored again,... and all but touched, and laid hold of it; and yet came not at it, nor touched nor laid hold of it. The very moment I was to become something other than I was, the nearer it approached me, the greater horror did it strike into me; yet it did not strike back at me, nor turn me away, but held me in suspense.

But the very toys of my youth, and vanities of vanities, my old mistresses, still held me; they plucked at my fleshy garment, and whispered softly, "Do you cast us off? and from that moment shall we no more be with you forever?"... What defilements did they suggest! What shame! And now I only half heard them, and they did openly show themselves nor contradict me, but muttering as it were behind my back, and gently plucking me as I was departing, to glance back on them. Yet they held me back, so that I hesitated to burst and shake myself free from them, and to spring over to where I was called: an old and violent habit saying to me, "Do you think you can live without us?"

But now the voices spoke very faintly and on that side where I had turned my face and where I trembled to go, there appeared to me the dignity of chastity, serene, yet not relaxed, happy, honestly alluring me to come and doubt no more. And stretching forth to receive and embrace me, her holy hands full of multitudes of good examples: there were so many young men and maidens here, a multitude of youth and every age, grave widows and aged virgins; and chastity herself in all, not barren, but a fruitful mother of children of joys, by you her husband, O Lord. And she smiled on me with a persuasive mockery, as though to say, "Can not you do what these youths do, what these maidens can?... Fear not, he will not withdraw himself from you that you should fall; cast yourself fearlessly upon him, he will receive, and will heal you." And I blushed exceedingly, for I still heard the muttering of those toys, and hung in suspense. And she again seemed to say, "Stop your ears against those your unclean members on the earth, that they may be mortified. They tell you of delights, but not as delight as does the law of the Lord your God." This turmoil in my heart was self against self only. But Alypius sitting close by my side, in silence, waited the decision of my emotion.

But when this deep consideration from the secret bottom of my soul had drawn together and heaped up all my misery in the sight of my heart; there arose in me a mighty storm, bringing a mighty shower of tears. When this happened, I rose and moved away from Alypius: solitude seemed to me more appropriate to the business of weeping. So I retired so far that even his presence could not be a burden to me. Thus it was with me, and he soon perceived something of it; for I suppose I had spoken and the tones of my voice appeared choked with weeping. He remained where we were sitting, extremely astonished. Somehow I cast myself down, under a certain fig-tree, giving full vent to my tears; and the floods of my eyes gushed out an acceptable sacrifice to you. And, not exactly in these words, I spoke to you: "O Lord, how long? How long, Lord, will you be angry forever? Remember not my former sins, for I felt that I was held by them." I sent up these sorrowful words: "How long, how long, tomorrow, or the next day? Why not now? Why not this be the hour to end my uncleanness?"

So I was speaking and weeping in this most bitter contrition of my heart, when I heard from a neighboring house a voice of a boy or girl, I know not, chanting, and repeating often: "Take up and read; Take up and read." Instantly, my countenance changed, and I began to think whether children normally sing such words in any kind of play and I could not remember ever hearing anything like this before. So holding back the torrent of my tears, I arose;

interpreting the words to be none other than a command from God to open the book, and read the first chapter I should find. For I had heard the story of Antony, that coming in during the reading of the Gospel, he received the admonition, as if what was being read was spoken to him: "Go, sell all that you have, and give to the poor, and you shall have treasure in heaven, and come and follow me," and by this sign he was converted to you. Eagerly then I returned to the place where Alypius was sitting, for there had I laid the volume of Paul I had been reading when I arose. I seized, opened, and in silence read that section on which my eyes first fell: "Not in reveling and drunkenness, not in lust and wantonness, not in quarrels and rivalries; but rather put on the Lord Jesus Christ, and give no thought to things of the flesh." No further would I read; nor did I need to read: for instantly at the end of this sentence, by a sudden light, as it were, of serenity infused into my heart, all the darkness of doubt vanished away.

Then putting my finger to mark the place, I shut the volume, and with a calm expression made it known to Alypius. What was troubling him I knew not. He asked to see what I had read: I showed him; and he read even further than I had read, and I did not know what followed. This is what followed: "... he that is weak in the faith, receive;" which he applied to himself, and disclosed to me. And by this sign was he strengthened... and without delay he joined me. Then we both went to my mother; we told her and she rejoiced; we related how it took place and she leaped for joy blessed you, O Lord, who are able to do more than that which we ask or even think; for she perceived that you had given her more by me than she was accustomed to ask. For you converted me to yourself, so that I sought neither wife, nor any hope of this world, standing in that rule of faith, where you had showed me to her in a vision, so many years before. And you converted her mourning into joy, more plentiful than she had desired....

15. Augustine, *Letters on True Faith*

*A*s bishop of Hippo in North Africa, Augustine devoted much
of his time and energy to purging Christianity of heresy. The Dona-
tists, the subject of the letter that follows, were radical Gnostics,
who maintained that they alone constituted the true church, and
denied the legitimacy of baptisms by orthodox clergy. Here he offers
guidelines as to how to deal with heretics. The principles he enunci-
ates would influence strongly later Christian attitudes and behavior
toward non-Christians, and help define the Christian position on
war.

To Vincentius

My Brother Dearly Beloved, Augustine sends greetings.

You are of the opinion that none should be compelled to follow
righteousness; and yet you read that the householder said to his
servants, "Whoever you shall find, compel them to come in." You
also read how he who was at first Saul, and afterwards Paul, was
compelled, by the great violence with which Christ coerced him,
to know and to embrace the truth; for you cannot but think that
the light which our eyes enjoy is more precious to men than money
or any other possession. This light, lost suddenly by him when he
was cast to the ground by the heavenly voice, he did not recover

until he became a member of the Holy Church. You are also of the opinion that no coercion is to be used with any man in order to secure his deliverance from the fatal consequences of error; and yet you see that, in examples which cannot be disputed, this is done by God, who loves us with more real regard for our profit than any other can; and you hear Christ saying, "No man can come to me unless the Father draws him," which is done in the hearts of all those who, through fear of the wrath of God, betake themselves to him. You know also that sometimes the thief scatters food before the flock that he may lead them astray, and sometimes the shepherd brings wandering sheep back to the flock with his rod.

Did not Sarah, when she had the power, choose rather to afflict the insolent bondwoman?... Those who have understanding may perceive that it is rather the Catholic Church which suffers persecution through the pride and impiety of those carnal men whom it endeavors to correct by afflictions and terrors of a temporal kind. Whatever therefore the true and rightful Mother [Church] does, even when something severe and bitter is felt by her children at her hands, she is not rendering evil for evil, but is applying the benefit of discipline to counteract the evil of sin, not with the hatred which seeks to harm, but with the love which seeks to heal. When good and bad do the same actions and suffer the same afflictions, they are to be distinguished not by what they do or suffer, but by the causes of each: e.g. Pharaoh oppressed the people of God by hard bondage; Moses afflicted the same people by severe correction when they were guilty of impiety. Their actions were alike, but they were not alike in the motive of regard to the people's welfare—the one being inflated by the lust of power, the other inflamed by love. Jezebel slew prophets, Elijah slew false prophets; I suppose that the desert of the actors and of the sufferers respectively in the two cases was wholly diverse.

Look also to the New Testament times, in which the essential gentleness of love was to be not only kept in the heart, but also manifested openly: in these the sword of Peter is called back into its sheath by Christ, and we are taught that it ought not to be taken from its sheath even in Christ's defense. We read, however, not only that the Jews beat the Apostle Paul, but also that the Greeks beat Sosthenes, a Jew, on account of the Apostle Paul. Does not the similarity of the events apparently join both; and, at the same time, does not the dissimilarity of the causes make a real difference? Again, God spared not his own Son, but delivered him up for us all. Of the Son also it is said, "who loved me, and gave himself for me;" and it is also said of Judas that Satan entered into him that he might betray Christ. Seeing, therefore, that the Father delivered up his Son, and Christ delivered up his own body, and Judas delivered up his Master, wherefore is God holy and man guilty in this delivering up of Christ, unless that in the one action which both did, the reason for which they did it was not the same? Three crosses stood in one place: on one was the thief who was to be saved; on the second, the thief who was to be condemned; on the third, between them, was Christ, who was about to save the one thief and condemn the other. What could be more similar than these crosses? What more unlike than the persons who were suspended on them? Paul was given up to be imprisoned and bound, but Satan is unquestionably worse than any jailer: yet to him Paul himself gave up one man for the destruction of the flesh, that the spirit might be saved in the day of the Lord Jesus. And what say we to this? Behold, both deliver a man to bondage; but he that is cruel consigns his prisoner to one less severe, while he that is compassionate consigns his to one who is more cruel. Let us learn, my brother, in actions which are similar to distinguish the intentions of the agents; and let us not, shutting our eyes, deal in groundless reproaches and accuse those who seek men's welfare as if they did them wrong...

If to suffer persecution were in all cases a praiseworthy thing, it would have sufficed for the Lord to say, "Blessed are they which are persecuted," without adding "for righteousness' sake." Moreover, if to inflict persecution were in all cases blameworthy, it would not have been written in the sacred books, "Whoever slanders his neighbor, him will I persecute..." In some cases, therefore, both he that suffers persecution is in the wrong, and he that inflicts it is in the right. But the truth is, that always both the bad have persecuted the good, and the good have persecuted the bad: the former doing harm by their unrighteousness, the latter seeking to do good by the administration of discipline; the former with cruelty, the latter with moderation; the former impelled by lust, the latter under the constraint of love. For he whose aim is to kill is not careful how he wounds, but he whose aim is to cure is cautious with his lancer; for the one seeks to destroy what is sound, the other that which is decaying. The wicked put prophets to death; prophets also put the wicked to death. The Jews scourged Christ; Christ also scourged the Jews. The apostles were given up by men to the civil powers; the apostles themselves gave men up to the power of Satan. In all these cases, what is important to notice is this: who were on the side of truth, and who on the side of iniquity; who acted from a desire to injure, and who from a desire to correct what was amiss?

You say that no example is found in the writings of evangelists and apostles, of any petition presented on behalf of the Church to the kings of the earth against her enemies. Who denies this? But at that time the prophecy...was not yet fulfilled.... Now, however, [the prophecy] is fulfilled which was prefigured... The earlier time...represented the former age of emperors who did not believe in Christ, at whose hands the Christians suffered because of the wicked; but now, believing in Christ,...the wicked suffer because of the Christians...

You now see therefore, I suppose, that the thing to be considered when any one is coerced, is not the mere fact of the coercion, but the nature of that to which he is coerced, whether it be good or bad—not that any one can be good in spite of his own will, but that, through fear of suffering what he does not desire, he either renounces his hostile prejudices, or is compelled to examine the truth of which he had been contentedly ignorant and under the influence of this fear repudiates the error which he was wont to defend, or seeks the truth of which he formerly knew nothing, and now willingly holds what he formerly rejected. Perhaps it would be utterly useless to assert this in words, if it were not demonstrated by so many examples. We see not a few men here and there, but many cities, once Donatist (a contemporary heresy), now Catholic, vehemently detesting the diabolical schism, and now ardently loving the unity of the Church; and these became Catholic under the influence of that fear which is to you so offensive...

I have therefore yielded to the evidence afforded by these instances which my colleagues have laid before me. For originally my opinion was, that no one should be coerced into the unity of Christ, that we must act only by words, fight only by arguments, and prevail by force of reason, lest we should have those whom we knew as avowed heretics feigning themselves to be Catholics. But this opinion of mine was overcome not by the words of those who controverted it, but by the conclusive instances to which they could point. For, in the first place, there was set over against my opinion my own town, which, although it was once wholly on the side of Donatus, was brought over to the Catholic unity by fear of the imperial edicts, but which we now see fined with such detestation of your ruinous perversity, that it would scarcely be believed that it had ever been involved in your error. There were so many others which were mentioned to me by name, that from facts themselves, I was made to own that to this matter the word of Scripture might be understood as applying: "Give opportunity to a wise man, and he win be yet wiser." For how many were already, as we assuredly know, willing to be Catholics, being moved by the indisputable plainness of truth, but daily putting off their avowal of this through fear of offending their own party! How many were bound, not by truth..., but by the heavy chains of inveterate custom, so that in them was fulfilled the divine saying: "A servant [who is hardened] will not be corrected by words; for though he understand, he will not answer." How many supposed the sect of Donatus to be the true Church, merely because ease had made them too listless, or conceited, or sluggish, to take pains to examine Catholic truth! How many would have entered earlier had not the calumnies of slanderers, who declared that we offered something else than we do upon the altar of God, shut them out! How many, believing that it mattered not to which party a Christian might belong, remained in the schism of Donatus only because they had been born in it, and no one was compelling them to forsake it and pass over into the Catholic Church.

...[Some] say: We knew not that the truth was here, and we had no wish to learn it; but fear made us become earnest to examine it when we became alarmed, lest, without any gain in things eternal we should be smitten with loss in temporal things: thanks be to the Lord, who has by stimulus of fear startled us from our negligence, that now being disquieted we might inquire into those things which, when at ease, we did not care to know! Others say: We were prevented from entering the Church by false reports which we could not know to be false unless we entered it; and we would not enter unless we were compelled; thanks be to the Lord, who by his scourge took away our timid hesitation, and taught us to find out for ourselves how vain and absurd were the lies which rumor had spread abroad against his Church!... Others say: We thought, indeed, that it mattered not in what communion we held the faith of Christ; but thanks to the Lord, who has gathered us in from a state of schism, and has taught us that it is fitting that the one God be worshiped in unity.

Could I therefore maintain opposition to my colleagues, and by resisting them stand in the way of such conquests of the Lord, and prevent the sheep of Christ which were wandering on your mountains and hills...from being gathered into the fold of peace, in which there is one flock and one Shepherd? Was it my duty to obstruct these measures in order that you might not lose what you call your own and might without fear rob Christ of what is his...? Nay verily; let the kings of the earth serve Christ by making laws for him and for his cause...

To His Brother Emeritus

Beloved and longed for,
Augustine sends greetings.

I know that it is not on the possession of good talents and a liberal education that the salvation of the soul depends; but when I hear of anyone who is thus endowed holding a different view from that which truth imperatively insists upon on a point which admits of very easy examination, the more I wonder at such a man, the more I burn with desire to make his acquaintance, and to converse with him; or if that be impossible, I long to bring his mind and mine into contact by exchanging letters, which wing their flight even between places far apart....

[But] the civil powers defend their conduct in persecuting schismatics by the rule which the apostle laid down: "Whoever resists the power, resists the ordinance of God; and they that resist shall receive judgment. For rulers are not a terror to good works, but to the evil. Will you then not be afraid of the power? Do that which is good and you shall have the praise of the same: for he is the minister of God to you for good. But if you do that which is evil, be afraid; for he bears not the sword in vain: for he is the minister of God, a revenger to execute wrath upon him that does evil." The whole question therefore is, whether schism is an evil work, or whether you have caused schism, so that your resistance of the powers that be is in a good cause and not in an evil work, whereby you would bring judgment on yourselves. Wherefore with infinite wisdom the Lord not merely said, "Blessed are they who are persecuted," but added, "for righteousness' sake."

I desire therefore to know from you, in the light of what I have said above, whether it be a work of righteousness to originate and perpetuate your state of separation from the Church. I desire also to know whether it be not rather a work of unrighteousness to condemn unheard the whole Christian world,... It is excusable for you either not to know the wickedness of your African colleagues [the Donatists] who are living beside you, and are using the same sacraments with you, or even to tolerate their misdeeds when known... [and] it is inexcusable for them, though they reside in most remote regions, to be ignorant of what you either know, or believe, or have heard, or imagine, concerning men in Africa. How great is the perversity of those who cling to their own unrighteousness, and yet find fault with the severity of the civil powers!

You answer, perhaps, that Christians ought not to persecute even the wicked. Be it so; let us admit that they ought not: but is it lawful to lay this objection in the way of the powers which are ordained for this very purpose? Shall we erase the apostle's words? Or do your [writings] not contain the words which I mentioned a little while ago? But you will say that we ought not to communicate with such persons. What then? Did you withdraw, some time ago, from communion with the deputy Flavianus, on the ground of his putting to death, in his administration of the laws, those whom he found guilty? Again, you will say that the Roman emperors are incited against you by us. Nay, rather blame yourselves for this, seeing that, as was long ago foretold in the promise concerning Christ, "Yea, all kings shall fall down before him," they are now members of the Church; and you have dared to wound the Church by schism, and still presume to insist upon rebaptizing her members. Our brethren indeed demand help from the powers which are ordained, not to persecute you, but to protect themselves against the lawless acts of violence perpetrated by individuals of your party, which you yourselves, who refrain from such things, bewail and deplore; just as, before the Roman Empire became Christian, the Apostle Paul took measures to secure that the protection of armed Roman soldiers should be granted him against the Jews who had conspired to kill him. But these emperors, whatever the occasion of their becoming acquainted with the crime of your schism might be, frame against you such decrees as their zeal and their office demand. For they bear not the sword in vain; they are the ministers of God to execute wrath upon those that do evil.

Finally, if some of our party transgress the bounds of Christian moderation in this matter, it displeases us; nevertheless, we do not on their account forsake the Catholic Church because we are unable to separate the wheat from the chaff before the final winnowing, especially since you yourselves have not forsaken the Donatist party on account of Optatus, when you had not courage to excommunicate him for his crimes.

You say, however, "Why seek to have us joined to you, if we be thus stained with guilt?" I reply: Because you still live, and may, if you are willing, be restored. For when you join yourselves to us, i.e. to the Church of God, the heritage of Christ, who has the ends of the earth as his possession, you are restored so that you live in vital union with the Root... If deserters carry with them the imperial standards, these standards are welcomed back again as they were, if they have remained unharmed, when the deserters are either punished with a severe sentence, or, in the exercise of clemency, restored. If, in regard to this, any more particular inquiry is to be made, that is, as I have said, another question; for in these things, the practice of the Church of God is the rule of our practice.

16. Augustine, *City of God*

The City of God *is Augustine's major philosophical work, in which he develops a philosophy of history that envisions fundamental conflict between good and evil. Augustine began this work just three years after Rome was sacked by the invading Goths, and it took him nearly thirteen years to complete. He started* City of God *to defend Christianity against its detractors who blamed Rome's fall on the Christians for their neglect of old Roman values.*

Augustine's political theory, as presented in the following selections from City of God, *center around his concept of "two cities," the earthly city and the city of God.*

On the City of God

We give the name of the city of God to that society which Scripture bears witness, which has the most perfect authority and preeminence among all other works.... For there it is said: "Glorious things are spoken of you, city of God" and in another place, "Great is the Lord and greatly to be praised, in the city of our God, even upon his holy mountain, increasing the joy of all the earth." And in the same psalm: "As we have heard, so have we seen in the city of the Lord of Hosts, in the city of our God; God has established it forever." And in another: "The rivers' streams shall make glad the city of God, the most high has sanctified his tabernacle, God is in the midst of it unmoved."

These testimonies, and thousands more, teach us that there is a city of God, and his inspired love makes us desire to be members. Citizens of the city of man prefer their gods instead of this heavenly city's holy founder, not knowing that he is the God of gods, not of those false, wicked, and proud gods.... The foes of this holy city, our former nine books (by the help of our Lord and king), I hope have fully affronted. And now, knowing what is expected next of me, as I promised earlier, that is, to show (as my poor talent stretches) how these two cities originated, progressed, and now exist in this world confusedly together. By the assistance of the same God and King of ours, I set pen to paper, intending first to show the beginning of these two cities, arising from the difference between the angelical powers....

God, desiring not only that the human race might be able by their similarity of nature to associate with one another, but also that they might be bound together in harmony and peace by the ties of relationship, was pleased to derive all men from one individual. And he created men with such a nature that the members of the race should not die, had not the first two (of whom one was created out of nothing and the other out of him) merited this with their disobedience; for by them so great a sin was committed, that by it human nature was altered for the worse, and was transmitted also to their descendants.

That the whole human race has been condemned in its first origin, this life itself bears witness by the host of cruel ills with which it is filled. Is not this proved by the profound and dreadful ignorance which produces all the errors that enfold the children of Adam, and from which no man can be delivered without toil, pain, and fear? Is not this proved by his love of so may vain and hurtful things, which produces gnawing cares, disquiet, griefs, fears, wild joys, quarrels, law suits, wars, treasons, angers, hatreds, deceit, flattery, fraud, theft, robbery, hatreds, perfidy, pride, ambition, envy, murders, parricides, cruelty, ferocity, wickedness, luxury, insolence, impudence, shamelessness, fornications, adulteries, incests, unnatural acts of both sexes, which it is shameful so much as to mention; sacrileges, heresies, blasphemies, perjuries, oppression of the innocent, calumnies, plots, falsehoods, false witnessing, unrighteous judgements, violent deeds, plunderings, and innumerable other crimes that do not easily come to mind, but that never absent themselves from the actuality of human existence? These are indeed the crimes of wicked men, yet they spring from that root error and misplaced love which is born with every descendant of Adam....

But because God does not wholly desert those whom he condemns, nor shuts up his tender mercies, the human race is restrained by law and education, which keep guard against the ignorance that besets us, and oppose the assaults of vice, but are themselves full of labor and sorrow.... But, besides the punishments of childhood, without which there would be no learning of what our parents wish—and the parents rarely wish anything useful to be taught—who can describe, who can conceive the number and severity of the punishments which afflict the human race—pains which are not only the accompaniment of the wickedness of godless men, but are a part of the human condition and the common misery? What fear and grief we suffer, all caused by losses and condemnations, by fraud and falsehoods, by false suspicions, and all the crimes and wicked deeds of other men!...

From this hell on earth, the deserved penalty of sin would have hurled all headlong even into the second death, of which there is no end, had not the undeserved grace of God saved some therefrom. And thus it came to pass, that though there are very many great nations all over the earth, whose rites and customs, speech, arms, dress, are distinguished by marked differences, yet there are no more than two kinds of human society, which we may justly call two cities, according to the language of our Scriptures. The one consists of those who wish to live after the flesh, the other of those who wish to live after the Spirit.

Of the first two parents of the human race, Cain was the first-born, and he belonged to the city of men; after him was born Abel, who belonged to the city of God. For as it is in individuals, the truth of the apostle's statement is made clear, "that is not first which is spiritual, but that which is natural is first, and afterward that which is spiritual." And so it comes to pass that each man, being derived from a condemned stock, is first of all born of Adam evil and carnal, and becomes good and spiritual only afterwards when he is grafted into Christ by regeneration; so it was in the human race as a whole. When these two cities began to run their course by a series of deaths and births, the citizen of this world was the first-born, and after him the stranger in this world, the citizen of the city of God, predestined by grace, elected by grace, by grace a stranger below, and by grace a citizen above....First the vessel to dishonor was made, and after it another to honor. For in each individual, as I have already said, there is first of all that which is evil, that from which we must begin but in which we need not remain; afterwards is that which is good, to which we may advancing attain, and in which, when we have reached it, we may abide forever. Whereupon it follows that no one can be good that has not first been evil, though all that are evil do not become good. But the sooner a man betters himself the quicker does the title "citizen of the city of God" follow him, abolishing the memory of the other. Accordingly it is recorded of Cain that he built a city, but Abel was a stranger and built none.

On Justice

This then is the place where I should return to Cicero's argument, and explain, as briefly as possible, that if we are to accept the definitions laid down in his *De Republica*, there never was a Roman republic; for he defines a republic as the commonwealth of the people. And if this definition be true, there never was a Roman republic, for the people's common benefit was never attained among the Romans. For the people, according to his definition, is an assemblage associated by a common acknowledgment of what is right [good] and by a community of interests. And what he means by an acknowledgment of what is right he explains, showing that a republic cannot be administered without justice. Where, therefore, there is no true justice there cannot exist what is called right. For what is rightly done is justly done, and what is unjustly done cannot be rightly done. For the unjust inventions of men are neither to be considered nor spoken of as something rightly done; for right is that which flows from the fountain of justice. Cicero and others deny the definition which is commonly given by those who misconceive the matter, that right is that which is useful to the stronger party. Thus, where there is not true justice there can be no assemblage of men associated by a common acknowledgment of what is right, and therefore there can be no people, as defined by Cicero; and if no people, there can be no commonwealth. Consequently, if the republic is the common-wealth of the people, and there is no people if it they are not associated by common acknowledgment of what is right, and if there is no common acknowledgment of what is right there can be no justice, then it most certainly follows that there is no republic where there is no justice.

Further, if justice is that virtue which gives everyone their due, where, then, is the justice of man when he deserts the true God and yields to impure demons?...

This same book, *De Republica*, advocates the cause of justice against injustice with great force and keenness....For it was laid down as an absolutely unassailable position that it is unjust for some men to rule and some to serve; and yet the imperial city to which the republic belongs cannot rule her provinces without having recourse to this injustice. It was replied in the behalf of justice, that this ruling of the provinces is just, because servitude may be advantageous to the provincials, and is so when rightly administered—that is to say, when lawless men are prevented from doing harm. And further, as they become worse and worse for so long as they were free, they will improve with subjection. To confirm this reasoning, there is added an eminent example drawn from nature: for "why," it is asked, "does god rule man, the soul the body, reason the passions and other vicious parts of the body?" This example leaves no doubt that, to some, servitude is useful; and, indeed, to serve God is useful to all. And it is when the soul serves God that it exercises a proper control over the body; and in the soul itself, reason must be subject to God if it is to govern as it ought the passions and other vices. Hence, when a man does not serve God, what justice can we ascribe to him, since in this case, his soul cannot exercise a just control over the body, nor his reason over his vices.

And if there is no justice in such an individual, certainly there can be none in a community composed of such persons. Here, therefore, there is not that common acknowledgment of what is right which makes an assemblage of men a people whose affairs we call a republic. And why need I speak of advantageousness, the common participation in which, according to the definition, makes a people? For although, if you chose to regard the matter attentively, you will see that there is nothing advantageous to those who live godlessly, as every one lives who does not serve God but rather demons, whose wickedness you may measure by their desire to receive the worship of men though they are most spirits. Yet what I have said of the common acknowledgment of what is right is enough to demonstrate that, according to the above definition, there can be no people, and therefore, no republic, where there is no justice....

And where there is not that justice whereby the one supreme God rules the obedient city according to his grace, so that it sacrifices to none but him, and where in all the citizens the soul rules the body and reason the vices in rightful order, so that, as in the individual man, so also in the community, the people live by faith, which works by love, the love whereby man loves God as he ought to be loved, and his neighbor as himself—there, I say, there is not an assemblage associated by an acknowledgment of what is right. And if there is not this, there is not a people, and therefore there is no republic; for where there is no people there can be no republic.

But if we discard this definition of a people, and, assuming another, say that a people is an assemblage of reasonable beings bound together by a common agreement as to the objects of their love, then, in order to discover the character of any people, we have only to observe what they love. Yet whatever it loves, if only it is an assemblage of reasonable beings and not of beasts, and is bound together by an agreement as to the objects of love, it is reasonably called a people; and it will be a superior in proportion as it is bound together by higher interests and love, and inferior in proportion as it is bound together by lower. According to this definition of ours, the Roman people are a people, and its commonwealth is without doubt a republic. But what happened to this republic and how it declined into sanguinary seditions and then to social and civil wars, and so burst asunder or rotted of the bond of concord in which the health of the people consists, history shows clearly. And what I say of this people and this republic I must be understood to think and say of the Athenians or any Greek state, of the Egyptians, of early Assyrian Babylon, and of every other nation, great or small, which had a public government. For in general, the city of the ungodly, which disobeys God's command that it should offer no sacrifice except to him alone, and which, therefore, cannot give to the soul its proper command over the body, nor to the reason its just authority over the vices, is void of true justice.

For though the soul may seem to rule the body admirably, and the reason the vices, if the soul and reason do not obey God, as God has commanded them to serve him, they have no proper authority over the body and the vices. For what kind of mistress of the body and the vices can that mind be which is ignorant of the true God, and which, instead of being subject to his authority, is prostituted to the corrupting influences of the most vicious demons?

Thus, in fact, true justice has no existence save in that republic whose founder and ruler is Christ...in this city is true justice, the city of which holy scripture says, "Glorious things are said of thee, O city of God."

On Slavery

Thus was nature's order defined, and man by God was thus

created: "Let them rule," he said, "over the fishes of the sea and the fowls of the air, and over every thing that creeps upon the earth." He made man with reason, and made him lord only over the unreasonable, not over man, but over beasts. And so it was that the first holy men were shepherds rather than kings, God showing in this example two things: the order of creation desired, and what sin merits. For justly was the burden of servitude laid upon the back of transgression. And, therefore, in all the Scriptures we never read the word servant, until such time as that just man Noah laid it as a curse upon his offending son. So that it was guilt, and not nature, that gave birth to that name.

The Latin word *servos* was first derived from the following: those that were taken in wars, being in the hands of the conquerors either to massacre or to preserve, if they saved them, then they were called *serri*, or *servo*, meaning "to save." But this did not happen in direct correspondence with the result of sin. For in the most just war, the sin of one side causes it; but if the victory falls to the wicked (as sometimes it may), it is God's decree to humble the conquered, either reforming their sins or punishing them for earlier sins. As an example, witness that holy man of God, Daniel, who, being in captivity, confessed to his Creator his sins, yet the sins of the people were the real cause of his captivity.

Sin, therefore, is the mother of servitude, and first cause of man's subjection to man, which only comes by the direction of God in whom there is no injustice, and who alone knows best how to proportionate his punishment for man's offenses. As he himself says, "Whosoever commits sin is the servant of sin," and therefore many religious Christians are servants of wicked masters, yet these wicked masters are not free men, for that to which a man is addicted is the same to which he is a slave himself. And it is a happier servitude to serve another man than lust, for lust (to omit all the other passions) practices extreme tyranny upon the hearts of those that serve it, be it lust after sovereignty or fleshly lust.

But in the peaceful orders of states, wherein one man is under another, as humility benefits the servant, so does pride damage the master. Man, as God created him at first, is neither slave to man nor to sin. But servitude had its beginning in the disturbance of nature's order, for if that law had not first been transgressed, servitude would never have been enjoined.

Therefore the apostle warns servants to obey their masters and to serve them with cheerfulness and good will. In this manner, if at least they cannot be made free by their masters, they make their servitude a freedom to themselves, by serving them, not in deceitful fear, but in faithful love, until iniquity is overcome, and all man's power and principality destroyed, and God alone rules.

Therefore, although our righteous forefathers had servants in their families and made a distinction between their servants and their children, yet in matters of religion (the fountain from which all eternal good flows), they provided for all their household with an equal respect for each member.

17. John of Salisbury, *Policraticus*

John of Salisbury (1115-1180) was an English political theorist. In this selection he defines the distinction between tyranny and legitimate government, and the hierarchical nature of society. The views expressed in The Policraticus *were widely held among medieval political thinkers.*

On the Difference between a Prince and a Tyrant

Between a tyrant and a prince there is a single difference: the latter obeys the law and rules the people by the dictates of the law, conducting himself as but their servant. It is by the virtue of the law that he makes his claim to the foremost place in the management of the affairs of the commonwealth and in the bearing of its burdens. Whereas private men are held responsible only for their private affairs, on the prince fall the burdens of the whole community. Thus there is conferred on him sufficient power over all his subjects in order that he may bring about the well-being of each individually, and of all collectively, so that the state of the human commonwealth may be ordered in the best possible manner, since each and all are members one of another. For we indeed but follow nature, the best guide for life; nature has gathered together all the senses of her microcosm or little world into its head, which is man,

319

and has subjected all the members in obedience to it so that they will all function properly as long as they follow the guidance of the head, and the head remains sane. Thus the prince stands on an exalted pinnacle, splendid with all the great and high privileges he deems necessary for himself. Rightly so, for nothing can be more advantageous to the people than that the needs of the prince be fully satisfied, since it is impossible that his will should be found opposed to justice. Therefore, the prince is the public power, and a kind of likeness on earth of the divine majesty. Indeed, a large share of the divine power exists in princes by the fact that at their nod men bow their heads and, for the most part, offer up their heads to the axe to be struck off and, as if by divine impulse, the prince is feared by each of those over whom he is set as an object of fear. And this I do not think could be, except as a result of the will of God. For all power is from the Lord God, and has been with him always, and will be forever. The power which the prince has is therefore from God, for the power of God is never lost, nor severed from him, but he merely exercises it through a subordinate hand making all things teach his mercy and justice. Whoever resists the ruling power, resists the ordinance of God, in whose hand is the authority of conferring that power, and when he so desires, of withdrawing it again, or diminishing it. For it is not the ruler's own act when his will is turned to cruelty against his subjects, but it is rather the dispensation of God for his good pleasure to punish or chasten them....If good men thus regard power as worthy of veneration even when it comes as a plague upon the elect, who should not venerate that power which is instituted by God for the punishment of evildoers and for the reward of good men, and which is promptest in devotion and obedience to the laws? For the authority of the prince depends upon the authority of justice and law; and truly it is a greater thing than imperial power for the prince to place his government under the laws, so as to deem himself entitled to do naught which is at variance with the equity of justice.

Having set forth the basic characteristics of the prince, it will be easier to make known the basic differences between a prince and a tyrant, for, in essence, a tyrant is one who oppresses the people by rulership based upon force, while he who rules in accordance with the laws is a prince. Law is the gift of God, the model of equity, a standard of justice, a likeness of the divine will, the guardian of well being, a bond of union and solidarity between peoples, a rule defining duties, a barrier against the vices and the destroyer thereof, a punishment of violence and all wrong-doing. The law is assailed by force or by fraud, and, as it were, either wrecked by the fury of the lion or undermined by the wiles of the serpent. In whatever way this comes to pass, it is plain that it is the grace of God which is being assailed, and that it is God himself who in a sense is challenged to battle. The prince fights for the laws and the liberty of the people; the tyrant thinks nothing done unless he brings the laws to nought and reduces the people to slavery. Hence the prince is a kind of likeness of divinity; and the tyrant, on the contrary, a likeness of the boldness of the Adversary, even of the wickedness of Lucifer, imitating him that sought to build his throne to the north and make himself like the Most High, with the exception of his goodness. For had he desired to be like him in goodness, he would never have striven to tear from him the glory of his power and wisdom. What he more likely did aspire to was to be equal with him in authority to dispense rewards. The prince, as the likeness of the deity, is to be loved, worshiped and cherished; the tyrant, the likeness of wickedness, is generally to be even killed. The origin of tyranny is iniquity, and springing from a poisonous root, it is a tree which grows and sprouts into a baleful pestilent growth, and to which the axe must by all means be laid. For if iniquity and injustice, banishing charity, had not brought about tyranny, firm concord and perpetual peace would have possessed the peoples of the earth forever, and no one would think of enlarging his boundaries. Then kingdoms would be as friendly and peaceful, according to the authority of the great father Augustine, and would enjoy as undisturbed repose, as the separate families in a well-ordered state, or as different persons in the same family; or perhaps, which is even more credible, there would be no kingdoms at all, since it is clear from the ancient historians that in the beginning these were founded by iniquity as presumptuous encroachments against the Lord, or else were extorted from him.

On the Nature of a Commonwealth

According to Plutarch in his "Instruction of Trajan," the prince is first of all to make a thorough survey of himself, and diligently study the condition of the whole body of the commonwealth of which he is the representative, and in whose place he stands. A commonwealth, according to Plutarch, is a certain body which is endowed with life by the benefit of divine favor, which acts at the prompting of the highest equity, and is ruled by what may be called the moderating power of reason. Those things which establish and implant in us the practice of religion and transmit to us the worship of God fill the place of the soul in the body of the commonwealth. And therefore those who preside over the practice of religion should be looked up to and venerated as the soul of the body. For who doubts that the ministers of God's holiness are his representatives? Furthermore, since the soul is, as it were, the prince of the body, and has rulership over the whole thereof, so those whom our author calls the prefects of religion preside over the entire body....The place of the head in the body of the commonwealth is filled by the prince, who is subject only to God, and to those who exercise his office and represent him on earth, even as in the human body the head is animated and governed by the soul. The place of the heart is filled by the Senate, from which proceeds the initiation of good and ill works. The duties of eyes, ears, and tongue are claimed by judges and governors of provinces. Officials and soldiers correspond to the hands. Those who attend upon the prince are likened to the sides. Financial officers may be compared with the stomach and intestines, which, if they become congested through excessive greed, and retain to tenaciously their accumulations, generate innumerable and incurable diseases, so that through their illness the whole body is threatened with destruction. Farmers correspond to the feet, which always cleave to the soil. They have special need for the care and foresight of the head, since they often risk stumbling over stones as they walk upon the earth doing service with their bodies. Since it is the feet who raise, sustain, and move forward the entire weight of the body, they especially deserve aid and protection. Take away the support of the feet from the strongest body, and it cannot move forward by its own power, but must creep painfully and shamefully on its hand, or else be move by means of brute animals....

John then examines the proper role of each segment of society in the well-functioning commonwealth, using the metaphor of the human body. The following describes the position of the most humble members of the commonwealth, analogous to the feet.

Those are called the feet who discharge the humbler offices, and by whose services the members of the whole commonwealth walk upon solid earth. Among these are included the husbandmen, who always cleave to the soil, working their plough-lands or vineyards or pastures or flower gardens. To them must be added the many species of cloth making, and the mechanical arts, those who work in wood, iron, bronze, and other metals; also the menial occupations, and the manifold forms of making a livelihood and sustaining life, or increasing household property, all of which, while they do not pertain to the authority of the governing power, are yet in the highest degree useful and profitable to the corporate whole of the commonwealth. All of these different occupations are so numerous in the commonwealth that its number of feet exceeds even the centipede, and because of their very multitude they cannot be fully enumerated; for while they are not infinite by nature, they are yet of so many different varieties that no writer on the subject of offices or duties has ever laid down particular precepts for each special variety. But it applies generally to each and all of them that in their exercise they should not transgress the limits of the law, and should in all things observe constant reference to the public utility. For inferiors owe it so their superiors to provide them with service, just as their superiors their turn owe it to their inferiors to provide them with all things needful for their protection and sustenance. Therefore Plutarch says that the commonwealth is to pursue a course that is advantageous to the humbler classes, that is to say, the multitude; for small numbers always yield to great. Indeed, the reason for the institution of magistrates was in order that subjects might be protected from wrongs, and the commonwealth itself might be strengthened by their service. For an afflicted people is a sign and proof of a diseased prince. The health of the commonwealth will be sound and flourishing only when higher members shield the lower, and lower members respond faithfully and fully in like measure to the just demands of their superiors, so that each and all are as it were members one of another by a sore of reciprocity, and each regards his own interest as best served by that which he know of be the most advantageous for the others.

18. Thomas Aquinas, *Summa Theologica, Treatise on Law*

Thomas Aquinas (1225-1274), the foremost philosopher of the Middle Ages, attempted to synthesize Aristotle and Christianity in his two massive works, the Summa Theologica *and the* Summa contra Gentiles. *With rigorous logic and precise language he addressed every aspect of Christian doctrine and traditional philosophy in one coherent presentation. Thomas Aquinas had a more favorable view of human nature and human reason than many of the theologians who had preceded him.*

The following selection on law is the classic Thomistic statement on the nature of law. It was a radical position for its time, for it relies on neither custom nor the consent of the governed. It is also a good example of the synthesis of Aristotelian thought with Christianity. The "Treatise on Law" is followed with Aquinas' succinct statement on "Just War," based largely on Augustine.

The Essence of Law

We have now to consider the extrinsic principles of acts. Now the extrinsic principle inclining to evil is the devil....But the extrinsic principle moving to good is God, who both instructs us by means of his Law, and assists us by his Grace.

Law pertains to reason:

Law is a rule and measure of acts, whereby a person is induced to act or is restrained from acting; for *lex* (law) is derived from *ligare* (to bind), because it binds one to act. Now the rule and measure of human acts is reason, which is the first principle of human acts.

Law is directed toward the common good:

The first principle in practical matters, the object of the practical reason, is the last end; and the last end of human life is happiness or beatitude. Consequently, law must concern itself mainly with the order that is in beatitude. Moreover, since one individual is a part of the perfect community, law must concern itself properly with the order directed to universal happiness.

Any person is not competent to make law:

A law, properly speaking, regards first and foremost the order to the common good. Now to order anything to the common good belongs either to the whole people, or to someone who is the vice-regent of the whole people. Hence the making of a law belongs either to the whole people or to a public personage who has care of the whole people.

Promulgation is essential to law:

As was stated above, a law is imposed on others as a rule and measure. Now a rule or measure is imposed by being applied to those who are to be ruled and measured by it. Therefore, in order that a law obtain the binding force which is proper to a law, it must be applied to those who are to be ruled by it. But such application is made by its being made known to them by promulgation. Therefore promulgation is necessary for law to obtain its force.

 Thus, from the four preceding articles, the definition of law may be gathered. Law is nothing else than an ordinance of reason for the common good, promulgated by that person who has the care of the community.

326

The Various Kinds of Law

Eternal law

As we have stated above, law is nothing else but a dictate of practical reason emanating from the ruler who governs a perfect community. Now it is evident, granted that the world is ruled by divine providence, that the whole community of the universe is governed by the divine reason. Therefore the very notion of the government of things in God, the ruler of the universe, has the nature of a law.

Natural law

Law, being a rule and measure, can be in a person in two ways: first, in the person that rules and measures; second, in that which is ruled and measured. Therefore, since all things subject to divine providence are ruled and measured by the eternal law, as stated above, it is evident that all things partake in some way in the eternal law, since from the eternal law they derive their respective inclinations to their proper acts and ends. Now among all others, the rational creature is subject to divine providence in a more excellent way, in so far as it itself partakes of a share of providence, by being provident both for itself and for others. Therefore it has a share of the eternal reason, whereby it has a natural inclination to its proper act and end; and this participation of the eternal law in the rational creature is called the natural law. Thus the light of natural reason, whereby we discern what is good and what is evil, which is the function of the natural law, is nothing else than an imprint on us of the divine light. It is therefore evident that the natural law is nothing else than the rational creature's participation of the eternal law.

Human law

A law is a dictate of the practical reason. Accordingly, human reason needs to proceed from the more general precepts of the natural law, common and demonstrable principles, to the more particular determination of certain matters. These particular determinations, devised by human reason, are called human laws, provided that the other essential conditions of law be observed.

Divine law

Besides the natural and the human law it was necessary for the directing of human conduct to have a divine law for four reasons. First, it is by law that human beings are directed how to perform their proper acts in view of their last ends. Now if humans were ordained to no other than that which is proportionate to their natural ability, there would be no need for them to have any further direction, on the part of their reason, in addition to the natural law and humanly devised law which is derived from it. But since humans are ordained to an end of eternal happiness which exceeds their natural ability, it was necessary that they should be directed to their end by a law given by God.

Secondly, different people form different judgments on human acts, especially on contingent and particular matters, because of the uncertainty of human judgment. As a result, different and contrary laws result. In order, therefore, that humans may know without any doubt what they ought to do and what they ought to avoid, it was necessary for them to be directed in their proper acts by a law given by God, for it is certain that such a law cannot err.

Thirdly, humans can only make laws in those matters they are competent to judge. But humans are not competent to judge hidden interior movements, only exterior acts that are observable; and yet for the perfection of virtue it is necessary for people to conduct themselves rightly in both kinds of acts. Consequently, human law could not sufficiently curb and direct interior acts, and it was necessary for this purpose that a divine law should supervene.

Fourthly, as Augustine says, human law cannot punish or forbid all evil deeds, since, while attempting to do away with all evils, it would do away with many good things, thereby hindering the advance of the common good. Therefore, that no evil might remain unforbidden and unpunished, it was necessary for the divine law to supervene, whereby all sins are forbidden.

The effect of law is to make human beings good:

A law is nothing else than a dictate of reason in the ruler by whom his subjects are governed. Now the virtue of any being that is a subject consists in its being well subordinated to that by which it is regulated. The virtue of the irascible and concupiscent powers consists in their being obedient to reason. In the same way, the virtue of every subject consists in his or her being well subjected to his ruler. But every law aims at being obeyed by those who are subject to it. Consequently it is evident that the proper effect of law is to lead its subjects to their proper virtue; and since virtue is that which makes its subject good, it follows that the proper effect of law is to make those, to whom it is given, good, either absolutely or in some particular respect. For if the intention of the lawgiver is fixed on a true good, which is the common good regulated according to divine justice, it follows that the effect of law is to make every person good absolutely. If, however, the intention of the lawgiver is fixed on that which is not good absolutely, but useful or pleasurable to the lawgiver, or in opposition to divine justice, then law does not make the person good absolutely, but in a relative way, namely, in relation to that particular government. In this way good is found even in things that are bad of themselves. Thus a man is called a good robber, because he works in a way that is adapted to his end.

Natural Law

Natural law contains several precepts:

The first principle in the practical reason is one founded on the nature of good, viz., that good is that which all things seek after. Hence this is the first precept of law, that good is to be done and promoted, and evil is to be avoided. All other precepts of the natural law are based upon this; so that all the things which the practical reason naturally apprehends as a human good belong to the precepts of the natural law under the form of things to be done or avoided.

Since, however, good has the nature of an end, all those things to which individuals have a natural inclination are naturally apprehended by reason as being good and objects of pursuit, and their contraries as evil and objects of avoidance. Therefore, the order of the precepts of the natural law is according to the order of natural inclinations. For there is in every person, first, an inclination to good in accordance with the nature which they share with all substances, the preservation of their own being, according to their nature. By reason of this inclination, whatever is a means of preserving human life, and of warding off its obstacles, belongs to the natural law. Secondly, there is in every person an inclination to those things that pertain to them according to that nature which they have in common with other animals; by virtue of this inclination, those things are said to belong to the natural law which nature has taught to all animals, such as sexual intercourse, the education of offspring and the like. Thirdly, there is in every person an inclination to good according to reason. Thus individuals have a natural inclination to know the truth about God, and to live in society; in this respect, whatever pertains to this inclination belongs to the natural law: e.g., to shun ignorance, to avoid offending those among whom one has to live, and other such things regarding the above inclination.

Natural law is the same for all persons.

To the natural law belong those things to which a man is inclined naturally, those things for which it is proper for man to be inclined according to reason....Consequently, we must say that the natural law, in its first common principles, is the same for all, both as to rectitude and as to knowledge. But in certain more particular aspects, which are conclusions, as it were, of those common principles, it is the same for all in the majority of cases; and yet in some few cases it may fail, both as to rectitude and to knowledge. The common principles will be found to fail more frequently as we descend towards the particular: it may happen, for example, that it would be injurious to return goods held in trust if they are claimed for the purpose of fighting against one's country. In the case of knowledge, reason may be perverted by passion, evil habit, or an evil disposition of nature.

Natural law is unchangeable:

The natural law is altogether unchangeable in its first principles. But in its secondary principles, which, as we have said, are certain detailed, proximate conclusions drawn from the first principles, the natural law is not changed so that what it prescribes be not right in most cases. But it may be changed in some particular cases of rare occurrence, through causes hindering the observance of such precepts.

Natural law cannot be abolished:

There belong to the natural law, first, certain most common precepts that are known to all; and secondly, certain secondary and more particular precepts, which are, as it were, conclusions following closely from first principles. As to the common principles, the natural law, in its universal meaning, cannot in any way be blotted out from the human heart. But it is blotted out in the case of a particular action, in so far as reason is hindered from applying the common principle to the particular action because of concupiscence or some other passion. But as to the other, i.e., the secondary precepts, the natural law can be blotted out from the human heart, either by evil persuasions, or by vicious customs and corrupt habits, as, among some peoples, theft, and even unnatural vices.

Human Law

The person has a natural aptitude for virtue. But the perfection of virtue must be acquired by some kind of training. It is difficult to see how individuals could suffice for themselves in the matter of this training, since the perfection of virtue consists chiefly in withdrawing from undue pleasures, pleasures to which above all human beings are inclined, especially the young. Consequently people need to receive this training from others in order to arrive at the perfection of virtue. For those young people who are inclined to acts of virtue by their good natural disposition or custom, (that is, by the gift of God), paternal training through admonition suffices. Some, however, are dissolute and prone to vice, and not easily amenable to words. It is necessary for them to be restrained from evil by force and fear so that they might desist from evil-doing and leave others in peace, and so that they themselves might be brought to do willingly what hitherto they did from fear, and thus become virtuous. Now this kind of training, which compels through fear of punishment, is the discipline of laws. Thus it was necessary for laws to be framed in order that people might have peace and virtue. As the Philosopher (Aristotle) says, just as man is the most noble of animals if he is perfect in virtue, so, too, he is the lowest of all if he is severed from law and justice. For humans can use their reason to devise means of satisfying their lusts and evil passions, which other animals are unable to do.

Human law is derived from natural law:

What is not just seems to be no law at all. Hence the force of a law depends on the extent of its justice. Now in human affairs a thing is said to be just from being right, according to the rule of reason. But the first rule of reason is the law of nature. Consequently, every human law has just so much of the nature of law as it is derived from the law of nature. But if in any point it departs from the law of nature, it is no longer a law but a perversion of the law.

But it must be noted that human law may be derived from the natural law in two ways. Some human laws are therefore derived from the common principles of the natural law by way of conclusions. For example, that one must not kill may be derived as a conclusion from the principle that one should harm no person. Other human laws are derived by way of determination. For example, the law of nature has it that the evil-doer should be punished, but that this evil-doer be punished in this or that way is a determination of the human law.

Both modes of derivation are found in human law. Those laws derived in the first way have some force from natural law as well.

But those laws derived in the second way have no other force than that of human law.

The binding of human law in conscience:

Laws framed by human beings are either just or unjust. If they are just they have the power of binding in conscience from the eternal law from which they are derived. Now laws are said to be just from their end (when they are ordained to the common good), from their author (when the law does not exceed the power of the lawgiver), and from their form (when burdens are laid on subjects according to an equality of proportion and with a view to the common good). For, just as a part, in all that it is, belongs to the whole, every person, in all that he is and has, belongs to the community. Moreover, nature inflicts a loss on the part in order to save the whole; for this reason, laws that impose proportionate burdens, are just and binding in conscience, and are legal laws.

On the other hand, laws may be unjust in two ways. First, they may be contrary to human good, in respect to their end, when an authority imposes on his subjects burdensome laws that serve his own cupidity or vainglory, not the common good; in respect to the author, when a ruler makes a law that goes beyond the power committed to him; or in respect to form, when burdens are imposed unequally on the community, even if with a view toward the common good. Such are acts of violence rather than laws, because, as Augustine says, a law that is not just seems to be no law at all. Therefore, such laws do not bind in conscience, except perhaps in order to avoid scandal or disturbance.

Secondly, laws may be unjust through being opposed to the divine good. Such are the laws of tyrants that induce idolatry, or anything else contrary to the divine law. Laws of this kind must in no way be observed.

Individual interpretation of human law:

Every law is directed to the common welfare of humankind, and derives the force and nature of it accordingly; but in so far as it fails to serve this common welfare, it is without binding power.

Now it often happens that the observance of some point of law is conducive to the common welfare in the majority of instances, and yet, in some cases, is very injurious. Since, then, the lawgiver cannot have in view every single case, he shapes the law according to what happens most frequently. Hence, if a case arise wherein the observance of that law would be injurious to the general welfare, it should not be observed.

Nevertheless, it must be noted that if the observance of the law according to the letter does not involve any sudden risk needing instant remedy, it is not permissible for every individual to determine what is useful and what is not useful to the state; rather those alone can do this who are in authority, and who, in the event of cases, have the power to dispense from the laws. If, however, the peril be so sudden as not to allow the delay involved in referring the matter to authority, the necessity itself carries with it a dispensation, since necessity knows no law.

* * *

On the Conditions of a Just War

In order for a war to be just, three things are necessary. First, the authority of the sovereign by whose command the war is to be waged. For it is not the business of a private individual to declare war, because he can seek for redress his rights from the tribunal of his superior. Moreover, it is not the business of a private individual to summon together the people, which has to be done in wartime. And as the care of the general welfare is committed to those who are in authority, it is their business to watch over the general welfare of the city, kingdom, or province subject to them. And just as it is lawful for them to have recourse to the sword in defending that general welfare against internal disturbances, when they punish evil-doers, it is their business to have recourse to the sword of war in defending the common good against external enemies....

Second, a just cause is required, namely that those who are attacked should be attacked because they deserve it on account of some fault. Thus Augustine says, "A just war is described as one that avenges wrongs, when a nation or state has to be punished, for refusing to make amends for the wrongs inflicted by its subjects, or to restore what it has seized unjustly."

Thirdly, it is necessary that the belligerent have a right intention, that is, either achieving the good, or avoiding evil. Thus Augustine says, "True religion looks upon as peaceful those wars that are waged not for motives of aggrandizement, or cruelty, but with the object of securing peace, of punishing evil-doers, and of uplifting the good." For it may happen that the war is declared by the legitimate authority, and for a just cause, and yet be rendered unlawful through a wicked intention. Hence Augustine says, "The passion for inflicting harm, the cruel thirst for vengeance, an unpeaceful and relentless spirit, the fever of revolt, the lust of power, and such like things, all these are rightly condemned in war."

Later writers added two additional conditions for just war: 1) There must be the likelihood of success; and 2) The means used must be proportionate to the desired end.

19. Thomas Aquinas, *On Kingship*

In his "Treatise on Law," Aquinas differentiates between human law and divine law. Both laws are necessary to help men and women achieve their natural, or moral, end as well as their supernatural end, or salvation. But these two ends are not independent of one another; they share a common authority.

In the following selection, Aquinas demonstrates that the state and the Church have a common interest in the moral virtue of their members.

To govern means to steer, and the nature of government is to be understood from the analogy of steering a ship. Government, like steering, consists in conducting its charge by the best route to its proper goal or end. Thus, a ship is said to be steered when the labor of the helmsman succeeds in conducting it direct to its port unharmed. If, therefore, anything is destined to an end beyond itself, as the ship is to the port, it will be part of the duty of the man in charge not only to preserve it unharmed in itself, but also to conduct it to its goal.

Now, if there were anything which had no goal or end outside itself, the care of its governor would be directed solely to the task of preserving it unharmed in its perfect condition. There is in fact nothing of such a kind, except God himself, who is the end of all things; but a thing which is destined to an end outside itself, requires a diversity of attentions from many different hands. It may well be the task of one man to preserve it in its present state of being, and of another to conduct it to a higher perfection. This is clearly illustrated in the example of the ship, from which the conception of government is derived. For the carpenter has the task of repairing any damage which may occur in the ship, while the helmsman has the responsibility of conducting the ship to its port. The case of a man is similar: it is the task of his physician to preserve his life in a condition of health, of his steward to supply him with the necessities of life, of the scholar to impart to him the knowledge of truth, of a moral teacher to instruct him in the conduct of his life according to reason.

Now, if man were not destined to a good beyond himself, these administrations would suffice for his well-being. But there is a good for man which is beyond him in this mortal life; namely, the final blessedness of the enjoyment of God which he expects after death. For, as the Apostle says in Corinthians, "while we are at home in the body, we are absent from the Lord." Therefore, the Christian man, for whom that blessedness has been won by the blood of Christ and who has received the pledge the Holy Spirit for the attainment of it, has need of another and a spiritual ministration by which he may be guided to the harbor of eternal salvation. This ministration is afforded to the faithful by the officers of the Church of Christ.

What is true concerning the end of the individual must be true also of a society of individuals. If the end of the individual were some good residing in himself, the final end of rule in a society would likewise be that the society should attain such a good and be preserved in the enjoyment of it. If such a final end, whether of individual or of society, were bodily, namely, the life and health of the body, it would be the task of the physician to secure it. If the ultimate ends were abundance of wealth, the man of business would be king of the society. If the good of knowledge were such that a multitude could attain to it, the king's task would be that of a teacher.

But it appears in fact that the end of a multitude gathered into society is a life according to virtue. For men associate for this purpose that together they may live well, which each living singly could not do. But to live well is to live according to virtue. Hence a life according to virtue is the end of human association.... But, since man is by a life according to virtue destined for the attainment of a further end, which consists as was said above, in the enjoyment of God, human society also must have the same end as the individual man. It is not, therefore, the final end of a society to live according to virtue, but by means of a virtuous life to attain the enjoyment of God.

If it were possible to attain this end by the virtue of human nature, it would belong to the function of the king to guide men towards this end. (For king is the title given to him who bears the highest authority in human matters; and an authority is higher in proportion to the end to which it is directed is higher. For we always find that the man whose task is the final end is in command over those whose work is about the means to the end. For example, the pilot, whose function it is to direct the sailing of the ship, gives orders to the ship maker as to the kind of ship which he shall make, so as to be fit for sailing; and the citizen, who uses arms, instructs the smith what kind of arms to make.) Since man attains the ultimate end, that is, the enjoyment of God, not by human but by divine virtue, conducting him to that end will be the part not of a human but of a divine governance. Such governance belongs to a king who is not man only, but God also, namely, to our Lord Jesus Christ who, by making men sons of God, has introduced them into the heavenly glory.

This government, therefore, which shall be incorruptible, was entrusted to Christ, and on this account he is called in the Scriptures not only priest but king, as Jeremiah says, "He shall reign as king and deal wisely." Hence the royal priesthood is derived from him, and, what is more, all Christ's faithful followers, in so far as they are members of him, are called kings and priests. The government of this kingdom, then, in order that spiritual things might be separated from earthly, was entrusted not to secular kings, but to priests, and above all to that High Priest, the successor of Peter and Vicar of Christ, the Pope of Rome, to whom all Christian peoples ought to be subject, as to their Lord Jesus Christ himself. For those into whose charge the care of subordinate ends has been committed ought to be subject to him whose charge is the supreme end, and to be directed by his authority.

20. Thomas More, *Utopia*

Thomas More (1478-1535) was typical of the Renaissance humanist in early sixteenth-century England. Lawyer, statesman, philosopher, man of affairs, he was an active participant in the affairs of his day. He refused to support Henry VIII's break from the Roman Church, and was subsequently beheaded for adhering to his principles, a story retold in our own time in A Man for All Seasons.

More's reputation as a humanist rests largely on his brief work, Utopia, *published in Latin in 1516. In it he uses a description of an imaginary kingdom, Utopia, to express his criticism of contemporary society and to outline possibilities for a better world.*

BOOK I

One day I came upon him talking with a stranger, who seemed past the flower of his age; his face was tanned, he had a long beard, and his cloak was hanging carelessly about him, so that by his looks and habit I concluded he was a seaman.

As soon as Peter saw me, he came and greeted me. He then took me aside, and pointing to the stranger with whom he had been speaking, said: "Do you see that man? I was just thinking of bringing him to you."

I answered, "He should have been very welcome on your account."

"And on his own too," replied he. "No one alive can give as full an account of unknown nations and countries as he can do; in which I know you are very much interested."

Then said I, "I did not guess amiss, for at first sight I took him for a seaman."

"But you are much mistaken," said he, "for he has not sailed as a seaman, but as a traveler, or rather a philosopher.... This Raphael—for that is his name—is quite a scholar...."

So we adjourned to the garden of my hotel, and began to talk freely. Raphael, it seems, had left the expedition of Americo Vespucci at a fort in the Indian Ocean. There he ingratiated himself with the local inhabitants, and had the opportunity to travel extensively.

After Raphael had spoken with great judgment on the many errors that were both among us and these far-off nations; had treated of the wise institutions both here and there, and had spoken of the customs and government of every nation through which he had passed as if he had spent his whole life in it, Peter, being struck with admiration, said: "I wonder, Raphael, how it comes that you do not enter a king's service, for I am sure there are none to whom you would not be very acceptable: for your learning and knowledge both of men and things, are such that you would not only entertain them very pleasantly, but be of great use to them...."

Upon this, said I: "I perceive, Raphael, that you neither desire wealth nor greatness; and indeed I admire such a man much more than I do any of the great men in the world. Yet I would think you would apply your time and thoughts to public affairs. Your learning, even without experience, and your experience, even without learning, would render you a very fit counselor to a king."

"You are doubly mistaken," said he, "Mr. More, both in your opinion of me, and in your judgment. Most princes apply themselves more to affairs of war than to the useful arts of peace; and in these I have neither the knowledge, nor the desire to acquire it. Princes are generally more set on acquiring new kingdoms, right or wrong, than on governing well those they possess. And among the ministers of princes, there are none who do not think themselves so wise as to imagine they have no need of counsel....Now if in such a court, where counselors envy all others but only admire themselves, a person should propose anything he had either read in history or observed in his travels, the rest would feel their reputation for wisdom threatened. As a result, they would call upon reverence for the past rather than adapt better things that might be proposed. I have met with these proud, morose, and absurd reactions in many places, particularly once in England."

"Were you ever there?" said I.

"Yes, I was," he answered, "some months not long after the rebellion in the west was suppressed by widespread slaughter of the poor people who were engaged in it. During my stay I was kindly treated by that reverend prelate, John Morton, Archbishop of Canterbury, Cardinal, and Chancellor of England, a man respected as much for his wisdom and character as for his prominence....

"One day there joined us at dinner an English lawyer, who took the occasion to observe with enthusiasm the large number of thieves who had recently been executed. 'They were hanged in such numbers,' he said, 'that there were sometimes twenty on one gibbet.' He wondered, however, how it came to pass, that since so few escaped, there were yet so many thieves left who were still robbing in all places. I boldly responded that there was no mystery, for executing thieves was neither just in itself nor in the public good. Hanging is too severe as a punishment, and ineffectual as a deterrent. Simple theft should not cost a man his life; no punishment, however severe, can deter those who have no other livelihood from stealing. 'In this,' I said, 'you English, like the rest of the world, imitate bad teachers who are more willing to punish their students than to teach them. Instead of enacting dreadful punishments against theft, it would be wiser to provide every man with a livelihood so that he would not find it necessary to steal and then to die for it.'

"'That has been provided for,' he said. 'There are trades, there is farming, by which they could support themselves rather than choosing a life of crime.'

"'It's not that simple,' I said. 'Let us ignore, for sake of argument, those who lose their limbs in civil or foreign wars, and return from service to their king and country mutilated. They can no longer follow their old trades, and are too old to learn new ones. But since war occurs only sporadically, let us consider those things that occur every day. There are many noblemen among you who are idle as drones, who subsist on other men's labor, who push their tenants to the limit by raising their rents. Indeed, this is their only frugality, for in everything else they are extravagant, even to the point of ruin. In addition, they surround themselves with idle retainers who know no trade. As soon as their lord dies or they themselves fall sick, these retainers are turned away, for your lords are readier to feed idle people than to take care of the sick. Eventually, they become hungry and turn to robbery. What else can they do? In wandering about, they wear out both their health and their clothes, and come to look ghastly. Men of quality will not employ them, and poor men dare not, since they know that one who has been bred in idleness and pleasure, accustomed to walking about with his sword and buckler, despising all about him with an insolent scorn, is not fit for honest work.'

"To this the lawyer answered: 'These are the sort of men we should encourage. They provide strength for our armies, since their birth inspires them with a greater sense of honor than is to be found among tradesmen or ploughmen.'

"'You may as well say,' replied I, 'that you must encourage thieves for the sake of wars, for you will never lack the one as long as you have the other. Just as robbers sometimes prove gallant soldiers, so do soldiers often prove brave robbers....'

"'Yet this alone,' I added, 'does not account for all robberies. There is another cause more peculiar to England.'

"'What is that?' said the cardinal.

"'Sheep,' said I. 'Your sheep, by nature docile creatures, may be said now to devour men, and depopulate not only villages, but towns. Wherever it is found that sheep will yield wool of fine quality, the nobility and gentry, even those holy men the abbots, are no longer content to live at ease off the rents from their farms. Rather than do no good for society, they resolve to do it harm. They stop the course of agriculture, destroy houses and towns, reserving only the churches, and enclose grounds for pasturing their sheep. These worthy countrymen turn the best inhabited places into places of solitude. When these insatiable wretches enclose many thousands of acres, owners and tenants alike lose all their possessions. Those poor unfortunates, both men and women, married and unmarried, old and young, with their poor but numerous families (since country business requires many hands), are forced to leave their homes with no place to go. They must sell their household belongings for almost nothing. When their little money is gone, what is left for them to do, but either to steal and so to be hanged (God knows how justly), or to go about and beg? And if they beg they are put in prison as idle vagabonds. In truth, they are willing to work, but no one will hire them, there being no need for farm labor, and no land left for agriculture. One shepherd can look after a flock of sheep on land that would require many hands if it were to be plowed and reaped. This also raises the price of grain.

"'The price of wool has also risen to the point where poor people who once made cloth are no longer able to buy it; this makes many of them idle as well. For since the increase of pasture, God has punished the avarice of the owners with a disease among the sheep, which has destroyed vast numbers of them. To be sure, it might have been more just if it had fallen on the owners themselves. Even if the number of sheep should increase, their price is not likely to fall. For the sheep are owned by a small number of very wealthy men, almost akin to a monopoly, who will never sell until they have raised the price as high as possible. Similarly, other kinds of cattle are expensive because many villages are depopulated and country labor is neglected; none make it their business to breed them. The rich do not breed cattle as they do sheep, but buy them lean, and at low prices; and after they have fattened them on their own pastures they resell them at a high price. The situation will grow even worse if cattle are consumed faster than they are bred. As a result, your island kingdom, once one of the happiest in the world, will suffer much by the cursed avarice of a few persons. The high price of food forces employers to dismiss their servants. What can those who are dismissed do, except beg or rob? A man of talent is more drawn to robbery than to begging.

"'Luxury exists along side poverty and misery; there is an excessive vanity in apparel, and great cost in diet, not only in noblemen's families, but among tradesmen, among the farmers themselves, and among all ranks of persons. You also have many brothels, taverns and alehouses; add to this dice, cards, tables, football, tennis, and quoits, in which money disappears quickly. Ultimately the participants lose everything, and must resort to robbery. Banish these vices, order those who have depopulated the countryside either to rebuild the villages they have destroyed or let someone else do it; put restraints on the accumulation of wealth, almost as evil as monopolies; reduce the need for idleness; restore agriculture; regulate the manufacture of the wool so as to create jobs for those currently forced to be thieves, and for idle vagabonds or useless servants who will certainly be forced to become thieves eventually. If you do not find a remedy to these evils, it is pointless to boast of your severity in punishing theft. Severe punishment, though it may have the appearance of justice, is in reality neither just nor productive. For if you allow your people to be ill-educated, systematically corrupted from their infancy, and then punish them for those very crimes their upbringing led them to commit, what else can one conclude but that you first make thieves and then punish them for being thieves?'

"'But, Raphael,' the Cardinal said he to me, 'why should theft not to be punished by death? What other punishment would be more useful to the public? If death does not restrain theft, what fear or force could? Would criminals not look on the mitigation of the punishment as an invitation to commit more crimes.'

"I answered: 'It seems to me a very unjust thing to take away a man's life for a little money; for nothing in the world can be of equal value to a human life. If it is not for the money that one suffers, but for his breaking the law, I must say extreme justice is an extreme injury; for we ought not to approve of these terrible laws that make the smallest offenses a capital one. Is there no difference between killing a man and taking his purse? God has commanded us not to kill, yet we kill so easily because of a little money? One might say that the law forbids only illegal killing. But what, then, can prevent people from enacting laws that permit adultery and perjury in some cases....?

"'Even under the harsh and severe Mosaic law, thieves were only fined, not put to death. We cannot imagine that in the new law of mercy, in which God treats us with the tenderness of a father, he has given us a greater license to cruelty than he did to the Jews. For these reasons I think putting thieves to death is not lawful; furthermore, it is absurd, and of ill consequence to society, that a thief and a murderer should be equally punished. If a robber sees that his punishment will be the same, whether he is convicted of theft or murder, he will more likely kill the person he otherwise would only have robbed, since there is less danger of discovery.

"'But as to the question, What would be a more effective punishment? The answer is far easier than to invent anything worse. Why not adopt the approach of the Romans, who understood so well the arts of government? They condemned those they found guilty of great crimes to work their whole lives in quarries, or to dig in mines with chains about them. However, the method I like best was what I observed in my travels in Persia, among the Polylerits, who are a considerable and well-governed people. They pay a yearly tribute to the King of Persia; but in all other respects they are a free nation, and governed by their own laws. They live in the hills, far from the sea; they are content with the production of their own country, which is very fruitful, and have little trade with other nations. Since, according to the genius of their country, they have no inclination to enlarge their borders, their mountains and the tribute they pay to the Persians secure them from all invasions.'

"'Thus they have no wars among them; they live in comfort rather than luxury, and may be called a happy nation, rather than an eminent or famous one. Those who are found guilty of theft are bound to make restitution to the owner, not, as in other places, to the prince, whom they reckon has no more right to the stolen goods than the thief. If what was stolen no longer exists, restitution is made from the property of the thief. What remains is given to the thief's wives and children. The thief himself is condemned to labor on public works, but is not imprisoned or chained except under extraordinary circumstances. They go about loose and free, working for the public. If they are idle or slow to work, they are whipped; but if they work hard, they are well treated. Only at night are they locked up. They endure no other punishment but a life of constant labor....

"'These, then, are their laws and rules for dealing with robbery. They are both constructive and humane. Vice is destroyed and the lives of the robbers are preserved; yet they appreciate the necessity of being honest, and spend the rest of their lives making reparation for the injuries they have done to society. There is no chance they will fall back to their old ways. Indeed, there is so little to be feared from them that travelers use them for guides. Since they are unarmed they cannot rob, and if money is found on them it proves they have robbed. Should they attempt to escape they are easily discovered since their clothing is unique. Punishment would be automatic....'"

The conversation then turned to whether such an approach could be implemented in England. The lawyer was dubious. After concluding his narrative of the conversation at the table of the Archbishop, Raphael reflects more generally on the nature of private property. To make his points, he refers to a well organized and happy kingdom he encountered in his travels, Utopia.

"In all candor, I must admit I am convinced that as long as there is any [private] property, as long as money is the standard of all other things, a nation cannot be governed justly or happily. Not justly, because the worst people will live the best; and not happily, because only a few will possess most of the wealth (and even these will not be completely happy), and everyone else will live in absolute misery. When I reflect on the wise and good constitution of the Utopians—who are well governed but with few laws; where virtue has its due reward, yet there is an equality whereby that every man lives in comfort—when I compare with them so many other nations that are constantly enacting new laws, and yet are not well-regulated to the point that men can earn, preserve or even identify what property is theirs; then I become more sympathetic to Plato, who resolved never to legislate for a community that did not adopt egalitarian principles. This wise man saw that only equality could make a nation happy, and equality cannot be obtained so long as there is private property. When every man tries to acquire for himself everything he can, it follows that regardless if how wealthy a nation may be, if a few divide the wealth among themselves, the rest must live in poverty.

"Thus there will be two classes of people whose fortunes should be reversed: the first useless, but wicked and ravenous; and the second sincere and modest men who by their constant industry serve the public more than themselves. Thus I am persuaded that until private property is abolished there can be no equitable or just distribution of things, nor can the world be happily governed. As long as property is maintained, the greatest and the far best part of mankind will be oppressed with a load of cares and anxieties. To be sure, the burden can be reduced, but it can never be eliminated. I confess that those pressures that lie on a great part of mankind may be made lighter; but they can never be quite removed. Laws might limit the amount of land or money a man could own....Such laws would have the effect of good diet and care on a sick man, whose situation is critical: they might allay and mitigate the disease, but he would never be quite healed. Nor will the body politic be restored to health as long as property remains...."

"On the contrary," answered I, "it seems to me that men cannot live comfortably where all things are owned in common: how can there be any plenty, where every man will excuse himself from labor? Just as the hope of gain does not motivate him, so the confidence that he has in other men's hard work may make him slothful. When shortages occur, violence and bloodshed would result.

"I do not wonder," said he, "that it appears that way to you, since you can't imagine how such a society would work. But if you had been in Utopia with me, and had seen their laws and rules, as I did, for the space of five years, you would have to acknowledge that you had never seen a people as well organized as they."

"You will not easily persuade me," said Peter, "that any nation in that new world is better governed than in our world. We are certainly as intelligent as they are, and our society is older."

"As for their relative antiquity," said he, "you cannot pass a true judgment until you read their histories. They had towns before Europe was inhabited. I do not deny that we are more ingenious than they, but they exceed us much in industry and application...."

Upon this I said to him: "I beg you to describe that island in detail for us."

"I will do it very willingly," said he, "for I have digested the whole matter carefully; but it will take up some time." He paused a little as if to collect himself, and began in this manner:

BOOK II

The island of Utopia is 200 miles across in the middle. It is narrower only at both ends. Its figure is like a crescent. Between the tips of the crescent is an entrance from the sea eleven miles wide. Inside this opening is a great bay, encircled by a 500 mile coastline, well secured from winds. Since there is no great current in the bay, the whole coast is, as it were, one continuous harbor, enabling all who live on the island access to commerce. The entry into the bay is made very dangerous by both rocks and shallows. In the middle of the opening there is a single rock appearing above water; at its peak is a tower in which a garrison is kept. Other rocks lie under water, and are very dangerous. The channel is known only to the natives, so that if any stranger should enter into the bay, without one of their pilots, he would run great danger of shipwreck....

On the other side of the island there are also many harbors, and the coast is so fortified, both by nature and art, that a small number of men can hinder the descent of a great army. There are reports (and there remain good marks of it to make it credible) that this was no island at first, but a part of the continent. Utopus (whose name it still carries) conquered it, and brought to the rude and uncivilized inhabitants such good government that they now far excel all the rest of mankind. After subduing the original inhabitants, he had a fifteen-mile channel dug to separate them from the continent. To avoid resentment from the natives, he forced his own soldiers as well as the inhabitants of the land to carry out his project. The project was completed quickly, to the amazement of residents of the mainland who had initially laughed at the undertaking.

There are fifty four cities on the island, all large and well built. Each has the same manners, customs, and laws, and each is built according to the same plan so that they all look exactly alike. The closest cities are at least twenty-four miles apart, and the most distant no more than a day's walk. The chief town of the island, located near the center and most convenient to all, is Amaurot. Every year each city sends three of its wisest Senators to Amaurot to consult about their common concerns. The jurisdiction of every city extends at least twenty miles; no town desires to enlarge its territories, for the people consider themselves more as tenants than as landlords. Throughout the countryside they have built farmhouses which are well designed and furnished with all things necessary for country labor. Inhabitants are sent by turns from the cities to dwell in them; each house accommodates a "family" of at least forty men and women plus the two slaves permanently attached to it. A master and a mistress run each household, and a magistrate rules over every thirty houses.

Every year twenty adults from each rural household return to their town, having spent two years in the country. Another twenty persons are sent from town in their place, so that they can learn country work from those that have been already there one year. In this manner all who dwell in those country farms become familiar with agricultural work, so that inexperience does not lead to mistakes and dangerous shortages. Although no one is compelled to do agricultural labor more than two years, some find such pleasure in it that they remain for many years. The farm workers till the ground, breed cattle and chickens, hew wood, and convey it to the towns, either by land or water, as is most convenient.

They breed very few horses, but those they have are full of mettle, and are kept only for riding practice, not for plowing or pulling carts. They use oxen for such heavy work, for they find oxen are less subject to disease. They sow grain only for bread, and know exactly how much each town will need. But they always produce more grain and livestock than they need so that they have plenty to spare for their neighbors. Whenever they need something from town, they simply request it without any sort of payment. When the time for harvest comes, the magistrates in the country let those in the towns know how many hands they will need for reaping the harvest. The number requested is sent immediately; often the harvest is completed within one day.

Of Their Towns, Particularly of Amaurot

If you know one of their towns you know them all, for they are all identical except where the lay of the land necessitates minor differences. Let me describe one of them, Amaurot, where I lived for five years. It is the most preeminent and the seat of their Supreme Council.

Amaurot lies upon the side of a modest hill. It is almost square, descending two miles from the top of the hill down to the river Anider. The Anider rises about eighty miles above Amaurot from a small spring. As it descends it is fed by many small streams, so that by the time it reaches Amaurot, it is a half mile wide. It continues to grow larger and larger until it runs into the ocean sixty miles below. At Amaurot there is a stone bridge consisting of many stately arches. Since this bridge crosses the river at the part of town furthest from the sea, ships can put in anywhere along its bank....

The town is surrounded by a high thick wall on which there are many towers and fortifications. The streets are well designed, and sheltered from the winds. Their buildings are well-built, and are so uniform that a whole side of a street looks like one house. There are gardens behind every house, enclosed by buildings on all sides; each house has a front door on the street, and a back door to the garden. Their doors easily swing open from either direction and shut of their own accord, so that anyone can freely enter any house—for there is no such thing as private property. The houses are allocated by lot, and changed every ten years.

They cultivate their gardens with great care, growing vines, fruits, herbs, and flowers in them. Never before have I seen gardens as fruitful and beautiful as theirs. There are competitions among the different blocks for the best maintained garden. The layout of the town was originally designed by Utopus, but it has been embellished by those who followed him. Their historical records, carefully preserved, run back 1,760 years. From these it appears that originally the houses were merely small cottages, built with mud walls and thatched with straw. But now their houses are three stories high: the fronts of them are faced with stone, plastering, or brick. The roofs are flat and covered with a sort of plaster, which costs very little, yet is resistant to fire and bad weather. Their windows they glaze with glass.

Of Their Magistrates

Each year every thirty households choose a magistrate known as a *syphogrant*; over every ten *syphogrants*, and the families subject to them, is another magistrate, the *tranibor*. The *syphogrants* of the city, who number 200, choose the mayor from a list of four, each named by the people of the four divisions of the city. However before the vote they take an oath to vote for the candidate they think most fit for the office. The vote is by secret ballot. The mayor serves for life unless he is removed by the people. The *tranibors* are newly chosen every year, but most serve several terms. All the other magistrates serve only a single year. The *tranibors* meet every third day, more often if necessary, and consult with the mayor both on affairs of the State in general and on private disputes that arise from time to time among the people. There are always two *syphogrants* called into the council chamber on an alternate basis. When anything of great importance is under consideration, it is sent to all the *syphogrants* so that they can consult with the families under their jurisdiction. It is a fundamental rule of their government that no decision can be made until it has first been debated three consecutive days in Council. This prevents Council members from acting rashly without consulting the public, and prevents the mayor and the *tranibors* from conspiring together to change the government and enslave the people.

Of Their Trades, and Manner of Life

Agriculture is so important that no person, either man or woman, is ignorant of it; they are instructed in it from their childhood, partly by what they learn at school, partly by practice. Children are taken into the fields about the town where they see others at work engage in it themselves. Besides agriculture, which is common to them all, every man has a particular trade of his own. All trades are held in equal esteem. Throughout the island everyone wears identical clothing, the only distinctions being those necessary to distinguish the two sexes, and the married and unmarried. The fashion never alters; their clothing is attractive, comfortable, and suitable for both summer and winter. Every family makes its own clothes; but every family member, women as well as men, learn another trade as well. Women, for the most part, deal in wool and flax, which best suits their weakness, leaving the heavier trades to the men. The same trade generally passes down from father to son, but if a young man's talent lies in another direction, he can be adopted into a family that deals in the trade to which he is inclined. And if after a person has learned one trade, he desires to acquire another, that is also allowed, and is managed in the same manner as the former. When he has learned both, he follows the one he likes best, unless the public has more need for the other.

The chief responsibility of the *syphogrants* is to make sure no one is idle. Yet the residents do not work from morning to night as if they were beasts of burden, as is so common among working people everywhere outside of Utopia. Six hours a day are devoted to work, three before dinner, three after. They then sup, and at eight o'clock go to bed and sleep eight hours. The time not taken up in work, eating and sleeping, is left to each individual's discretion; yet they are not to abuse this discretionary time with luxury or idleness, but must employ it in some useful exercise according to their inclinations, usually reading. There are public lectures every morning before daybreak; although none are obliged to attend, both men and women of all ranks attend lectures of one sort or another, according to their interests. Others, less inclined toward intellectual pursuits, use that time to pursue their trade. After supper, they spend an hour in some diversion, in summer in their gardens, and in winter in the halls where they eat, entertaining each other with music or discourse. They do not know dice, or other foolish and mischievous games, but do have two sorts of games not unlike our chess. One is between several numbers, in which one number, as it were, consumes another; the other resembles a battle between the virtues and the vices. You may think that with so little time devoted to labor, there would be many scarcities. But this is not the case; indeed, there are considerable surpluses. This makes sense, of course, when you consider how many in most societies are idle.

First, women, half the population, generally do little work; and if some few women are diligent, their husbands are idle. Then consider idle priests, and members of religious orders; how much work do they do? Add to these all rich men, particularly those who have estates in land, who are called noblemen and gentlemen, together with their households of idle persons, kept more for show than use. Add to these beggars. All in all, you will find that the number of people whose labor supplies basic human needs is much less than you might have imagined. Then consider how few of those who do work are employed in labor that is of real service. We who measure all things by money promote trades that are vain and superfluous, and serve only to support luxury and waste. If all those who work were employed only in producing necessities of life, there would be such an abundance that prices would sink below what tradesmen need to support themselves. If all those who labor about useless things were to engage in more profitable employments, and if all who languish out their lives in sloth and idleness, each consuming as much as any two men who work, were forced to labor, it is easy to see that only a small amount of time would be needed to produce what is necessary for a comfortable life—especially if pleasure is kept within appropriate bounds.

This is all very evident in Utopia. In a great city and the surrounding territory it is difficult to find even 500 men or women who are capable of labor but not engaged in it. Even the *syphogrants*, excused by law, engage in labor to set a good example. A similar exemption is granted to a selected few so that they might apply themselves entirely to study. Sometimes even a mechanic, for example, who has used his leisure hours for study, is exempted from labor and ranked among their learned men. From among their learned men they choose ambassadors, priests, *tranibors*, even the mayor himself.

Since few among them are either idle or engaged in fruitless labor, you can easily estimate how much can be done in those few hours in which they are obliged to labor. In addition, necessary tasks require less work than anywhere else. Among us the building and repair of houses requires many hands, often because a thriftless heir allows a house his father built to fall into disrepair. As a result, his successor must repair at great cost what might have been maintained with little effort. Sometimes a house built by one man is neglected by another only because the latter thinks he has a more delicate sense of architecture and wants to build another house from scratch. But among the Utopians all things are so regulated that men very seldom build upon a new piece of ground. They are quick to repair their houses, and show foresight in preventing decay. As a result, their buildings are preserved with little labor.

Labor is similarly saved on clothing. While at work they wear simple leather overalls which last seven years. When they appear in public they put on an outer garment over their overalls, always of a single color, the natural color of the wool. As a result they consume less wool and what they do consume is less costly to produce....Thus, since they are all employed in some useful labor, and since they content themselves with fewer things, there is a great abundance of all things. At times, when the need for work is limited, vast numbers are sent out to repair the highways. At other times, when no public undertaking is necessary, the work day is reduced. The magistrates never require unnecessary labor, since the purpose of their constitution is to require only what labor is necessary, and to allow everyone as much time as possible to improve their minds, the basis, they believe, of true happiness.

Social Arrangements

Let me now describe their social arrangements, how they behave with each other, and the rules by which property is distributed among them.

Just as their cities are composed of households, so their households are made up of those who are closely related to each other. When a woman grows up and marries she moves in with her husband's family, but all males, both children and grandchildren, remain in the same household, living under the authority of the oldest male—unless he has become senile, in which case the next oldest male takes over. But to avoid the possibility that any city become too large or too small, provision is made that no city may contain more than 6,000 families, not counting those in the surrounding countryside. No family, in turn, may include fewer than ten or more than sixteen adults. This rule is easily followed by removing some of the adult children of a more fruitful couple to a smaller household.

By the same rule, they move residents of larger cities to those with a smaller population; and if the population of the whole island grows excessively, they send people from several towns to unpopulated regions on the mainland. This new colony welcomes local inhabitants as long as they are willing to live under Utopian institutions. When this happens, natives and Utopians quickly form a single society. But if the natives refuse to conform themselves to Utopian laws, they drive them out of the colony, and use force if they resist. They believe this is a just cause for war, for a nation that prevents others from using land that lies idle and uncultivated violates the law of nature. If the population of all the towns decreases to a dangerous degree, they recall citizens from the colonies.

But to return to their society. The oldest male in every family, as has been already said, is its governor. Wives serve their husbands, and children their parents, and always the younger serve the older. Every city is divided into four equal districts; at the center of each district there is a marketplace. Each family brings what it produces to warehouses there. When a family needs something, the father simply takes whatever the family needs without paying for it or leaving anything in exchange. There is no reason to refuse any person's need, since there is plenty of everything; and there is no danger of a man's asking for more than he needs since he knows their needs will always be met. It is fear of privation that makes animals greedy and ravenous; in the case of man, in addition to fear, there is a pride that makes him want to excel over others in pomp and excess. But the laws of the Utopians prohibit this. Near these markets are sold other sorts of provisions—herbs, fruits, bread, fish, fowl, and cattle.

Outside the towns, near running water, are places for slaughtering animals. This is done by their slaves; they prohibit their own citizens from killing cattle, because they think that sensitivity and pity, fine qualities with which we are born, will be impaired by butchering animals....

In every street there are great halls, each with its own name. Here the *syphogrants* live, and here the thirty families under his jurisdiction take their meals. The stewards for each hall go to the marketplace every day at an appointed hour, and receive provisions according to the number who belong to the hall.

The Utopians give special priority to their sick, who are lodged and provided for in public hospitals. The hospitals are furnished and equipped with everything necessary for their care and treatment; and those that are put in them are looked after with tender and watchful care by skillful physicians and nurses. No one is sent to a hospital against their will, but few people would not choose a hospital over lying sick at home.

After the steward of the hospitals has taken for the sick whatever the physician prescribes, the best things left in the market are distributed equally among the halls, in proportion to their numbers. Only the mayor, the chief priest, the *tranibors*, the ambassadors, and strangers, if there are any, receive special treatment. At the hours of dinner and supper, the sound of a trumpet calls together the whole *syphogranty*, who meet and eat together. But after the halls are supplied, no one is prevented from taking goods home from the marketplace, for they know there must be good reason. Within the halls all the unpleasant and disagreeable services are performed by slaves; but the actual preparing and cooking the food, and planning the menu, is left to the women; women from each household take turns with these responsibilities....

Every child is nursed by its own mother. All the children under five years old sit among the nurses. Older children of both sexes serve the adults or, if they are not old enough, stand quietly, accepting what is given to them from the table. Seating throughout the hall is arranged in such a way that everyone sits with others of their own age, but in such a way that the young are always in close proximity with the old. The oldest are served first, though all receive the same fare. Both dinner and supper are preceded with a lecture on morality; but it is short and not tedious. The older people then start discussing important issues, but always allow the young to contribute to the conversation. At the evening meal there is always music.

Of the Traveling of the Utopians

If a Utopian wishes to visit friends in another town, or desires to travel and see the rest of the country, he can easily obtain permission from the *syphogrant* or *tranibor* at a time when there is no need for him to remain at home. Travelers carry with them a passport, which both certifies that a license was granted for traveling, and limits the time they can be away. They are furnished with a wagon, and a slave who drives the oxen and looks after them. While on the road, they carry no provisions with them for everywhere travelers are treated as if they were at home. However, if one leaves his city without permission and is found wondering without a passport, he is severely treated, punished as a fugitive, and sent home in disgrace; if he repeats the offense he is condemned to slavery. If a man wishes to travel within his own city, he may freely do so as long as he has the consent of his father and his wife. But if he expects to be entertained at a country home, he must labor with them and conform to their rules. There are no idle persons among the population. There are no taverns, no alehouses nor any other occasions of license. Since everything is distributed among all the people, no man has want, or is obliged to beg.

In their great Council at Amaurot, to which three delegates are sent from every town once a year, they examine what towns enjoy surpluses and what towns suffer from any scarcity. Transfers are made freely from one town to another, without any sort of exchange, as if the entire island were one family. After providing for their whole country storing reserves sufficient for two years, they export what is left. One seventh of surplus is given freely to the poor of the countries to which they send them; the rest are sold at moderate prices. This trade supplies those few things not produced at home. Over time they have accumulated a substantial reserve of gold and silver.

The only purpose of this reserve is to engage in warfare. In times of emergency they hire foreign troops, whom they pay generously, knowing that they are more exposed to danger than their own people. They will also attempt to bribe potential enemies. Since they have no use for money among themselves, but only keep it in reserve against events that seldom happen, they value gold and silver less than iron, since men can no more live without iron than without fire or water. Only human folly has enhanced the value of gold and silver because of their scarcity....

Although few are wholly excused from labor in order to engage in studies, all children, both boys and girls, receive a basic education. In addition, most of the nation spends those hours in which they are not obliged to work in reading, which becomes a lifetime habit. All their learning is in their own tongue, which has a rich vocabulary and a pleasant sound, and in which a man can fully express his mind. Although they had never heard of those philosophers who are so famous in this part of the world, they had made the same discoveries as the Greeks, in music, logic, arithmetic, and geometry....They are expert in astronomy, and familiar with the motions of the heavenly bodies....

As to moral philosophy, they debate the same issues we do. They examine what is properly good both for the body and the soul, and whether any external thing can be called truly good, or if that term belongs only to the endowments of the soul. They inquire likewise into the nature of virtue and pleasure; but their chief concern is human happiness, and of what it consists? They seem generally inclined toward the conviction that the greatest good for human happiness is pleasure; indeed, they defend this proposition with arguments from religion.

The first principle in their religion is that the soul of man is immortal, created by God, and intended to be happy. Secondly, God has ordained that there be rewards for good and virtuous actions, and punishments for vice, distributed after this life. They believe that these principles of religion are supported by reason as well as tradition.

They do not identify happiness with all pleasure, but only in those things that are themselves good and honest. They believe that our natures are conducted by virtue to happiness, the greatest human good. They define virtue as living according to nature, and think that we are made by God for that end. A man follows the dictates of nature when he pursues or avoids things according to reason. The first dictate of reason is love and reverence for the Divine Majesty, to whom we owe both all that we have and all that we can ever hope for. Reason also directs us to keep our minds as free from passion and as cheerful as we can, and to do our utmost to insure happiness of all other persons. In other words, man must advance the welfare and comfort of the rest of mankind, there being no greater virtue than easing the miseries of others....Piety is to prefer the public good over one's private concerns; but it unjust for a man to seek pleasure for himself by snatching pleasures from another....

Thus they argue that all actions, and even all virtues, culminate in pleasure as in our chief end and greatest happiness. They define pleasure as any activity or state, whether physical or mental, that is naturally enjoyable. Thus they cautiously limit pleasure only to those appetites to which nature leads us; and nature leads us only to those delights inspired by reason as well as the senses, and by which we neither injure any other person nor lose the possession of greater pleasures....

They divide true happiness into two categories, mental and physical. The pleasures of the mind lie in knowledge, in the contemplation of truth, in the joyful reflection on a well spent life, and the assured hopes of a future happiness. They divide the pleasures of the body into two sorts. The first consists of fulfilling physical needs and filling the whole organism with a sense of enjoyment....The second is good health, the greatest of all bodily pleasures....

Of Their Slaves, and of Their Marriages
They do not make slaves of prisoners of war, except those that are taken in battle. Nor are there slaves by birth, or slaves purchased in foreign markets. The only slaves among them are those who have been condemned to that state for the commission of some crime,

or convicted criminals from other countries who have been purchased at low rates. Slaves are kept at perpetual labor, and are always chained; they treat Utopians worse than foreigners, since the former had the advantage of an excellent education. Another group of slaves are the poor from neighboring countries, who voluntarily prefer slavery in Utopia to poverty at home. This latter group can leave the country whenever they wish.

I already spoke of the care with which they look after their sick. They do everything possible to ease the discomfort of those with incurable diseases. If, however, someone is taken with a torturing and lingering pain, so that there is no hope of recovery or comfort, the priests and magistrates come and exhort them, saying you can no longer live a constructive life, you are a burden to yourself and those around you, and encourage them to choose death over a life of misery. Since by choosing to end their life they lose none of the pleasures but only the pain, they think it is not only reasonable but consistent with religion and piety. But no man is forced to end his life; and if he cannot be persuaded, he will still be treated with kindness and care. Although they believe a voluntary death, when officially sanctioned, is honorable, if a man takes his life without the approbation of the priests and the Senate, they give him none of the honors of a decent funeral, but throw his body into a ditch.

Their women do not marry before eighteen, nor their men before twenty-two. Anyone who engages in premarital sex is severely punished, and denied the privilege of marriage unless pardoned by the mayor. Such behavior casts much disgrace upon the master and mistress of their family, for it demonstrates they have failed in their duty. The reason for such severe punishment is that if such powerful appetites were not restrained, few would enter into the state of marriage, where one must live his or her entire life with one person, accepting occasional frustration.

In choosing their wives they use a method that would appear to us very absurd and ridiculous, but one that makes great sense to them. Before marriage the bride is presented naked to the bride-groom; and the bridegroom is presented naked to the bride. We indeed both laughed at this, and condemned it as very indecent. But they, on the other hand, wondered at the folly of men of all other nations, who, when buying a horse will insist on seeing every part of him, but when choosing a wife, relies on seeing only her face despite the fact that his decision will determine how happy he is for the rest of his life.

Regulations were also required on these matters because they are the only people in that part of the world who prohibit both polygamy and divorce, except in the case of adultery or insufferable perverseness. In these cases the Senate dissolves the marriage, and grants the injured person permission to marry again; but the guilty must live in disgrace, prohibited from engaging in a second marriage. No one is allowed to put away his wife against her will under any condition, for it is the height of cruelty and treachery to abandon a spouse when he or she is in most need of tender care. Frequently a married couple will agree to separate by mutual consent and then find other persons with whom they hope they may live more happily. Yet this cannot be done without first obtaining permission of the Senate, which grants a divorce only after both the Senators and their wives make thorough inquiries. Adultery is severely punished. If both parties are married they are divorced, and the injured party may remarry; but the adulterer and the adulteress are condemned to slavery. If the injured person does not wish to leave his or her guilty spouse, they may continue to live together but in that condition to which the slaves are condemned. Sometimes the repentance of the condemned, together with the forgiveness of the innocent and injured person, has led the mayor to let both go free. But the punishment for a second conviction is death.

Their law does not determine the punishment for other crimes; rather the Senate assigns punishment according to the circumstances of particular case. Husbands are entitled to correct their wives, and parents to chastise their children, unless the offense is so great that a public punishment is deemed necessary as a deterrent to others. Slavery is the most common punishment for serious crimes; it is no less terrible than death for the criminals, and of greater utility to society. The sight of their misery also serves as a deterrent to others. If slaves rebel, or will not perform the labor demanded of them, they are treated like wild beasts and put to death. But if they bear their punishment patiently and demonstrate repentance, their sentence might be reduced by the mayor or by a vote of the people.

He that attempts to seduce a married woman to adultery is no less severely punished than he who commits adultery. They believe that the attempt to commit a crime is just as evil as the crime itself, since failure to succeed does not render a person less guilty....

In addition to punishments designed to deter crime, the Utopians also reward virtuous behavior with public honors. They erect statues to the memories of those who have served their country in the marketplaces, both to perpetuate their memory and to urge others to follow their example. Anyone who actively seeks public office is disqualified from holding it. Magistrates are never insolent or cruel to the people, and are affectionately referred to as fathers.

The Utopians have few laws because their society does not require many. Indeed, they condemn nations whose laws swell up many volumes, for they think it is unreasonable to oblige men to obey laws that cannot be easily read and understood by every subject.

They have no lawyers among them, a profession whose purpose they believe is to disguise the truth. They think it is much better for every man to plead his own case, and entrust it to the judge, as in other places the client entrusts it to a lawyer. By this means they eliminate many delays, and discover the truth with greater certainty....

Of Their Military Discipline

The Utopians detest war as a brutal, subhuman activity, even though it is more practiced by men than by any beast. Unlike every other nation, they believe that there is nothing more inglorious than that glory that is gained by war. Although they receive military training—men and women alike—they do not engage in war except to defend themselves or their friends from unjust aggressors, or to assist an oppressed nation in shaking off the yoke of tyranny....

Of the Religions of the Utopians

There are several different religions, not only in different parts of the island, but even within every town. Some worship the sun, others the moon or one of the planets; some worship men from former times known for their virtue or glory. Most, however, worship one eternal, invisible, infinite, and incomprehensible deity who is beyond our comprehension and diffused throughout the whole universe in his power and virtue. All agree that there is one Supreme Being who made and governs the world, even though they disagree on his nature.... One of the most basic principles of their society is religious toleration.

Their priests are men of great piety....They are elected by secret ballot by all the people just as the magistrates are; and once chosen they are consecrated by the College of Priests. They are charged with the care of all sacred things, the worship of God, and an inspection into the manners of the people. They can only exhort and admonish, however, for the power of correcting and punishing wicked men belongs to the magistrates. The severest thing that a priest can do is to exclude the wicked from joining in worship. Priests are also responsible for educating the young, especially in developing their sense of morality. Priests marry; their wives are some of the most extraordinary women in the country. Women sometimes become priests themselves....

They have magnificent temples, spacious and imposing. Though the people vary in their religious beliefs, they all agree on the main point, worshiping the Divine Essence. Nothing can be seen or heard in their temples that would be offensive to any particular belief; there are no images of God so that everyone may think of him according to the way of his own religion.

They meet in their temples on the evening of the festival that concludes a season, and thank God for their success during that year or month. The next day, which begins the new season, they meet early in their temples, to pray for prosperity in the future. In the festival that concludes the period, before they go to the temple, both wives and children fall on their knees before their husbands or parents, and confess everything in which they have either erred or failed in their duty, and beg pardon for it. Thus all little discontents in families are removed, so that they might offer up their devotions with a pure and serene mind. In the temples, the two sexes are separated, the men on the right hand, and the women to the left. Care is taken to assure that the young sit next to the old, since if the young were all together they might waste time playing childish games....

* * *

Thus have I described to you as accurately as possible what I think is the best country in the world, and the only one deserving to be called a republic. In all other places people talk of a commonwealth, but in reality seek individual wealth. But in Utopia, where no man possesses any property, all men zealously pursue the public good. This distinction is not surprising: in other commonwealths, every man knows that unless he provides for himself, he will die of hunger no matter how prosperous the commonwealth may be. He has no choice but to place his own needs over those of the society. But in Utopia, where every man has a right to everything, they all know that if care is taken to keep the public stores full, no individual will be wanting for any necessity. There, where the distribution of goods is equal, no one is poor, no one lives in need; and though no one owns anything, everyone is rich. The citizen of Utopia need not fear their children will live in poverty, and knows that he and his wife, his children and grandchildren, to as many generations as he can imagine, will live happy and prosperous lives.

How can you compare the justice of Utopia with that in any other land? Where is justice where a nobleman, a goldsmith, a banker, or anyone who does nothing at all, or at whose employment has no social utility, should live in great luxury and splendor, while a laborer, a carter, a smith, or a ploughman, who works harder even than the beasts themselves, and whose labors are so necessary that no society could survive without them, earns so poor a livelihood and leads so miserable a life that the condition of beasts is better? These poor souls live in anxiety about the future, depressed by a barren and fruitless employment, and tormented with the worry over their old age.

Is not a society unjust that is so generous in its rewards to those that are called gentlemen, who are idle, or live by flattery; and on the other hand, takes no care of those of a meaner sort, such as plowmen, colliers, and smiths, without whom it could not subsist? Even worse, when they come to be oppressed with age and sickness, all the labors and the good they have done is forgotten; their reward is that they are left to die in poverty. Indeed, the rich are often endeavoring to bring down the wages of the poor, not only by their fraudulent practices, but by the laws they enact with that in mind....

I can only conclude that in every other society the rich are engaged in a conspiracy to protect their own fortunes under pretense of managing the public welfare. They devise countless ways to preserve their ill-gotten wealth and then make sure the poor will be forced to toil and labor for them at wages as low as possible. Once these contrivances become established under the show of public authority, they assume the force of law. A wicked and greedy minority divides among itself what would be sufficient for the entire population. Our people are far from that happiness that is enjoyed by the Utopians. Think of the crime and misery that would be eliminated with the elimination of money and the desire for it. Human fears, worries, cares, labors, and distress would all perish with the disappearance of money; even poverty itself would disappear....

I am sure even rich men are aware of this; they know well it is better to want for nothing necessary than to abound in luxury. The entire world would have adopted the laws of the Utopians, if pride, that plague of human nature, that source of so much misery, did not stand in the way. For pride does not measure happiness by what it has as much as by what others do not have. Pride thinks its own happiness shines brighter by comparing it with the misfortunes of others. Utopia has succeeded by rooting out of the hearts of men all ambition and faction and pride.

21. Martin Luther, *On Temporal Authority*

*W*hen Martin Luther (1483-1546) began his revolt against the Roman Catholic Church in 1517, he challenged not only existing theological doctrines but also traditional notions of authority within the Church and within society as a whole. His theology argued that faith alone justifies human beings before God and enables them to achieve salvation; good works, from pious acts to obedience to authority, might flow from faith but do not in themselves accomplish salvation.

Some interpreted Luther's teaching to mean that obedience to authority and to human law was no longer necessary. In this selection Luther addresses the role of secular authority in human society for believers and nonbelievers alike. It represents a significant departure from medieval Catholic thinking on the Christian in civil society.

Part I: The Basis for Temporal Authority

First, we must provide a sound basis for the civil law and sword so no one will doubt that they are in the world by God's will and ordinance. The passages which do this are the following: Romans 𝐴 13, "Let every soul be subject to the governing authority, for there is no authority except from God; the authority which everywhere exists has been ordained by God. He then who resists the governing authority resists the ordinance of God, and he who resists

God's ordinance will incur judgment." Again, in I Peter 2, "Be subject to every kind of human ordinance, whether it be to the king as supreme, or to governors, as those who have been sent by him to punish the wicked and to praise the righteous."

The law of this temporal sword has existed from the beginning of the world. For when Cain slew his brother Abel, he was in such great terror of being killed in turn that God even placed a special prohibition on it and suspended the sword for his sake, so that no one was to slay him [Gen. 4]. Abel would not have had this fear if he had not seen and heard from Adam that murderers are to be slain. Moreover, after the Flood, God reestablished and confirmed this in unmistakable terms when he said in Genesis 9, "Whoever sheds the blood of man, by man shall his blood be shed." This cannot be understood as a plague or punishment of God upon murderers, for many murderers who are punished in other ways or pardoned altogether continue to live, and eventually die by means other than the sword. Rather, it is said of the law of the sword, that a murderer is guilty of death and in justice is to be slain by the sword. Now if justice should be hindered or the sword become negligent so that the murderer dies a natural death, Scripture is not on that account false when it says, "Whoever sheds the blood of man, by man shall his blood be shed." The credit or blame belongs to men if this law instituted by God is not carried out; just as other commandments of God, too, are broken.

Afterward it was also confirmed by the law of Moses, Exodus 21, "A life for a life, an eye for an eye, a tooth for a tooth, a foot for a foot, a hand for a hand, a wound for a wound, a stripe for a stripe."....Hence, it is certain and clear enough that it is God's will that the temporal sword and law be used for the punishment of the wicked and the protection of the upright.

Second. There appear to be powerful arguments to the contrary. Christ says in Matthew 5, "You have heard that it was said to them of old: An eye for an eye, a tooth for a tooth. But I say to you, Do not resist evil; but if anyone strikes you on the right cheek, turn to him the other also. And if anyone would sue you and take your coat, let him have your cloak as well. And if anyone forces you to go one mile, go with him two miles," etc. Likewise Paul in Romans 12, "Beloved, defend not yourselves, but leave it to the wrath of God; for it is written, Vengeance is mine; I will repay, says the Lord.'" And in Matthew 5, "Love your enemies, do good to them that hate you." These and similar passages would certainly make it appear as though in the New Testament Christians were to have no temporal sword.

Hence, the sophists also say that Christ has thereby abolished the law of Moses. Of such commandments they make "counsels" for the perfect. They divide Christian teaching and Christians into two classes. One part, they call the perfect, and assign to it such counsels. The other they call the imperfect, and assign to it the commandments. This they do out of sheer wantonness and caprice, without any scriptural basis. They fail to see that in the same passage Christ lays such stress on his teaching that he is unwilling to have the least word of it set aside, and condemns to hell those who do not love their enemies. Therefore, we must interpret these passages differently, so that Christ's words may apply to everyone alike, be he perfect or imperfect. For perfection and imperfection do not consist in works, and do not establish any distinct external order among Christians. They exist in the heart, in faith and love, so that those who believe and love the most are the perfect ones, whether they be outwardly male or female, prince or peasant, monk or layman. For love and faith produce no sects or outward differences.

Third. Here we must divide the children of Adam and all mankind into two classes, the first belonging to the kingdom of God, the second to the kingdom of the world. Those who belong to the kingdom of God are all the true believers who are in Christ and under Christ, for Christ is King and Lord in the kingdom of God....

Now observe, these people need no temporal law or sword. If all the world were composed of real Christians, that is, true believers, there would be no need for or benefits from prince, king, lord, sword, or law. They would serve no purpose, since Christians have in their heart the Holy Spirit, who both teaches and makes them to do injustice to no one, to love everyone, and to suffer injustice and even death willingly and cheerfully at the hands of anyone. Where there is nothing but the unadulterated doing of right and bearing of wrong, there is no need for any suit, litigation, court, judge, penalty, law, or sword. For this reason it is impossible that the temporal sword and law should find any work to do among Christians, since they do of their own accord much more than all laws and teachings can demand, just as Paul says in I Timothy, "The law is not laid down for the just but for the lawless."

Why is this? It is because the righteous man of his own accord does all and more than the law demands. But the unrighteous do nothing that the law demands; therefore, they need the law to instruct, constrain, and compel them to do good. A good tree needs no instruction or law to bear good fruit; its nature causes it to bear according to its kind without any law or instruction. I would take to be quite a fool any man who would make a book full of laws and statutes for an apple tree telling it how to bear apples and not thorns, when the tree is able by its own nature to do this better than the man with all his books can describe and demand. Just so, by the Spirit and by faith all Christians are so thoroughly disposed and conditioned in their very nature that they do right and keep the law better than one can teach them with all manner of statutes; so far as they themselves are concerned, no statutes or laws are needed.

You ask: Why, then, did God give so many commandments to all mankind, and why does Christ prescribe in the gospel so many things for us to do? To put it here as briefly as possible, Paul says that the law has been laid down for the sake of the lawless [I Tim.], that is, so that those who are not Christians may through the law be restrained outwardly from evil deeds....Now since no one is by nature Christian or righteous, but altogether sinful and wicked, God through the law puts them all under restraint so they dare not wilfully implement their wickedness in actual deeds. In addition,

Paul ascribes to the law another function, that of teaching men to recognize sin in order that it may make them humble unto grace and unto faith in Christ.

Fourth. All who are not Christians belong to the kingdom of the world and are under the law. There are few true believers, and still fewer who live a Christian life, who do not resist evil and indeed themselves do no evil. For this reason God has provided for them a different government beyond the Christian estate and the kingdom of God. He has subjected them to the sword so that, even though they would like to, they are unable to practice their wickedness, and if they do practice it they cannot do so without fear or with success and impunity. In the same way a savage wild beast is bound with chains and ropes so that it cannot bite and tear as it would normally do, even though it would like to; whereas a tame and gentle animal needs no restraint, but is harmless despite the lack of chains and ropes.

If this were not so, men would devour one another, seeing that the whole world is evil and that among thousands there is scarcely a single true Christian. No one could support wife and child, feed himself, and serve God. The world would be reduced to chaos. For this reason God has ordained two governments: the spiritual, by which the Holy Spirit produces Christians and righteous people under Christ; and the temporal, which restrains the un-Christian and wicked so that...they are obliged to keep still and to maintain outward peace....

If anyone attempted to rule the world by the gospel and to abolish all temporal law and sword on the plea that all are baptized and Christian, and that, according to the gospel, there shall be among them no law or sword —or need for either—pray tell me, friend, what would he be doing? He would be loosing the ropes and chains of the savage wild beasts and letting them bite and mangle everyone, meanwhile insisting that they were harmless, tame, and gentle creatures; but I would have the proof in my wounds. Just so would the wicked under the name of Christian abuse evangelical freedom, carry on their rascality, and insist that they were Christians subject neither to law nor sword, as some are already raving and ranting.

To such a one we must say: Certainly it is true that Christians, so far as they themselves are concerned, are subject neither to law nor sword, and have need of neither. But take heed and first fill the world with real Christians before you attempt to rule it in a Christian and evangelical manner. This you will never accomplish; for the world and the masses are and always will be un-Christian, even if they are all baptized and Christian in name. Christians are few and far between (as the saying is). Therefore, it is out of the question that there should be a common Christian government over the whole world, or indeed over a single country or any considerable body of people, for the wicked always outnumber the good. Hence, a man who would venture to govern an entire country or the world with the gospel would be like a shepherd who should put together in one fold wolves, lions, eagles, and sheep, and let them mingle freely with one another, saying, "Help yourselves, and be good and peaceful toward one another. The fold is open, there is plenty of food. You need have no fear of dogs and clubs." The sheep would doubtless keep the peace and allow themselves to be fed and governed peacefully, but they would not live long, nor would one beast survive another.

For this reason one must carefully distinguish between these two governments. Both must be permitted to remain; the one to produce righteousness, the other to bring about external peace and prevent evil deeds. Neither one is sufficient in the world without the other.

Fifth. But you say: if Christians then do not need the temporal sword or law, why does Paul say to all Christians in Romans 13, "let all souls be subject to the governing authority," as quoted above? Answer: I have just said that Christians, among themselves and by and for themselves, need no law or sword, since it is neither necessary nor useful for them. Since a true Christian lives and labors on earth not for himself alone but for his neighbor, he does by the very nature of his spirit even what he himself has no need of, but is needful and useful to his neighbor. Because the sword is most beneficial and necessary for the whole world in order to preserve peace, punish sin, and restrain the wicked, the Christian submits most willingly to the rule of the sword, pays his taxes, honors those in authority, serves, helps, and does all he can to assist the governing authority, that it may continue to function and be held in honor and fear. Although he has no need of these things for himself—to him they are not essential—nevertheless, he concerns himself about what is serviceable and of benefit to others.

Just as he performs all other works of love which he himself does not need—he does not visit the sick in order that he himself may be made well, or feed others because he himself needs food—so he serves the governing authority not because he needs it but for the sake of others, that they may be protected and that the wicked may not become worse.

Sixth. You ask whether a Christian too may bear the temporal sword and punish the wicked, since Christ's words, "Do not resist evil," are so clear. Answer: You have now heard two propositions. One is that the sword can have no place among Christians; therefore, you cannot bear it among Christians or hold it over them, for they do not need it. The question, therefore, must be referred to the other group, the non-Christians, whether you may bear it there in a Christian manner. Here the other proposition applies, that you are under obligation to serve and assist the sword by whatever means you can, with body, goods, honor, and soul. For it is something which you do not need, but which is very beneficial and essential for the whole world and for your neighbor. Therefore, if you see that there is a lack of hangmen, constables, judges, lords, or princes, and you find that you are qualified, you should offer your services and seek the position, that the essential governmental authority may not be despised and become enfeebled or perish, the world cannot and dare not dispense with it....

Christ is not abrogating the law when he says, "You have heard that it was said to them of old, An eye for an eye'; but I say to you: Do not resist evil," etc. [Matt. 5]. On the contrary, he is expounding the meaning of the law as it is to be understood, as if he were to say, "You Jews think that it is right and proper in the sight of God to recover by law what is yours. You rely on what Moses said, 'An eye for an eye,' etc. But I say to you that Moses set this law over the wicked, who do not belong to God's kingdom, in order that they might not avenge themselves or do worse but be compelled by such outward law to desist from evil, in order that by outward law and rule they might be kept subordinate to the governing authority. You, however, should so conduct yourselves that you neither need nor resort to such law. Although the temporal authority must have such a law by which to judge unbelievers, and although you yourselves may also use it for judging others, still you should not invoke or use it for yourselves and in your own affairs. You have the kingdom of heaven; therefore, you should leave the kingdom of earth to anyone who wants to take it."

There you see that Christ does not interpret his words to mean that he is abrogating the law of Moses or prohibiting temporal authority. He is rather making an exception of his own people. They are not to use the secular authority for themselves but leave it to unbelievers. Yet they may also serve these unbelievers, even with their own law, since they are not Christians and no one can be forced into Christianity. That Christ's words apply only to his own is evident from the fact that later on he says they should love their enemies and be perfect like their heavenly Father. But he who loves his enemies and is perfect leaves the law alone and does not use it to demand an eye for an eye. Neither does he restrain the non-Christians, however, who do not love their enemies and who do wish to make use of the law; indeed, he lends his help that these laws may hinder the wicked from doing worse.

Thus the word of Christ is now reconciled, I believe, with the passages which establish the sword, and the meaning is this: No Christian shall wield or invoke the sword for himself and his cause. In behalf of another, however, he may and should wield it and invoke it to restrain wickedness and to defend godliness....

Here you inquire further, whether constables, hangmen, jurists, lawyers, and others of similar function can also be Christians and in a state of salvation. Answer: If the governing authority and its sword are a divine service, as was proved above, then everything that is essential for the authority's bearing of the sword must also be divine service. There must be those who arrest, prosecute, execute, and destroy the wicked, and who protect, acquit, defend, and save the good. Therefore, when they perform their duties, not with the intention of seeking their own ends but only of helping the law and the governing authority function to coerce the wicked, there is no peril in that; they may use their office like anybody else would use his trade, as a means of livelihood. For, as has been said, love of neighbor is not concerned about its own; it considers not how great or humble, but how profitable and needful the works are for neighbor or community.

NEW
discussion

Part II: How Far Temporal Authority Ends

We come now to the main part of this treatise. Having learned that there must be temporal authority on earth, and how it is to be exercised in a Christian and salutary manner, we must now learn how far its arm extends and how widely its hand stretches, lest it extend too far and encroach upon God's kingdom and government. It is essential for us to know this, for where it is given too wide a scope, intolerable and terrible injury follows; on the other hand, injury is also inevitable where it is restricted too narrowly. In the former case, the temporal authority punishes too much; in the latter case, it punishes too little. To err in this direction, however, and punish too little is more tolerable, for it is always better to let a scoundrel live than to put a godly man to death. The world has plenty of scoundrels anyway and must continue to have them, but godly men are scarce.

It is to be noted first that the two classes of Adam's children—the one in God's kingdom under Christ and the other in the kingdom of the world under the governing authority, as was said above—have two kinds of law. For every kingdom must have its own laws and statutes; without law no kingdom or government can survive, as everyday experience amply shows. The temporal government has laws which extend no further than to life and property and external affairs on earth, for God cannot and will not permit anyone but himself to rule over the soul. Therefore, where the temporal authority presumes to prescribe laws for the soul, it encroaches upon God's government and only misleads souls and destroys them. We want to make this so clear that everyone will grasp it, and that our fine gentlemen, the princes and bishops, will see what fools they are when they seek to coerce the people with their laws and commandments into believing this or that.

* * *

Furthermore, every man runs his own risk in believing as he does, and he must see to it himself that he believes rightly. As nobody else can go to heaven or hell for me, so nobody else can believe or disbelieve for me; as nobody else can open or close heaven or hell to me, so nobody else can drive me to belief or unbelief. How he believes or disbelieves is a matter for the conscience of each individual, and since this takes nothing away from the temporal authority the latter should be content to attend to its own affairs and let men believe this or that as they are able and willing, and constrain no one by force. For faith is a free act, to which no one can be forced. Indeed, it is a work of God in the spirit, not something which outward authority should compel or create....

You must know that since the beginning of the world a wise prince is a mighty rare bird, and an upright prince even rarer. They are generally the biggest fools or the worst scoundrels on earth; therefore, one must constantly expect the worst from them and look for little good, especially in divine matters which concern the salvation of souls. They are God's executioners and hangmen; his divine wrath uses them to punish the wicked and to maintain outward peace. Our God is a great lord and ruler; this is why he must also have such noble, highborn, and rich hangmen and constables. He desires that everyone shall copiously accord them riches, honor, and fear in abundance. It pleases his divine will that we call his hangmen gracious lords, fall at their feet, and be subject to them in all humility, so long as they do not ply their trade too far and try to become shepherds instead of hangmen. If a prince should happen to be wise, upright, or a Christian, that is one of the great miracles, the most precious token of divine grace upon that land.

* * *

But you might say, "Since there is to be no temporal sword among Christians, how then are they to be ruled outwardly? There certainly must be authority even among Christians." Answer: Among Christians there shall and can be no authority; rather all are alike subject to one another, as Paul says in Romans 12: "Each shall consider the other his superior." Among Christians there is no superior but Christ himself, and him alone. What kind of authority can there be where all are equal and have the same right, power, possession, and honor, and where no one desires to be the other's superior, but each the other's subordinate? Where there are such people, one could not establish authority even if he wanted to, since in the nature of things it is impossible to have superiors where no one is able or willing to be a superior. Where there are no such people, however, there are no real Christians either.

Part III: How the Prince Should Use His Authority

Now that we know the limits of temporal authority, it is time to inquire also how a prince should use it. We do this for the sake of those very few who would also like very much to be Christian princes and lords, and who desire to enter into the life in heaven.

First. He must give consideration and attention to his subjects, and really devote himself to it. This he does when he directs his every thought to making himself useful and beneficial to them; when instead of thinking, "The land and people belong to me, I will do what best pleases me," he thinks rather, "I belong to the land and the people, I shall do what is good for them ..."

Second. He must beware of the high and mighty and of his counselors, and so conduct himself toward them that while he does not despise them, he does not trust them enough to leave everything to them. God cannot tolerate either course....

Third. He must take care to deal justly with evil-doers. Here he must be very wise and prudent, so he can inflict punishment without injury to others.... Let this be his rule: Where wrong cannot be punished without greater wrong, there let him waive his rights, however just they may be. He should not have regard to his own injury, but to the wrong others must suffer in consequence of the penalty he imposes. What have the many women and children done to deserve being made widows and orphans in order that you may avenge yourself on a worthless tongue or an evil hand which has injured you?

Fourth. Here we come to what should really have been placed first, and of which we spoke above. A prince must act in a Christian way toward his God also; that is, he must subject himself to him in entire confidence and pray for wisdom to rule well. Thus we will close with this brief summation, that a prince's duty is fourfold: First, toward God there must be true confidence and earnest prayer; second, toward his subjects there must be love and Christian service; third, with respect to his counselors and officials he must maintain an untrammeled reason and unfettered judgment; fourth, with respect to evil-doers he must manifest a restrained severity and firmness. Then the princes job will be done right, both outwardly and inwardly; it will be pleasing to God and to the people. But he will have to expect much envy and sorrow on account of it; the cross will soon rest on the shoulders of such a prince.

22. Machiavelli, *The Prince*

Nicolò Machiavelli (1469-1527) lived at the height of the Italian Renaissance in Florence. Throughout his life he was fascinated with the nature of political power, not as an ideal, but as how it works in the real world. He is often considered the first political scientist.

The Prince, his most famous work, was written in 1513. In it Machiavelli, a Florentine patriot, offers advice, a formula for successful rule, to his prince, Lorenzo de Médici, ruler of Florence. His arguments are essentially empirical; each point is supported by many historical examples, of which only a few are included in the excerpts that follow. His empiricism disregards many of the most basic principles of earlier writers.

CHAPTER I

How Many Kinds of Principalities There Are, and by What Means They Are Acquired

All states, all powers, that have ever held and that now hold rule over men have been and are either republics or principalities.

Principalities are either hereditary, in which the family has been long established; or they are new.

The new are either entirely new, as was Milan to Francesco Sforza, or they are, as it were, members annexed to the hereditary state of the prince who has acquired them, as was the kingdom of Naples to that of the King of Spain.

Such dominions thus acquired are either accustomed to live

under a prince, or to live in freedom; and are acquired either by the arms of the prince himself or of others, or else by fortune or by *virtù*.

CHAPTER II

Concerning Hereditary Principalities

I will leave out all discussion on republics, since I have written of them at length elsewhere, and will address only principalities. In doing so I will keep to the order indicated above, and discuss how such principalities are to be ruled and preserved.

I would say at once there are fewer difficulties in holding hereditary states, and those long accustomed to the family of their prince, than new ones; for it is sufficient only not to avoid violating the customs of his ancestors, and to deal prudently with circumstances as they arise. A prince of average powers can maintain himself in this state, unless he be deprived of it by some extraordinary and excessive force; and if he should be so deprived of it, whenever anything sinister happens to the usurper, he will regain it.

We have in Italy, for example, the Duke of Ferrara, who could not have withstood the attacks of the Venetians in '84, nor those of Pope Julius in '10, unless he had been long established in his dominions. For the hereditary prince has less cause and less necessity to offend; hence it happens that he will be more loved; and unless extraordinary vices cause him to be hated, it is reasonable to expect that his subjects will be naturally well disposed towards him; and in the antiquity and duration of his rule the memories and motives that make for change are lost, for one change always leaves the longing for another.

CHAPTER VI

Concerning New Principalities Which Are Acquired by One's Own Arms and Virtù

Let no one be surprised if, in speaking of entirely new principalities as I shall do, I use the highest examples both of prince and of state. Men who walk almost always in the paths of others and imitate their deeds are yet unable imitate their ways completely or attain to the *virtù* of those they imitate. Yet a wise man ought always to follow the paths of great men, and to imitate those who have been supreme, so that if his *virtù* does not equal theirs, he will at least taste of it. Let him act like the clever archers who, designing to hit the mark which appears too distant, and knowing the *virtù* of their bow, take aim much higher than the mark, so that the arrows will reach it not by their strength, but by the aid of an aim so high.

I would say, therefore, that in entirely new principalities with a new prince, that prince will have more or less difficulty in keeping them in proportion to his *virtù*. Now, as the act of becoming a prince presupposes either *virtù* or fortune, it is clear that one or the other of these two things will mitigate in some degree many difficulties. Nevertheless, he who has relied least on fortune will be the strongest. Further, it facilitates matters when the prince, having no other state, is compelled to reside there in person.

Among those who became princes by their own *virtù*, not through fortune, Moses, Cyrus, Romulus, Theseus, and others are excellent examples. Although Moses was a mere executor of the will of God, he ought to be admired, if only because he was worthy of speaking with God. But in considering Cyrus and others who have acquired or founded kingdoms, all were admirable; their particular deeds and conduct were not inferior to those of Moses, although he had so great a preceptor. And in examining their actions and lives one can see that they owed nothing to fortune beyond opportunity, which brought them the material to mold into the form which seemed best to them. Without that opportunity their *virtù* of mind would have been extinguished, and without their *virtù* the opportunity would have come in vain.

It was necessary, therefore, that Moses find the people of Israel enslaved and oppressed in Egypt, which disposed them to follow him out of bondage. It was necessary for Cyrus that the Persians were unhappy under the government of the Medes, and that the Medes were soft and effeminate after a long period of peace. These opportunities made those men fortunate, and their high *virtù* enabled them to recognize the opportunity. As a result, their countries were ennobled and made famous.

Those who by a *virtuose* manner become princes, like these men, have difficulty acquiring a principality, but they hold on to it with ease. The difficulties they have in acquiring it arise in part from the new rules and methods they are forced to introduce in order to establish their government and its security. Nothing is more difficult to initiate, more perilous to conduct, or more uncertain in its success, than to take the lead in the introduction of a new order of things. The innovator has as enemies all those who have done well under the old conditions, and only lukewarm defenders in those who may do well under the new. Their lack of enthusiasm arises partly from fear of the opponents, who have the laws on their side, and partly from the incredulity of men, who do not readily believe in new things until they have had a long experience of them. Thus it happens that whenever those who are hostile have the opportunity to attack they do so aggressively, while the defenders act lukewarmly, so that the prince is endangered along with them.

It is necessary, therefore, to inquire whether these innovators can rely on themselves or have to depend on others: that is to say, whether they have to beg or use force to succeed? In the case of begging, they always succeed badly, and never accomplish anything; but when they can rely on themselves and use force, then they are rarely endangered. For this reason armed prophets have won, and the unarmed ones have always been destroyed. In addition, human nature is fickle; while it is easy to persuade them, it is difficult to make them stand fast in that position. And thus it is necessary to take measures so that when they no longer believe voluntarily, force will make them believe.

If Moses and Cyrus had been unarmed they could not have enforced their rule for long—as happened in our time to Fra Girolamo Savonarola, whose new order of things was ruined as soon as the multitude no longer believed in him, and who had no means of keeping steadfast those who believed, or of making the unbelievers believe. Those who are successful [those who use force] have great difficulties in consummating their enterprise, for there are dangers in the ascent; yet with *virtù* they will overcome them. And once in power, when those who envied them their success are exterminated, they will begin to be respected, and they will be secure in their rule, powerful, secure, honored, and happy.

CHAPTER VIII

Concerning Those Who Have Obtained a Principality by Wickedness

A prince may rise from a private station in two ways, neither of which can be entirely attributed to fortune or *virtù*. The first method of ascending to a principality is by wicked and nefarious deeds; and the second is by winning favor of one's fellow-citizens. Let me give two examples of the first method for those who might be inclined to follow them.

Agathocles, the Sicilian, became King of Syracuse from a low and abject position. This man, the son of a potter led an infamous life no matter how much his fortunes changed. Nevertheless, he accompanied his infamies with so much *virtù* of mind and body that he rose through the military ranks to become praetor of Syracuse. Once in that position, he was determined to make himself prince and to seize power by violence without acquiring any obligation to others. To achieve this, he came to an understanding with Hamilcar, the Carthaginian, who, with his army, was fighting in Sicily. One morning he assembled the people and senate of Syracuse on the pretense of discussing issues of state. At a given signal the soldiers killed all the senators and the wealthy citizens, then seized and held the princedom of that city without any civil commotion. And although he was twice routed by the Carthaginians, and ultimately besieged, he was not only able to defend his city but also to attack Africa and lay siege to Syracuse. The Carthaginians were compelled to come to terms with Agathocles, and depart from Sicily.

He who considers the actions and the genius of this man can attribute little or nothing to fortune, for he achieved his position not with the aid of anyone else, but by progressing successfully step by step in the military profession through a thousand troubles and perils. Yet it cannot be called *virtù* to slay fellow-citizens, to deceive friends, to be without faith, without mercy, without religion; such methods may gain empire, but not glory. Still, if one considers the *virtù* of Agathocles in entering into and extricating himself from dangers, and his brilliance of mind in enduring overcoming hardships, why should he not be as esteemed as the most notable captain. Nevertheless, he is not celebrated among outstanding men because of his barbarous cruelty and inhumanity. What he achieved cannot be attributed either to fortune or to *virtù*.

Some may wonder how Agathocles, and his like, after infinite treacheries and cruelties, can live securely in his country, defend himself from external enemies, and never be conspired against by his own citizens; after all, other cruel leaders have never been able to cling to power even in peaceful, much less in times of war. I believe the explanation lies in whether the cruelty was used badly or properly. Cruelty may be called properly used (if one can speak of using evil well) if it is applied at one blow for one's security, and is not used repeatedly afterwards unless for one's subjects' advantage. Cruelties badly employed are those which, even if few in the beginning, increase rather than decrease over time. Those who follow the first approach can justify their rule, as Agathocles did. Those who follow the second approach find it impossible to remain in power.

Hence before seizing a state, the usurper ought to examine closely all those injuries he must inflict, and to do them all at once so as not to have to repeat them daily. By not unsettling men he will be able to reassure them, and win their support. He who does otherwise, either from timidity or evil advice, is always compelled to keep his knife in his hand; he can neither rely on his subjects nor win their loyalty. Injuries must be committed all at one time; having been experienced less often, they cause less offense. Benefits, on the other hand, should be bestowed little by little, so that the appreciation of them will last longer.

Above all, a prince ought to behave consistently with his sub-

388

jects, permitting no unexpected events, whether of good or evil, to change his behavior. If it becomes necessary to change one's behavior in troubled times, it is too late for harsh measures, and generous measures will not help you, for you will be seen as acting under compulsion, and no one will feel grateful to you for them.

CHAPTER XV

Concerning Things for Which Men, and Especially Princes, Are Praised or Blamed

It remains now to examine the appropriate rules of conduct of a prince towards subject and friends. Although many have written on the subject, it is my intention to describe what shall be useful to the reader, to examine the truth of the matter, rather than what might be imagined. Many have described republics and principalities that in fact have never existed, because how one lives in the real world is so different from how one ought to live. He ignores what really happens for what ought to happen will destroy, not preserve, himself, for a man who wishes to act completely *virtuosemente* will be destroyed by the great number of men who are not *virtuose*.

Hence a prince wishing to maintain his power must know how to do wrong, and to use that knowledge when necessary. Let us therefore put aside those imaginary qualities of a prince and discuss what is real. When men, especially princes, are discussed, they are considered remarkable for those qualities that bring them either blame or praise. Thus one is considered generosity, another miserly; one is reputed magnanimous, one rapacious; one cruel, one compassionate; one faithless, another faithful; one effeminate and cowardly, another bold and brave; one affable, another haughty; one lascivious, another chaste; one sincere, another cunning; one hard, another soft; one grave, another frivolous; one religious, another unbelieving, and so forth. I know every one agrees that it is admirable for a prince to exhibit every quality considered good; but given human nature, which can never possess or exhibit those qualities completely, a prince only has to be sufficiently prudent to avoid disgrace for those vices that would cost him his state; only then should he try to guard against those vices that would not cost him his state. But if he cannot prevent the latter, he should not be overly concerned. In addition, he need not worry over incurring criticism for those vices necessary to preserve the state; after all, what appears to be *virtù* could result in his ruin, while what appears like vice can bring security and prosperity.

CHAPTER XVI

Concerning Generosity and Stinginess

Beginning with the first set of qualities mentioned above, I say that a reputation for generosity is fine, but generosity that earns you that reputation can cause you great harm. For generosity exercised *virtuosemente* and honestly, as it should be exercised, harms you, for it will not be known and you cannot avoid criticism for meanness. A prince wishing to be considered generous among men must make a grand display of it, consuming all his property, and ultimately burdening his people with heavy taxes to acquire money. This will soon make him hated by his subjects; once he has become poor he will be held in little esteem by anyone. As a result, having offended many and rewarded few, he will be in danger at the first sign of trouble. And as soon as he tries to change, he will immediately be labeled stingy.

Therefore, since a prince cannot exercise this *virtù* of generosity in such a way that it is recognized without considerable cost, he should not fear a reputation of stinginess. In time he will be held in greater esteem than if he were generous since people will see that his revenues are sufficient to defend against all attacks, and to engage in worthy enterprises without burdening his people. As a result, he will have exercised generosity towards those from whom he does not take, who are many, and stinginess toward those few to whom he does not give.

We have not seen great things done in our time except by those who have been considered stingy; the rest have failed. A prince, therefore, should not worry about a reputation for miserliness, provided he has not to rob his subjects, can defend himself, and does not become poor and abject, for it is one of those vices that enable him to govern.

Nothing is so wasteful as liberality, for even while you exercise it you lose the power to do so, becoming either poor and despised, or to avoid poverty, rapacious and hated. A prince should guard above all else against being despised and hated; and liberality leads to both. Therefore it is wiser to have a reputation for meanness which brings criticism without hatred, than to incur a reputation for rapaciousness, which results in both criticism and hatred, by seeking a reputation for liberality.

CHAPTER XVII

Concerning Cruelty and Clemency, and Whether it Is Better to Be Loved than Feared

Turning to other sets of qualities mentioned above, I would say that every prince ought to desire to be considered clement and not cruel, yet should to take care not to misuse this clemency. Cesare Borgia, for example, was considered cruel; yet his cruelty reconciled the Romagna, unified it, and restored it to peace and loyalty. In truth, he ultimately was much more merciful than the Florentine people, who, to avoid a reputation for cruelty, permitted Pistoia to be destroyed. Therefore a prince, so long as he keeps his subjects united and loyal, should not mind criticism that he is cruel, because he will ultimately be more merciful than those who, through too much mercy, allow disorders to arise, and the murders or robberies that follow. This injures the whole people, whereas executions ordered by a prince offend only the individual.

Nevertheless a prince should be slow to believe rumors and to act upon them. He must not show fear, but proceed in a temperate manner with prudence and humanity. He must neither let overconfidence make him incautious, nor too much distrust render him intolerable.

Another question follows: is it be better to be loved than feared, or better to be feared than loved? One might wish to be both, but since it is difficult to unite them in one person, it is much safer to be feared than to be loved. Human nature is in general ungrateful, fickle, false, cowardly, covetous. As long as your rule is successful and danger is distant, they are yours entirely; they will offer you their blood, property, life and children. But when danger approaches, they will turn against you. A prince who relies entirely on the promises of the people, and neglects other precautions, is ruined; friendships that are bought by payments, not by greatness or nobility of mind, may indeed be earned, but they are not secure; in times of need they are unreliable. Men have less scruple in offending one who is beloved than one who is feared, for love is preserved by the link of obligation which, owing to the baseness of men, is broken at every opportunity. But a fear based on dread of punishment never fails.

Nevertheless, a prince ought to inspire fear in such a way that, if it does not win love, avoids hatred. He can endure very well being feared if he is not hated, a condition that will endure as long as he abstains from taking property from his subjects. When it is necessary for him to take someone's life, he must do so with proper justification and for manifest cause. And above all things he must keep his hands off the property of others, because men more quickly forget the death of their father than the loss of their inheritance. Besides, there are always pretexts for taking someone's property; once one has begun to live by robbery, he will always find pretexts for seizing what belongs to others. But reasons for taking life, on the contrary, are more difficult to find.

When a prince is at the head of his army he must disregard any concern for a reputation of cruelty, for without it he would never hold his army together. Hannibal, for example, who led an enormous army, composed of many various races of men, to fight in foreign lands, allowed no dissension among them or against the prince, whether things went well or not. This he achieved through his inhuman cruelty alone, which, with his boundless *virtù*, rendered him revered and awesome in the eyes of his soldiers. Without that cruelty, his other *virtùs* would not have been sufficient to produce this effect. Ironically, shortsighted writers admire his deeds but condemn what made them possible.

Thus I conclude on the question of being feared or loved that men choose to love of their own will, but fear according to the will of the prince. Since a wise prince should establish himself on what he can control, not what is under the control of others, he must endeavor only to avoid hatred.

CHAPTER XVIII

Concerning the Way in Which Princes Should Keep Their Word

Every one acknowledges that it is praiseworthy for a prince to keep his word, to live with integrity not craftiness. Yet experience shows that those princes who have done great things have held good faith of little account, and have known how to manipulate the minds of men with deception, and in the end have overcome those who have kept their promises. You know there are two ways of fighting: by the law, and by force. One is proper to men, the other to beasts, but because the first is frequently not sufficient, it is necessary to have recourse to the second. Therefore a prince must understand how to play upon both the beast and the man, both aspects of human nature.

Since the prince must know how to use the character of beasts, he should choose as models the fox and the lion. A lion cannot defend himself against traps, and a fox cannot defend himself against wolves. Therefore, one must be a fox to discover the traps and a lion to terrify wolves. Those who only adopt the role of the lion do not understand what they are about. Therefore a wise lord cannot, and should not, keep his word when it might be turned against him, and when the reasons that motivated a promise no longer. If all men were good this precept would not hold, but because they are bad, and will not keep faith with you, you should not feel bound to keep it with them. Legitimate reasons for violating a promise will always exist.

But one must know well how to disguise this characteristic, and be an effective liar and hypocrite. Men are so simple, so concerned with present needs, that anyone who seeks to deceive them will always find some who want to be deceived.

Therefore it is unnecessary for a prince to have all the good qualities I have enumerated, but it is very necessary to appear to have them. To have them and always to observe them is injurious, but to appear to have them is useful; to appear merciful, faithful, humane, religious, upright, and to be so, is good. But you should always be of a state of mind ready to behave oppositely. A prince, especially a new one, cannot always observe all those things for which men are esteemed, for in order to maintain the state he is often forced to act contrary to faith, friendship, humanity, and religion. Therefore he must be flexible, ready to change as the winds and variations of fortune demand; he must not avoid the good if possible, but if forced, must know how to set about it.

For this reason a prince ought to take care that he never utter any words that are not replete with the above named five qualities, so that he appears to all who see and hear him merciful, faithful, humane, upright, and religious. Nothing is more important than to appear to have than this last quality, for men judge generally more by the eye than by the hand, since all will see you, but few will come in touch with you. Every one sees what you appear to be, but few really know what you are; and those few dare not challenge the opinion of the many, who have the majesty of the state to defend them. As long as a prince receives the credit for conquering and maintaining his state, the means he used will always be considered honest. The masses will praise him because they are always more influenced by appearances and results.

CHAPTER XIX

That One Should Avoid Being Despised and Hated

Having discussed the most important characteristics of a successful prince, let me turn more briefly to others. As we have seen, a prince must consider how to avoid those things that will make him hated or contemptible. To the extent he succeeds he will have done well, and need not fear other criticisms.

A prince is most hated when he seizes the property or women of his subjects; he must abstain from both. Since the majority of men are content as long as their property and women are secure.

Thus the prince must concern himself only with the ambition of a few, whom he can easily control in many ways.

A prince is contemptible if he is considered fickle, frivolous, effeminate, mean spirited, or irresolute, from all of which he must protect himself as from a rock. He should endeavor to exhibit in his actions greatness, courage, gravity, and fortitude; in his private dealings he should demonstrate that his judgments are irrevocable, and maintain himself in such a way that no one can hope to deceive or control him.

Any prince who conveys this impression of himself will be held in high esteem, and he who is held in high esteem is not easily conspired against. If he is known as an excellent man and revered by his people, he can be attacked only with difficulty. For this reason a prince ought to have two fears, one from within (his subjects), the other from without (external powers). From the latter he can defend himself by a strong army and good allies; if he is well armed he will have faithful allies, and there will be internal peace as long as there is external peace unless disturbed by conspiracy. Even if he faces an external threat, he need not despair as long as he is well-prepared and remains sensibly.

But in the case of his subjects, he need only fear that they will conspire secretly against him at times of external threats. The prince can defend himself against this possibility by taking care that he is not hated and despised, and by keeping himself in the popular favor, for conspirators expect popular support for their efforts. But when a conspirator knows he will offend public opinion, he will not have the courage to take such a course, knowing the infinite difficulties he will face. History records many conspiracies, but few successful ones: a conspirator cannot act alone, and can seek supporters only from those he believes to be malcontents. Once the conspirator has explained his plot to a malcontent he have given him the means to find contentment, for by denouncing the conspirator he can hope for special favors. Rare is the individual who will sacrifice guaranteed rewards for a dubious proposition filled with risks. For the conspirator faces nothing but fear, jealousy, prospect of punishment and terror; but on the side of the prince there is the majesty of the state, the laws, the protection of friends and the state to defend him.

Thus a prince need not worry extensively about conspiracies when his people hold him in esteem. But when public opinion is hostile and bears hatred towards him, he ought to fear everything and everybody. One of the most important goals a prince must set in order to secure a well-ordered state is to take care not to drive the nobles to desperation, and to keep the people satisfied and contented.

Among the best ordered and governed kingdoms of our times is France, which possesses many good institutions to protect the liberty and security of the king. The first of these is the parliament and its authority. The founder of the kingdom, cognizant of the ambition and boldness of the nobility, knew he needed a bit in their mouths to restrain them. He also knew how much the people feared and hated them. The founder wished to protect the nobles without appearing biased, for he knew his vulnerability to the nobles accusing him of favoring the people and the people accusing him of favoring the nobles. Parliament, then, was an arbiter that could keep the nobles in their place. This was a prudent arrangement, a source of security for the king and kingdom. From this one can draw two additional conclusions: princes should leave affairs of reproach to the management of others, and keep those of grace in their own hands. And second, princes should cherish the nobles, but not so much as to make themselves hated by the people.

CHAPTER XXI

How a Prince Should Conduct Himself So As to Gain Renown

Nothing makes a prince so much esteemed as great enterprises and a fine example. We have in our time Ferdinand of Aragón, the present King of Spain. He can almost be called a new prince, because he has risen, by fame and glory, from being an insignificant king to be the foremost king in Christendom; and if you will consider his deeds you will find them all great and some of them extraordinary....

A prince is also respected when he is either a true friend or an outright enemy, that is, when, he declares himself in favor of one party or against the other without reservation. Such a course will always be more advantageous than remaining neutral, for if two of your powerful neighbors go to war and one of them prevails, you have either to fear him or not. In both cases the most advantageous course is to declare yourself in support of one side and declare war on that side's behalf. If you do not take sides, you will invariably fall prey to the conqueror because he who conquers does not want ambivalent friends who will not come to his support in times of danger. And he who loses will not harbor you because you did not willingly come to his support with sword in hand....

Never let a Government think that it can choose perfectly safe courses; rather let it expect to have to take very uncertain ones. In the course of human affairs one cannot avoid one source of trouble without running into another. Prudence consists in knowing how to distinguish the importance of different challenges, and the wisdom to choose the lesser evil.

A prince should also to show himself a patron of *virtù*, and honor those who are proficient in every art. He should also encourage his citizens to practice their callings peaceably, whether in commerce, agriculture, or other endeavor. They should not hesitate to increase their wealth out of fear that he will lose them to taxes. Indeed, the prince should offer rewards to those who do these things and bring to honor his city or state.

Further, he ought to entertain the people with festivals and spectacles. He should hold in esteem the various guilds and societies of the cities and associate with them, without, of course, compromising the majesty of his position.

CHAPTER XXV

What Fortune Can Effect in Human Affairs, and How to Withstand Her

Many hold, and still hold, the conviction that the affairs of the world are governed by Fortune, and that men, however wise, cannot control them, nor even influence them. They would argue it is pointless to try to influence events that should be left to chance. This opinion has been more prominent in our own time because of the great changes that have occurred. Although I appreciate this point of view, I would argue that Fortune controls half of our actions, but that she leaves us free to control the other half.

I compare Fortune to a raging river, which when in flood overflows the plains, sweeps away trees and buildings, carries the soil from place to place. Everything flies before it, yielding to its violence, without being able to withstand it. But it does not follow that when the weather clears, men should build defenses against future floods. It is the same with Fortune, who shows her power when *virtù* has not prepared to resist her; she turns her power where she knows no barriers or defenses have been raised to constrain her.

To be sure, a prince may be seen happy today and ruined tomorrow without having shown any change of disposition or character. This, I believe, occurs in the first instance from causes I have already been discussed: the prince who relies entirely upon Fortune is lost when it changes. I believe also that he will experience success whose actions are guided by the spirit of the times, and that he whose actions are not guided by the spirit of the times will not be successful. Men achieve what they seek, glory and riches, by various methods: one with caution, another with haste; one by force, another by skill; one by patience, another by impatience; each succeeds differently. One can find examples of one cautious man who reaches his goal and another who fails; and of two men, one cautious, the other impetuous, who are both successful. These differences in outcome are simply result of whether or not their actions conform to the spirit of the times.

Changes in circumstances are also influenced by the times. If one who governs with caution and patience, and the times favor these qualities so that his administration is successful, his fortune is made; but if times and circumstances change, he who does not change his behavior is ruined. But a man can rarely accommodate himself to change, first because nature has inclined him a certain way, and second, because having prospered according to one course of action, he finds it difficult to adopt a different course. As a result, the cautious man does not know how to become reckless, and hence he is ruined; but had he changed his conduct with the times his fortune would not have declined.

I conclude therefore that since Fortune is constantly in flux but men are steadfast in their ways, men are successful when their actions complement the times, but unsuccessful when they do not. For my part, I consider that it is better to be adventurous than cautious, because fortune is a woman. If you wish to control her you must beat and abuse her; she allows herself to be mastered by the aggressive, not by those who come to her coldly. She is, therefore, always womanlike, a lover of young men, because they are less cautious, more violent, and with more audacity command her.